Brian R. Farmer

Understanding Radical Islam

Medieval Ideology in the Twenty-First Century

PETER LANG
New York • Washington, D.C./Baltimore • Bern
Frankfurt am Main • Berlin • Brussels • Vienna • Oxford

Library of Congress Cataloging-in-Publication Data

Farmer, Brian R.
Understanding radical Islam: medieval ideology
in the twenty-first century / Brian R. Farmer.
p. cm.
Includes bibliographical references and index.
1. Islam and politics. 2. Terrorism—Religious aspects—Islam.
3. Religion and politics—Islamic countries. 4. Islam—21st century. I. Title.
BP173.7.F37   320.5'57—dc22   2006022466
ISBN 978-0-8204-8843-1

Bibliographic information published by **Die Deutsche Bibliothek**.
Die Deutsche Bibliothek lists this publication in the "Deutsche
Nationalbibliografie"; detailed bibliographic data is available
on the Internet at http://dnb.ddb.de/.

Cover design by Joni Holst

The paper in this book meets the guidelines for permanence and durability
of the Committee on Production Guidelines for Book Longevity
of the Council of Library Resources.

© 2007, 2008 Peter Lang Publishing, Inc., New York
29 Broadway, 18th floor, New York, NY 10006
www.peterlang.com

Printed in the United States of America

Understanding
Radical Islam

PETER LANG
New York • Washington, D.C./Baltimore • Bern
Frankfurt am Main • Berlin • Brussels • Vienna • Oxford

Contents

Acknowledgments

Perhaps no discussion of Islamism is complete and the selection of material for discussion on the subject would not be completely satisfactory to everyone; consequently, the material presented within these pages is not exhaustive, but was chosen somewhat subjectively at the discretion of the author. Similarly, conceptualization of Islamism is by nature somewhat imprecise, and scholars are not always in complete agreement. In this, Islamism is no different than other ideologies, such as Marxism, about which scholarly debate fills entire libraries with unending barrages of conflicting arguments. It is my hope and belief, however, that the essence of Islamism has been sufficiently captured within these pages so that readers can gain a much greater understanding of what has become the most important ideology challenging the Western liberal paradigm in the early twenty-first century.

The ideas for this book are largely not my own, but were borrowed from the cumulative knowledge of hundreds of other scholars of ideology, Islam, and politics in the Islamic realm. I only hope that I have interpreted their writings correctly and used them fairly in my effort to construct a synthesis of Islamism as it exists in 2006. To all of those scholars whose works I have used, I want to express my greatest appreciation.

I also want to thank those in my personal life for their tolerance and support of my academic pursuits. First and formost, I owe my entire academic career to Denise, who not only put me through school, both graduate and undergradutate, but continues to grant me the space for my academic pursuits. I also want to thank my division chair, Jerry Moller, my colleagues, Dr. Jim Powell and Dr. Alan Kee who provide both friendship and intellectual stimulation, and the "two Cheryls" in the Department of Social Sciences at Amarillo College for their tolerance and exemplary administrative support. Finally, I also need to thank Bobbie Hyndman, Sherri Hromas, and Arthur Castillo for their invaluable technical support.

Introduction

The late twentieth and early twenty-first centuries witnessed a revival of the role of religious political ideology on the global political stage. Radical Islam or the ideology of "Islamism" (as it will be referred to in this book) presently merits attention due to the prevalence of Islamism as an important facet of the rise in religious ideology across the globe, and its recent emergence as the primary challenge to the primacy of the Western democratic capitalist model. Islamism also merits attention due to its obvious association with terrorism. For instance, a study by the International Policy Institute for Counterterrorism in 2001 concluded that suicide terrorism in particular often is a product of indoctrination into Islamic fundamentalism (Pape, 2005, p.16). The rise in Islamic suicide terror in turn appears associated with a general rise in religious terrorism in the latter part of the twentieth century. In 1980, for example, the US State Department's list of international terrorist groups included very few religious groups, however, at the end of the twentieth century, more than half of the groups on the list were religious in character, suggesting that religious political ideology had not only become more important in global politics, but also more dangerous (Juergensmeyer, 2003, p.6). Although religion may not be the only factor contributing to the rise in international terrorism, it is also clear that religion does make a difference and religious ideology is a contributor to violence when it becomes intertwined with other factors such as poverty, pride, and culture clash (Juergensmeyer, 2003, p.10).

In cases of political conflict, religious differences tend to make it more difficult for diverse groups to reach across the fence and achieve a compromise. Religion is often extremely exclusive and intolerant, and believers often cannot abandon religious principles without not only offending their own community, but also (in their minds) God himself. Religion is often more divisive than other factors such as language, for instance, because one may learn another's language without social sanction, but it is much more difficult for the faithful to convert to the religion of another. In the words of Robert Pape (2005, p.90), "Religion typically claims to possess superior insight into ultimate truths, from which it follows that devotees of any other religion must be misguided, amoral, immoral, or even actively evil."

Importance of Islamism

At present, one of the largest groups of people in the world that do not appear to be satisfied with the political and economic status quo at the beginning of the twenty-first century describe themselves as Muslims, and that discontent has become politically active in the form of Islamism. Furthermore, that radical Islam played a major role in the worst terrorist attacks in American history on 9/11/01 is beyond dispute. For example, the final instructions found in the luggage of several hijackers instructed them to make,

> an oath to die ... When the confrontation begins, strike like champions who do not want to go back to this world ... Check your weapons long before you leave ... you must make your knife sharp and must not discomfort your animal during the slaughter ... Afterwards, we will all meet in the highest heaven. (Quoted in Pape, 2005, p.5)

How much of a role radical Islam played in the attacks and what the proper responses should be, however, are matters of dispute. For instance, Robert Pape (2005, p.4) argues that religion only plays the role of a recruiting tool and that the real cause of Islamist terrorism and violence is American occupation of foreign lands. Pape further argues that suicide terrorism, which is often associated with radical Islam, is most likely when the religion of the occupying power differs from the religion of the occupied peoples (Pape, 2005, p.22). Given that the non-Islamic United States is the chief "occupying power" in the Islamic world, suicide terrorism is the result. In support of his argument that it is occupation that produces suicide terrorism rather than Islamism itself, Pape cites Osama bin Laden's oft-repeated demand that the United States withdraw from the Persian Gulf region (Pape, 2005, p.21).

Pape's argument that the real culprit is military occupation, however, does not appear to hold up under closer scrutiny since the United States has invaded dozens of lands since its "age of Imperialism" dawned in the nineteenth century (including Cuba, Panama, Haiti, Dominican Republic, etc., not to mention Europe and Japan following World War II), but the instances of terrorism stemming from the invasions were few. Instead, the explaining factor for terrorist violence appears to be not simply occupation, but occupation only when combined with Islamist religious ideology. This suggests that the control variable is actually American occupation and that the more important factor in explaining suicide terror is the ideology of Islamism.

The rise in Islamist-driven terrorism in the early twenty-first century clearly has emerged as a primary policy concern of Western governments, as evidenced not only by the two major American wars in the first decade of the new millennium (in Afghanistan and Iraq) that were launched in response to the 9/11 attacks, but also by the incidents of Islamist violence and terrorism all over the globe in the years since the 9/11 attacks.

In the United States, the "War on Terror" that has raged since 9/11 has dominated the foreign policy and political campaign strategy of the Bush administration, with mixed results. Bush's heavy-handed military response has led to the toppling of two brutal regimes in Islamic countries and helped Bush secure reelection in the United States, however, both the terrorist attacks and the wars that followed have resulted in thousands of deaths, billions of dollars in economic costs, and perhaps incalculable human suffering, commensurate with the deaths and destruction produced by the terrorism and the Western war against it. Furthermore, the American invasions do not appear to have significantly reduced Islamic terror. In the two years following the 9/11 attacks, al-Qaeda conducted 15 suicide terrorist attacks, more than had been attributed to the group in all the years prior to the 9/11 attacks (Pape, 2005, p.6). The increases in attacks, rather than decreases since President Bush launched his War on Terror, suggest that Islamism merits further study since military invasion does not appear to be a foolproof method for transforming radical Islam. At this writing, the failure of President Bush to subdue radical Islamists through military means appears to be a major contributor to his slide in approval ratings from approximately 90% to barely a third.

Islamism is also important as a focus of study due to the fact that the War on Terror appears to be a war without the limitations of the twentieth-century conflicts. Unlike World War II, which was sure to end with the destruction of Imperial Japan and Nazi Germany, and unlike the cold war, which ended after the economic and political collapse of the communist bloc states, there is no predictable end to the War on Terror because it is not a conflict between states, but a war of ideas. In such a war, as the war in Vietnam in the 1960s and 1970s has already demonstrated, the superiority of Western economics and technology does not guarantee triumph.

The War on Terror also thus far has been without limits, in that it appears to be bound by no particular rules of war. Islamic terrorists clearly pay no attention to the Geneva Convention or any other set of West-constructed international rules, because they are constrained only by their own interpretations of Islam. Consequently, they abuse and execute prisoners and kill civilians at will without concern for any set of international rules governing such conduct. Concurrently, the United States has selectively abandoned the provisions of the Geneva Convention on the conduct of war, arguing that its tenets are outdated and not in conformity with the new type of warfare that includes non-state actors. The United States has further incentive to abandon the Geneva Convention from a practical standpoint, since it is not expected that large numbers of American fighters in the War on Terror will actually fall into enemy hands, and even if they do, the Islamic terrorists are not expected to adhere to any tenets of the Geneva Convention regardless of whether their Western counterparts adhere to its provisions or not. Clearly, there is danger of an escalation of violence in such a war without limits that may only be in its beginning stages; consequently, Islam needs to be better understood in the West, so as to avoid as many mistakes as possible and hopefully find an ultimate solution to the conflict.

Islamism is also an important field of study at present due to the sheer numbers of Muslims in the world and the fact that Islamist ideology is present in varying degrees not only in all of the world's predominantly Muslim countries, but also among Muslims living in Western industrialized democracies. Most Muslims obviously are not radical Islamists, but approximately one fifth of the world's human inhabitants (1.2 billion) are adherents of Islam, and the Islamic religion ranks second only behind Christianity in terms of the number of followers. If only a very small percentage subscribe to the radical Islamist ideology that induces its adherents to terrorism, murder, and mayhem, then Islamism has the potential to present the world with perhaps its greatest challenge of the new millennium. To put it another way, if only one tenth of 1% of Muslims are radical Islamists that would resort to terrorism against the West, then there are 1.2 million potential radical Islamic terrorists living in the world, more than 150,000 of whom are living in the West already (Ingersoll et al., 2001, p.251).

To exacerbate the potential even further, more recent advancements in communications (cell phones, satellite television, and the Internet) have helped radical Islamists to develop into what Martin Kramer (1993, p.38) describes as the emergence of a "global village" of Islamism, interconnected by both ideology and technology. The advances in communications technology has increased the access of the world's radical Islamists to each other and thus provided greater tools, connections, and resource availability for Islamists who desire to form a global Islamist movement.

As if that is not reason enough to merit study, the gap in numbers between the adherents of Christianity and Islam is likely to diminish in subsequent decades, since populations in Islamic countries are growing much faster than those in the developed "Christian" West. While growth rates in the developed West typically range between 1% and 1.5% annually, population growth in the Islamic world is often more than 3%. For example, in the next fifteen years, it is estimated that Egypt will grow by 25%, Syria by 39%, Jordan by 44%, Saudi Arabia by 56%, and Palestine (Gaza and the West Bank) by 64%. In the decade of the 1990s, while Europe moved ever closer to zero population growth, the growth rate in the Arab Islamic world was 3.4%, the highest growth rate of any world region (Benjamin and Simon, 2002, p.176).

The fact that much of the world's Islamic population, including those in Indonesia (the world's most populous Muslim country with over 200 million people), also sits atop the world's largest reserves of petroleum means that the West and the world of Islam will be inextricably linked as long as Western societies are dependent on petroleum for fuel. Western withdrawal from the Islamic realm does not appear to be an option; thus, contact between the West and the realm of Islam appears to be unavoidable. Regrettably, the interaction between the Western societies and the Muslim world currently can be expected to produce continued conflict due to economic differences alone, even if cultural factors were not involved. After all, one should expect those with the oil to desire greater profits for their nonrenewable resource, while one should also expect the consumers of that same commodity to desire lower prices. When cultural misunderstanding and religious differences are combined with the economic mix, however, the potential for conflict in the contact between the developed West and the realm of Islam perhaps increases exponentially. One could hope that cultural conflict between the West and the realm of Islam could diminish in the increasingly multicultural world village, but unfortunately, cultural misunderstanding between the West and the realm of Islam has been endemic to their interaction throughout the previous century, and shows few signs of abating.

Instead, the cultural misunderstanding thus far has been nothing if not consistent. For example, Meg Greenfield (Quoted in *Newsweek*, March 26, 1979, p.26), argued during the Iranian Revolution that "No part of the world is more hopelessly, systematically and stubbornly misunderstood in the West than that complex of religion, culture and geography known as Islam." A quarter century later, the Western bewilderment over the terrorist attacks of 9/11 (along with numerous other subsequent terror attacks, including bombings of the London transit system in July 2005) and the fact that many Westerners were surprised when Islamists rejected the two wars of "liberation" launched by American President George W. Bush in Islamic countries, are evidence that little has changed since Greenfield's writing. The widespread rejection by the Islamic world of the Bush administration's approach to the problem of Islamist terrorism reflects the fact that Western culture and hegemony has not achieved legitimacy in most of the Islamic world (Sayyid, 2003, p.xvii)

Similarly, neoconservatives in the Bush administration (and those that supported them) were evidently surprised when Iraqi citizens did not greet the US military invasion with sweets and flowers when they arrived to "liberate" the Iraqi people from Saddam Hussein. Furthermore, the wave after wave of insurgents that have relentlessly attacked Americans and other Iraqis in Iraq since the American invasion of 2003 were evidently unanticipated by President Bush and the top advisors in his administration, thus suggesting more cultural misunderstanding and confusion. The insurgents have continued to mystify the American leadership since Bush's declaration of "mission accomplished" May 1, 2003, with continued attacks that have included seemingly incomprehensible (to Westerners) suicide bombings (Phillips, 2005 Diamond, 2005 Shadid, 2005 Packer, 2005).

If the Islamists in each of these situations have appeared irrational to the leaders and peoples of the West, perhaps the Western leaders can find some solace in the fact that it is not rational analysis that drives the Islamic insurgents and terrorists, but ideology, and all ideology, not just that of the Islamists, is antithetical to rational analysis and critical thinking. Consequently, to fully understand what drives the terrorists and Iraqi insurgents to such seemingly irrational actions, it is necessary to understand their underlying ideology.

Ideology

Ideologies are belief systems through which people view and interpret reality. In the words of Milton Rokeach (1972, p.5), "Ideology refers to more or less institutionalized set of beliefs—the views someone picks up." Ideologies are not reality, but instead produce simplified versions of reality for those who view the world through ideological frameworks. Ideology interprets and explains what is wrong with society in simplistic terms and provides simplistic prescriptions purported to solve all societal ills. In general, people are very good at identifying someone else's ideology and noting the flaws in their precepts, but they may not even recognize that they themselves are normally just as ideological as others.

Whether one is discussing the United States, Europe, or the Islamic world, there are scores of differing ideologies within each society, some mainstream, and some on the political "fringe." The fringe ideologies, such as Islamism, are easily recognizable as ideologies by the masses and generally scorned for their "heretical errors" and deviations from social mores and accepted norms. If we consider, for example, the racist Nazi ideology of Germany in the 1930s, we will find that the ideology simplistically taught that, "all of the world's problems" were created by "subversive Jews" and other minorities. The simplistic solution of the Nazis in Germany during World War II therefore included the genocide of Jews and others that the Nazis considered societal "problems," with the disastrous result that over 10 million people died in the Nazi death camps. Islamism is similar in that it often reduces all of societal problems to a battle between good, (represented by radical Islam) and evil (represented by a collaborative effort between infidels Israel and the United States against Islam), and the solution is therefore to "kill every American, everywhere" (www.washingtonpost.com/ac2/wp-dyn?). Though Islamism is not normally considered representative of the mainstream in Islamic societies, the strength of Islamism in the Islamic world at present was demonstrated in the most recent elections in Palestine, where the Islamist group, Hamas, won control of the Palestinian Authority.

Islamism, of course, is only a fringe ideology in the United States and Europe and therefore is not itself an important force in American or European Party politics at the moment, but its presence has had tremendous impact on Western politics, not only by spawning a "war on terror," but also by fuelling reactionary movements in Europe and the United States. In the United States, a company from the United Arab Emirates was forced to give up its bid to take control of the management of several American ports in the spring of 2006, due to public fears of violence spawned by radical Islam. The United States also erupted in perhaps its largest mass demonstrations since the 1960s, in the spring of 2006, over proposed changes to immigration policies. While Latinos and other immigrants paraded in the streets in favor of more relaxed immigration laws, conservatives called for more stringent immigration laws, at least partially as an effort to curb Islamic terror. Meanwhile, a reactionary conservative group known as the "Minutemen," patrols the US-Mexican border to ward off illegal immigrants.

In France, far-right candidate Jean Marie Le Pen, who opposes Muslim immigration to France, once referred to the holocaust as a "detail" of World War II, and has repeatedly declared his belief in the inequality of races, came in second in the French Presidential election of 2002 with almost 17% of the vote, a testimony to the negative reaction of a large segment of the French population to the presence of a large and ever-expanding number of Islamic citizens in their midst (www.wikipedia.org/wiki/Jean-Marie_Le_Pen#quotes).

Although Le Pen lost 83% of the French vote, it should be remembered that Nazism was only a fringe ideology in Germany as late as 1928. The fact that the Nazis came from political "nowhere" to assume power in Germany a mere five years later, and then overran virtually all of Europe within a dozen years, is a testimony to the mobilizing power of ideology. Furthermore, as proven by the terror attacks of 9/11 and the War on Terror that has followed, the continuing Arab/Israeli conflict in Palestine, and the continued insurgency against the United States in Iraq, a fringe ideology can have tremendous impact on global politics even if it is not the ideology of the vast majority. Although there are clearly other elements involved in the aforementioned conflicts, including economic inequality and the conflict between great powers and those in lesser developed areas, it is also clear that ideology plays a central, if not overriding role. If global politics has become more ideological, rather than more practical in recent years, then it clearly has also become more dangerous, since ideology tends to be uncompromising.

Conservative Political Ideology

As previously stated, radical Islamism is an extremist form of traditional conservative ideology. Thus, to understand Islamism, one must understand conservative political ideology in general as well as the ideology of traditional conservatism in particular. Samuel Huntington (1957) argues that conservatism as an ideology is best understood not as an inherent theory, but as a positional ideology. According to Huntington,

> When the foundations of society are threatened, the conservative ideology reminds men of the necessity of some institutions and the desirability of the existing ones. (Quoted in Huntington, 1957, p.455)

Huntington contends that ideological conservatism arises from an anxiety that develops when people perceive valuable institutions to be endangered by contemporary developments or proposed reforms, and the awareness that perceived useful institutions are under attack then leads conservatives to attempt to provide a defense of those institutions. Islamism thus clearly fits well with Huntington's conception since Islamists view the foundations of their society as threatened and call for return to the societal structures of the past, including veils, beards, and traditional gender roles. The globalization of Western mass-consumption society and culture into the Islamic world has served to fuel the reactionary conservatism that has emerged in the Islamic world as new technology and fashions from abroad, as well as new ways of thinking have served to alter traditional societies. Other more forceful precipitants, such as the Persian Gulf War and forward placement of American troops in Islamic countries along with the more recent American invasion and occupation of Iraq have obviously intensified the perception of many in the Islamic world that Islam is under attack. The reaction of the Islamists is therefore to defend their cultures and traditions against the foreign encroachments and corruptions from within (Shadid, 2005, p.397).

Samuel Huntington (1957, p.456) explains that the ideology of conservatism is an extremely situational ideology due to the different societal institutions in different societies at different times that people may desire to conserve. In the words of Huntington,

> because the articulation of conservatism is a response to a specific social situation. ... The manifestation of conservatism at any one time and place has little connection with its manifestation at any other time and place. (Quoted in Huntington, 1957, p.456)

In other words, conservatives at one time or another have sought to conserve just about every institution ever invented, from monarchies, to aristocracies, to slavery, to tariffs, to free trade, to capitalism, to the defense of communism in the late 1980s in the Soviet Union.

In the case of radical Islam, the institutions that the Islamists seek to conserve are those of traditional religion. Islamists essentially do not recognize that society and its institutions may continually change, develop, evolve, or improve in response to changing circumstances. The Islamists also object to the Western attempts to impose new cultural values that were derived in the non-Muslim world, such as democracy, for example, on Islamic societies. The Islamists believe that there are no values higher than those provided by Islam; consequently, Western values of the free market, democracy, and freedom of choice, that were not derived from Islam, must therefore be inferior (Ingersoll et al., 2001, p.270). For example, Bediuzzaman Said Nursi, a Turkish Islamist of the early twentieth century, condemned the educational reforms of Kemal Ataturk, who put education under direct state control, as "irreligious materialist philosophy" that neglected religious concerns and therefore inadequately prepared people for life's challenges (Nursi, 1997, pp.495–496). Similarly, Hassan al-Banna, the founder of the Islamist Muslim Brotherhood in Egypt, denounced

Western-style education reforms in Egypt as "mental colonization" that would erode Islamic traditions (Quoted in Abu-Rabi, 1996, p.80).

Conservatism, however, is forced to be selective concerning what traditions and legacies must be retained and which ones may be discarded. In what Edmund Burke referred to as the "choice of inheritance," one may expect disagreement even among conservatives as to which societal institutions are absolutely essential and must be preserved, which ones may be altered and how, and which ones should be abolished completely (Muller, 1997, p.31). For example, radical Islamists tend to reject Western decadence, Western music, and Western dress, along with all forms of lavish spending, yet Saudi Arabian Princes are known for their lavish spending, including gambling and prostitutes, and Osama bin Laden operated with cell phones, desired Western military technology, and provided luxury Toyota Land Cruisers for his Mujahadeen warriors in Afghanistan (Benjamin and Simon, 2002 Baer, 2003, pp.25-28).

The term "conservative" itself dates back to 1818 as the title of a French weekly journal, *Le Conservateur*, that was purposed to "uphold religion, the King, liberty, the Charter and respectable people" (Muller, 1997, p.26). If "Allah" and "Koran" are inserted for the words "King" and "Charter," then one may see that the fundamental elements of conservatism in France in 1818 are still present in the form of radical Islam in the twenty-first century. Other aspects of conservative thought that have remained constant throughout the centuries that are present in radical Islam are presented below.

Transcendent Moral Order

In spite of the diversity of institutions that conservatives throughout the centuries have sought to defend, a set of assumptions and themes behind conservatism have endured. Among those is the assumption that there exists a transcendent moral order to which humans should attempt to conform to in society (Kirk, 1982, p.17). Conservatism therefore tends to be skeptical of new and abstract theories that may attempt to mold society to a new morality, because in the views of the conservatives, the existing order, whatever it may be, arose and exists now as it does due to its consistency with the transcendent and true morality. Consequently, any theory of a "new" morality represents "immorality" or it would have already emerged as accepted morality through the human experiences of the ages. In the Islamic world, conservatism has therefore adhered to strict readings of the Koran and viewed its moral teachings of the seventh century as absolute, transcendent, and nonnegotiable. Consequently, Islamists have opposed the "abstract theories" of democracy and capitalism as un-Islamic and decadent violations of the transcendent moral order established by Islam.

Negative View of Human Nature

Conservative ideologies typically emphasize human imperfections and depravity, especially those of common individuals. Typically, humans are viewed as naturally bad, selfish, uncooperative, untrustworthy, and incapable of honorable behavior unless coerced. Christian religious conservatives in particular tie the negative view of human nature to the doctrine of original sin in the Bible, and argue that human nature has been flawed ever since sin first came into the world in the Garden of Eden. In this perspective, it is impossible for humans to be good without divine assistance (Muller, 1997, p.31). It is because of this belief in a flawed human nature that conservatives also view human attempts to create a "just society" through reason, as Plato prescribed in *The Republic,* as unrealizable. Thus, movements in the West such as "secular humanism" are viewed by Western religious conservatives as doomed to failure, if not immoral as well. Similarly, Islamists generally accept the view of humans as morally depraved and reject human reasoning for the Word of God as spoken by the prophet Mohammed in the Koran (Smith, 1991, p.232).

Focus on Order

Conservatives in general are skeptical of a society without constraints on the "fallen humans" and argue that institutional measures must be taken to ensure order. Conservatives therefore can be expected to clash with liberals over the expansion of rights and the utility of existing institutions (such as the Church) that conservatives view as necessary to control human passions and disorder. In the words of Edmund Burke in *Reflections on the Revolution in France* "the restraints on men, as well as their liberties, are to be reckoned among their rights" (Quoted in Muller, 1997, p.11). Burke therefore argued for retention of customary moral rules, even if those rules had not been subject to rational justification. After all, flawed human reasoning would be unlikely to rationally determine definitively whether customary mores were rationally justified or not. Even if such things could be known, conservatives' low regard for ordinary humans leads them to believe that most people would lack the time, energy, and intellect to reevaluate societal mores anyway. Therefore, conservatives argue that humans have a duty to abide by existing societal rules in most cases (Muller, 1997, p.11). Edmund Burke argues that because the dissolution of the social order would also destroy the societal institutions by which human passions are restrained, the individual has no right to opt out of obligation to the State and community (Muller, 1997, p.11).

In Islamism (as in all Islam), the focus on order is directed by the adherence to the Koran and the sharia (Islamic law) that is derived from the Koran and the Hadiths (traditions of the Prophet). Given that the Koran is viewed by Islamists as the literal, inerrant Word of God, any deviation from the societal rules as set down in the Koran would be considered to be against the Word of God, forbidden, and disorderly (Smith, 1991, p.232). Similarly, the rights of men are limited by the unchanging sharia, and are not open to negotiation.

Emphasis on History and Existing Institutions

Conservatives place a major emphasis on history and the history of human institutions. For conservatives, the survival of a human institution throughout history, whether one speaks of religion, marriage, aristocracy, or the free market, proves that the institution itself must serve a human need (Kristol, 1983, p.161). The need that is met by the institution, however, may not necessarily be the need for which the institution was created. For example, the practice of the burial of deceased human bodies may have arisen for purposes of sanitation; however, the institution of the funeral and burial serves the purpose of aiding the psychological well-being of the living. The fact that humans at any given time may not recognize the utility of existing institutions is a reflection of the human limitations of the critics of the institutions rather than any flaws in the institutions themselves. The ongoing existence of the institutions themselves is sufficient to indicate their superiority in meeting human needs. Conservatives typically point to the family as the most important societal institution, but a major emphasis is also placed on religion. Conservatives typically defend religion under these pretenses and ignore the fact that religion from time to time throughout human history has been the cause of much discord, death, and oppression. For conservatives, it is less important whether religion is true or false, and more important that it offers humans hope and thus helps to diffuse discontent that could disrupt the societal order (Muller, 1997, p.13).

Radical Muslims also emphasize family, religion, and history, but the religion they focus on is the Islam of the seventh century, the family relations they focus on are those of traditional Islam, and the history they emphasize is Islamic history, with a focus on Mohammed and those who carried the torch of Islam known as "the four caliphs" (Abu Bakr, Umar, Uthman, and Ali) after his death in the seventh century. Muslims regard Mohammed's migration (known as the Hijra) from Mecca to Yathrib (Medina) in 622 AD. to be the turning point in world history, and it is this year from which they date their calendar (Smith, 1991, p.230). Muslims commemorate the Hijra through the practice of Ramadan, the month in the lunar calendar when Mohammed received his revelations, and the month during which he made the Hijra ten years later. During Ramadan, Muslims neither eat, drink, nor smoke during the sunlight hours (Smith, 1991, p.247).

Additionally, Shiite Muslims (in addition to the life of Mohammed), focus on the lives of Mohammed's cousin and son-in-law, Ali (the fourth caliph), who was stabbed in Kufa in southern Iraq in 661 and buried in Najaf. Currently, Najaf is home to a gold-domed shrine that serves as Ali's tomb and one of Shiite Islam's most Holy sites of pilgrimage (Shadid, 2005, pp.160–161). Shiites also focus on the life of Mohammed's grandson (and Ali's son), Hussein, who was killed and decapitated in battle near the Iraqi city of Karbala in 680 AD. Shiites view Hussein as the rightful heir to the caliphate, being a direct descendent of Mohammed, who was slaughtered along with his greatly outnumbered army of 72 men by the army of the "illegitimate" caliph, Yazid (Hashim, 2006, pp.233–234).

In Shiism, Hussein's death evokes emotions similar to the sentiments inspired by the crucifixion of Jesus among Christians. Hussein's historical life and death are symbols to Shiite Muslims of service to God, suffering, and martyrdom (Shadid, 2005, p.57). To devout Shiites, Ashura, the anniversary of Hussein's martyrdom, is the most tragic and sorrowful day of the year, complete with ritual frenzied mourning and self-mutilation to commemorate Hussein's suffering. The grief of Ashura commemorates the Shiites' history of dispossession and injustice and intersects with the perceived dispossession and injustice of the present (Shadid, 2005, p.162). For Shiites, the suicidal fight waged by Hussein against the superior forces of his adversary, Yazid, at Karbala in 680 AD is the perfect model of self-sacrifice (Benjamin and Simon, 2005, p.73).

Ashura in some respects resembles the Jewish Passover in that the Shiites prepare large quantities of food, feast, and stay up together until dawn while waiting and watching for the spirit of Imam Hussein to pass by (Packer, 2005, p.270). In other respects, it resembles the perfect sacrifice and martyrdom of Jesus in terms of its symbolism. Islamist suicide bombers need look no further than the example of Hussein for inspiration and justification of their deeds. Although it is certainly true that most Muslims do not resort to suicide attacks against non-Muslims, it is also true (according to survey data) that the majority of Muslims in many Islamic countries approve of suicide bombings against Westerners in Iraq (Benjamin and Simon, 2005, p.75).

Skepticism of Altruistic Efforts

Western conservatives typically oppose liberal moral "do-gooders" and scoff at the efforts of those who attempt to improve the lives of those less fortunate. In general, Western conservatives argue that such efforts only encourage laziness and dependency among the recipients. Furthermore, conservatives argue that such efforts have unintended and unforeseen negative consequences. For instance, a government welfare program that increases aid based on the number of children in a family may be designed to eliminate malnutrition, but would be expected by conservatives to lead to the birth of more welfare-recipient children, as people take advantage of the larger government stipend. Conservatives typically view income inequalities as legitimate and natural and therefore attempts at redistribution to the poor are not only "casting one's pearls before swine," but also a violation of the natural order (Muller, 1997, p.18).

Although the Koran requires the giving of alms (2.5% of one's net worth), and charity is one of the "five pillars of Islam" and, therefore, central to Islamist thought, Islamists generally reject Western charity (at least in rhetoric) due to what is perceived as its corrupting influence rather than due to any disincentive to work it might induce. The "corrupting" influence of Western charity that Islamists reject is instead its connection to Western culture that violates the "natural order" of Islam. For example, Iranian philosopher Jalal Al-e Ahmad (1982, pp.15–16) argues that such contact with the West would lead inexorably to cultural corrosion and, therefore, must be avoided. Ayatollah Khomeini (1981, pp.35–36) offered a similar argument in his writings on Islam and revolution. Khomeini not only denounces Western charity as corrosive to society, but argues that the solution to societal problems lies in faith and morals rather than in material power, wealth, and technology, which he believed had no impact on the relief of human misery.

Islamic extremist groups, however, tend to use the Islamic command to give alms to their advantage by engaging in charity work and, therefore, setting themselves up as legitimate "charities" rather than terrorist organizations so that devout Muslims may contribute to them ostensibly to further the good works of God. For example, Egypt's Muslim Brotherhood, Lebanon's Hezbollah, and Palestine's Hamas, all generally categorized in the West as Islamic extremist terror groups, are often considered Islamic "charities" in the Muslim world and have generated support in the Islamic world for their social work, providing logistical and financial help for Muslim weddings, funerals, the pilgrimage to Mecca, and funding kindergartens, orphanages, sports clubs, and libraries (Shadid, 2005, pp.185,186).

Role of the State in Conservative Thought

The role of the state in Western conservative thought is primarily for security and the protection of property and the free market. Western conservatives, therefore, emphasize a strong military and favor other coercive measures, such as police, to ensure order, the security of property, and the efficient operation of the free market. The state is also expected to protect and support the important societal institutions of Church and family. For example, religious conservatives in the United States call for American laws to be based on biblical laws and for government-funded school voucher systems to support parochial schools.

It is these latter functions (state support of religion and family) where Islamism is consistent with Western conservatism. Islamists argue that the state must be subordinate to Islam and Islamic law, but the state must also enforce Islamic law. In Saudi Arabia, for example, there are official religious police that arrest individuals for activities that they view as inconsistent with the sharia. Where the state does not support sharia to the satisfaction of the Islamists (as in Iraq at present), religious vigilant groups or militias form to roam the streets for the purpose of enforcing sharia and destroying anything and any activity that they view as un-Islamic (Bradley, 2005, pp.76–77). The role of the clergy (known as ulama) in the traditional Islamic model, however, is not to rule, but to ensure that the state conforms to Islamic law or sharia. In this model, the ulama neither make the laws nor enforce them, but exercise veto power over the state if it strays from sharia. In fact, with the exception of Iran, no clergy served as heads of state in Islamic countries until the ascension of the Taliban to power in Afghanistan in the 1990s (Roy, 1994, pp.29–30). It must be noted, however, that there technically are no clergy in Islam (although scholars frequently refer to Islamic religious leaders as such), but instead, what are referred to in the West as "clergy" in Islam are actually a body of learned men, or "doctors of the law," known as the *ulama*, who reside in the *madrassas* (theological schools) in the Islamic world. The term *ulama* is used to designate those that are officially acknowledged (by diploma) as scholars of the Koran (the sacred text of Islam), the Hadith (the traditions of the Prophet), and the full body of Islamic common law jurisprudence (Kepel, 2003, p.47).

The ulama perform various roles, including their functions as interpreters, teachers, and keepers of Islamic law, but also serve the roles of judges and imams (prayer leaders) in the Mosques. The ulama differ from mullahs, in that mullahs typically have no higher religious preparation, but serve as imams in their local mosques either due to family lineage or their ability to memorize larger segments of the Koran better than others at the same mosque, though in some Islamic countries, the mullahs are chosen by a mufti or shaykh designated by the state. In any case, the primary responsibility of the ulama is to ensure the adherence to sharia or Islamic law (Roy, 1994, pp.28–29). It must be noted, however, that Muslim societies throughout history have been sociologically diverse and there has been a broad range of opinion among Islamic scholars as to the correct political and social implications of Islam and the Koran (Roy, 1994, vii).

In general, the state in the Islamist ideology is merely a component of the "Nation of Islam," which is both a political and religious community based on the model of Mohammed, who was the sole interpreter of divine will and the divine law that governed all human activities. The concept of the "state" in radical Islam is not conceptualized as a territorialized nation-state, but instead consists of the entire community of the faithful (the umma), wherever they exist in the world (Roy, 1994, p.13). For Islamists, the goal is to create a global Islamic society that is Islamic in its foundation, structure, and organizing principles, not just a society composed of Muslims. Everything that is not Islamic must be eliminated (Roy, 1994, p.36).

Islamists envision a society that is headed by a strong leader or "amir" and an Islamic advisory council (shura). The amir serves as both the political and religious leader of the community and would rise to the position of amir according to God's will, and the will of God that he serve as amir would be recognizable to all. The amir would be a pious man of God and a model of behavior that would also have the right of Koranic interpretation (Roy, 1994, pp.42–43). The role of the council or shura would be to advise the amir in the name of Islamic principles (Sivan, 1985, pp.73–74). In any case, the Koran is viewed by Islamists as the ultimate constitution and authority in all matters and the amir and the council are subject to the Koran (Esposito, 1983, p.248).

The Islamists' paradigm is one based on the example of Mohammed of the divinely inspired charismatic leader that unites the world under Islam. This is the model for revolutionary Iran as well as other radical Islamic movements, including the Taliban, al-Qaeda, and the radical Islamic government of the Sudan. The notion of segmentation of the community into ethnicities, tribes, political parties, etc., is rejected by Islamists as an affront to Islamic unity and a violation of God's will to unite all humans under Islam. Islamists view unity, or the concept of "divine oneness," as the very foundation of Islam, and argue that society must be a reflection of that divine oneness; hence, any form of societal division or segmentation is an affront to Islam under the sovereignty of God (Roy, 1994, pp.40–41). Consequently, the Western concepts of democracy and elections are inconsistent with the unity of the umma (body of believers) and therefore viewed by Islamists as inconsistent with Islam (Roy, 1994, p.43). Furthermore, since Islamists view sovereignty as belonging only to God, the notion of "popular sovereignty" is viewed as un-Islamic (Esposito, 1983, p.243). In the words of Kramer (1993, p.38),

> The sharia, as a perfect law, cannot be abrogated or altered, and certainly not by the shifting moods of an electorate. Accordingly, every major fundamentalist thinker has repudiated popular sovereignty as a rebellion against God, the sole legislator. In the changed circumstances of the 1990s, some activists do allow that an election can serve a useful one-time purpose, as a collective referendum of allegiance to Islam, and as an act of submission to a regime of divine justice. But once such a regime gains power, its true measure is not how effectively it implements the will of the people but how efficiently it applies Islamic law.

Given that Islamists view sharia as "perfect law" that "cannot be abrogated or altered," they also have a different view of human rights than those espoused by the West. In short, Islamists argue that where individual freedoms and sharia are in conflict, the rights of the individual must give way to what Islamist view as the will of God. In the words of Ann Elizabeth Mayer (1991, p.91), who compared the views of Islamists with Western views of human rights,

> the sharia criteria that are employed to restrict rights are left so uncertain and general that they afford no means for protecting the individual against deprivations of the rights that are guaranteed by international law. Thereby the stage is set not just for the diminution of these rights but potentially for denying them altogether.

Nowhere are individual freedoms more absent in the Islamist conception than in the area of freedom of religion. According to Bernard Lewis (1988, p.85), Islamists consider Muslims who abandon the faith to be traitors and apostates and therefore worthy of death. Although there are Western parallels with the Islamists in that there are Christian fundamentalists who espouse basing civil and criminal law on "God's Law" as outlined in the Bible, there are simply no Western democracies that still execute people for religious heresy in the twenty-first century, and there is no serious mainstream discussion of replac-

ing Western civil and criminal codes with the ancient laws of Leviticus. In the final analysis, one can only conclude that Islamists not only
reject the democratic principle of the sovereignty of the people in a
way that Western societies do not, but they also reject the notion of
the rights of the people, specifically freedom of thought and religion,
all central to Western conceptions of freedom and democracy, to
measures that are extreme in comparison with their Western fundamentalist counterparts.

The problem of Muslim unity, however, creates problems for
Islamists, who themselves often create disunity with their extremist
positions while theoretically striving for Islamic unity, and go so far as
to create political parties while opposing the very concept of political
parties under the premise that they cause disunity of the umma. For
example, a slogan of Iranian Hezbollah (literally, Party of God), is that
"there is no other party than the Party of God"; consequently, Hezbollah attacked the headquarters of other political parties in Iran during
the Iranian Revolution. Similarly, Hassan al-Banna, the leader of the
Egyptian Muslim Brotherhood (that eventually morphed into outright
political parties in the Islamic world), called on King Farouk of Egypt
to dissolve political parties (Esposito, 1983, p.248).

A major source of state power in the Islamic model is in the fact
that the umma or Islamic community are obligated to obey the state
as long as it is subservient to the ulama, institutes sharia, and defends
the Nation of Islam against its enemies. Early versions of this Islamic
tradition are offered by Ibn Shurhabil al-Shabi al-Kufi in the eighth
century, who argued that the umma should "obey the caliph even if he
is a black slave." Similarly, Ibn Hanbal, a founder of a strict school of
Islamic law, argued in the ninth century that, "You should obey the
government and not rebel against it. ... Do not support strife, neither
by hand nor by your tongue" (Quoted in Sivan, 1985, p.91). Because
the state defends Islam and implements God's will, the state is given
the right to coin money and have Friday prayers said in its name (Roy,
1994, pp.14–15).

In any case, there simply is no model in the Islamists' conception
where the state could be completely separate from religion; consequently, Islamists view the separation of state and religion imposed by
Kemal Ataturk in Turkey as an abomination. Instead, Islamists typically agree with the arguments of Ibn Taymiyya, a thirteenth-century
Muslim theologian, who argued for obedience to the state as long as
the state would consult with the ulama to ensure that it remained consistent with Islamic law (Benjamin and Simon, 2002, p.48). In severe
cases of state neglect of sharia, however, Islamists call for revolt
against the state itself. Hassan al Banna, the founder of the Muslim
Brotherhood, for instance, argued that if the government should be-

come so alien as to transcend the sharia, then the individual has the right and obligation to revolt (Quoted in Esposito, 1983, p.249). In doing so, Islamists deviate from the traditional Islamic model by intervening directly in politics so as to seize control of the state, as in Iran and Afghanistan, for the purpose of enforcing the sharia and imposing a pure Islamic society from above.

The Islamist conception of the unity of Islam and the state has not been realized in practice in the Islamic realm, where an autonomous political space has developed in virtually all areas. In fact, from the very beginning of Islamic history, a separation of the political power between sultans and amirs and the religious power of the caliph developed and was institutionalized. To argue, for instance, that Hosni Mubarak in Egypt, Bashir Assad in Syria, Saddam Hussein in Iraq, or Moammar Qadafi in Libya are truly subservient to the ulama (Islamic clergy) is such a stretch of reality as to border on absurd. It is this fact of an autonomous political space that Islamists denounce and reject. To Islamists, the role of the state is to defend Islam and the sharia. Otherwise, the power of the sovereign is to intervene only in what lies outside the domain of the sharia, which essentially is very little, and certainly nothing essential (Roy, 1994, p.14). Since numerous Islamic leaders clearly fail to fully implement sharia and operate outside of their sphere designated by Islam, Islamists protest state violations of sharia and the violations of Islamic unity that are produced through state-centered nationalism (Roy, 1994, p.20).

In the Islamist model of religion and state, subservience of the state to Islam is expected to end the corruption, selfishness, and dishonesty of politics by subordinating the state to the ulama, and, therefore, to the will of God. Iran has attempted to conform to this model since the Islamic Revolution of 1978, and even though the Iranian system includes democratically elected politicians, they are limited to legislation that is consistent with Islam in the eyes of the ulama. Similarly, Ayatollah Sistani, the highest ranking Shiite cleric in Iraq, has, since the fall of Saddam Hussein, consistently called for a democratically elected government in Iraq, with the caveat that a democratically elected government would look to the Islamic clergy (him) for guidance. In fact, a problem for the Iraqi Governing Council since its inception during the American occupation of Iraq has been the fact that Council members, most of whom are Shiites, view themselves as bound by Ayatollah Sistani's opinions. Consequently, when Sistani opposed President Bush's transition plans for Iraq, all of the Shiites on the Council also opposed Bush's transition plans (Phillips, 2005, pp.178–180).

In spite of the fact that Islam is viewed by Islamists as a "total system," and they argue that no law is needed except the sharia, which is viewed as total and complete, Islam actually provides no practical way of governing. In other words, the Koran does not provide a road map for Islamists who desire to seize political power, exactly how it is that they will be able to, for instance, make the trains run on time, make sure the garbage is collected, and find answers to the problems of sewage disposal.

Diversity of Conservative Ideology

Ideological conservatism in general is an extremely diverse area of political thought, and Islamic conservatism is no exception to this rule. Although some facets of conservatism (as well as some individual conservatives themselves) are more ideological than others, it is certainly a fact that most Islamic conservatives are driven by religious ideology rather than rational analysis, whether it be one coherent ideology or a combination of several. Islamism appears to conform well to the observations of Winston Churchill concerning conservatism when he stated that, "It is stirred on almost all occasions by sentiment and instinct rather than by worldly calculations" (Quoted in Manchester, 1983, p.3). Although Churchill's comments were made concerning Western conservatism, they are most certainly applicable to Islamic conservatism since it is driven by religion and, therefore, based on "sentiment" rather than "worldly calculations." In a similar vein, Clinton Rossiter argues that the American conservative "feels more deeply than he thinks about political principles, and what he feels most deeply about them is that they are a gift of great old men" (Rossiter, 1982, p.74). The same could be said for Islamists, but in addition to the "gifts of great old men," Islamist ideology is also viewed by its adherents as a gift from God, and therefore unassailable. Nevertheless, the fact that virtually anyone with inspiration is allowed to interpret the Koran means that one should expect tremendous disagreement and variety within Islam, and Islamism is merely one of those varieties, although it appears to be perhaps the most extreme and dangerous variety at present.

Traditional Conservatism

The Islamist ideology prevalent in Islamic societies is not just Islamic conservatism, but the Islamic form of the ideology known in a generic sense in the West as traditional conservatism. Consequently, there are numerous distinct parallels between the traditional conservatives of Islamic Societies and those in the West, in general, but in particular, in the United States since the United States is the most religious of the world's advanced industrialized democracies. Traditional conservatism in American history emerged out of the religious foundations established by the Pilgrims and Puritans of the seventeenth century and has continued as an ideological force in American politics through the Christian Coalition and other social conservatives of the present. Similarly, the traditional conservative Islamist ideology of Islamic societies has emerged from its religious foundations from the seventh century under Mohammed and continues through the Islamic traditional conservative groups of the present, including the Muslim Brotherhood, Iranian Hezbollah, Taliban, and al-Qaeda. The ideology of traditional conservatism as it exists in the West, and the United States in particular, will be explained below and the Islamic parallels will be noted.

Negative View of Human Nature

Traditional conservatives tend to espouse the "realist" negative view of human nature and a low view of the average person's intelligence. In other words, traditional conservatives tend to view humans as naturally bad, uncooperative, untrustworthy, and, in some instances, just plain stupid. As a consequence, traditional conservatives tend to view government and politics (both permeated with those corrupt and dull-minded people) with great skepticism (Schumaker et al., 1996, p.90). After all, if people are naturally bad, they can therefore be expected to be extra bad when they are entrusted with political power.

The popular quote from Lord Acton that "power corrupts, but absolute power corrupts absolutely" is consistent with traditional conservative ideology.

In the Islamic realm, this negative view of human nature is reflected in the Islamists' call for state submission to the interpretation of God's law (sharia) from the ulama and the enforcement of the sharia by the state, so as to ensure that all Muslims are on the correct path. Implicit in this call is the assumption that people will deviate from the straight path if not coerced. Islamism also reflects Lord Acton and traditional conservatism in the denunciation of current political regimes as "apostates" and un-Islamic, for straying from what the Islamists view as pure Islamic principles established by God. In other words, the Islamists view those that are currently in power as "corrupt absolutely" (Sivan, 1985, pp.4–5).

Society Is in Decay

Traditional conservatives view the current society as in decay, depraved, and decadent. The government within that society in the here and now is equally flawed, but the government and society of the past are viewed as virtuous and glorious. As such, traditional conservatives in the United States have disdain for current politicians such as former President Bill Clinton, whom they view as a corrupt product of the current flawed society, but reverence for the politicians of the past, such as George Washington, Abraham Lincoln, and Thomas Jefferson (Hoover, 1994, pp.47–51). Traditional conservatives also condemn what they view as the corrupting influences of pop culture. Consistent with their Western counterparts, traditional conservatives of the Islamic realm denounce "apostate" governments of the Islamic realm for their failure to implement God's laws, and condemn Western television, music, dress, and the Internet (as well as a host of other Western influences and technologies) for replacing God with lust and carnality (Sivan, 1985, pp.4–5).

Intolerance and Demonization of Enemies

The adherence to moral absolutes also creates intolerance among traditional conservatives against those that think differently and leads to demonization of the enemies of traditional conservatism. Those that think differently are considered not only as political opponents, but as "evil" individuals that may be exterminated. This is perhaps especially true when religion is mixed with political ideology as in Islamism. In the words of Robert Pape,

> Religious difference can enable extreme demonization—the belief that the enemy is morally inferior as well as militarily dangerous, and so must be dealt with harshly. To most people brought up in any religion, the dogmas and practices of any other religion will seem strange, perhaps inexplicable or pointless, and possibly immoral. (2005, p.90)

The very meaning of the word "heresy," for which the Catholic Church executed, tortured, and brutalized thousands for centuries, is "to think differently." Traditional conservatives that kill others in the twenty-first century because the others "think differently" include Osama bin Laden and the Islamic extremists that carried out the 9/11 attacks on the United States. Osama bin Laden and other Islamists have been so successfully able to portray America as an evil infidel that suicide terrorists can believe that God will be happy with his "martyrs" for flying airplanes into buildings and killing thousands of innocent people.

A closer look at traditional conservatives in the United States, however, reveals some striking similarities. For example, American Evangelist Pat Robertson called for the assassination of Venezuelan President Hugo Chavez on his Christian television program. Another group, known as the Westboro Baptist Church in Topeka, Kansas has an antihomosexual Web site (www.godhatesfags.com/) and denounces homosexuals not only as "workers of iniquity" and "abominable," but also includes a memorial celebration of the number of days that Matthew Shepard (a gay man murdered by exposure in Wyoming) "has been in hell." In such a mindset there is only good and evil, white and black, with us or against us, and no "grey areas" or anything in between. Osama bin Laden and the Taliban are obviously fabulous examples of this ideology, but then so is the Westboro Baptist Church in Topeka, Kansas.

The views of the Westboro Baptist Church, however, are not unique in American society. For example, in a letter to the editor of the *Amarillo Globe News* on June 28, 2004 (p.8a), a West Texas traditional conservative citizen complained that Senator "Teddy" Kennedy should be executed for treason for his statement that "Abu Ghraib prison is still open, all that has changed is the management." Furthermore, the writer went on to argue that the Iraqi people are a "bunch of animals" and that the torture at Abu Ghraib prison was therefore fitting punishment for them. Obviously, the political enemies according to this traditional conservative are so dehumanized that they are not only considered to be "animals," but worse than animals since they should be tortured and executed. When the enemy is thus dehumanized, torture and killing are prescribed with little violation of conscience. The parallels from Islamists with such thinking, such as Osama bin

Laden's famous fatwa urging Muslims to "kill any American, any-where" are legion.

On the subject of the extreme forms of religious traditional conservatism that produce religious terror, Bruce Hoffman (1995) argues that religious terrorists are different than other types of terrorists because they are not constrained by the same factors that inhibit other types. Hoffman argues that religious terrorists (Islamists included) view their world as a battlefield between the forces of light and darkness, and winning is not described in terms of political gains. Instead, the enemy must be totally destroyed. Hoffman argues that religious terrorists see killing as a sacramental act and the purpose of their operation is to kill the enemies of God, and in so doing please God. In doing so, religious terrorists necessarily demonize their enemies, thus making murder much easier because the enemies are no longer people, but are instead equated with the ultimate source of evil. Enemies are devilish and demonic and in league with the forces of darkness. Consequently, it is not enough to simply defeat them. Instead, they must be completely eradicated. Similarly, Chip Berlet (1998) argues that the demonized enemy becomes a scapegoat for all problems and it becomes possible for the group to believe that all evil is the result of some sort of conspiracy involving their scapegoat and the evil entity. Hence, Islamists demonize Israel and the United States and blame both for all of the calamities that afflict the Islamic world. The Ayatollah Khomeini, therefore, categorized the United States not only as a political enemy of Iran, but as "the Great Satan." Similarly, American traditional conservative Jerry Falwell blamed the devastation of the city of New Orleans by Hurricane Katrina in 2005 on homosexuality in the United States.

Low Social Trust

The negative view of human nature espoused by traditional conservatives translates into low social trust. As a consequence, traditional conservatives tend to favor rule through coercion and advanced security measures by means of a strong military, a strong police force, and an emphasis on personal self-defense. For traditional conservatives, a strong military is necessary because foreign entities cannot be trusted not to attack. A strong internal police force is also needed because the "naturally bad" humans cannot be trusted and otherwise will not behave. Measures for personal defense, such as the right to bear arms, are required for the same reasons (Hoover, 1994, pp.60–61).

In traditional conservatism, policies for dealing with crime are slanted heavily toward retribution and punishment, with incarceration and corporal and capital punishment favored over rehabilitation programs. Essentially, since humans are naturally bad, the only thing they might understand is pain (Territo et al., 1989, pp.387–388). The traditional conservative view on punishment is reflected in numerous passages in both the Koran and the Bible. In the words of Mohammed in the Koran (5:38), "And the man who steals and the woman who steals, cut off their hands as a punishment for what they have earned." Similarly, Moses writes in Exodus 21:23–24,

> If there is serious injury, you are to take life for life, eye for eye, tooth for tooth, hand for hand, foot for foot, burn for burn, wound for wound, bruise for bruise.

Again, the parallels between Islamists and their Western counterparts are many. Much as Mosaic law prescribed "eye for eye and tooth for tooth," based on the prescriptions from the Koran, the Islamist societies, such as that of Saudi Arabia and the Taliban in Afghanistan in the 1990s, have imposed brutal corporal and capital punishments, including executions, stonings, amputations, and religious police.

Reverence for Symbols, Institutions, History

In spite of the negative view of human nature and the disdain for government and politics of the present, traditional conservatives have an extreme reverence for symbols, institutions, and history, both religious and patriotic (Dunn and Woodard, 1991, pp.31, 48). Traditional conservatives in the United States generally view the United States as the greatest country in the history of mankind, the American form of government as the greatest ever invented (if not handed to the founding fathers directly from God himself), and those that criticize the American form of government are, in some cases, viewed not just as critics, but as traitorous abominations before God that should be shipped out of the country. Furthermore, the great American figures of history, such as Lincoln, Washington, Jefferson, and Franklin are viewed as endowed with brilliance, leadership, wisdom, integrity, and virtue that simply cannot be matched in the present time. Historical figures are placed on a pedestal and the "revisionist" historians that would write such things as the accusation that Jefferson slept with his slaves or that George Washington is not generally regarded as a great military strategist, are not only wrong (the DNA evidence on Jefferson and Sally Hemings being invented by those liberal scientists), but are also just plain evil people who should be silenced. Furthermore, the mere suggestion to the traditional conservatives that the First Amendment protects burning the American flag as an exercise of free speech is absolutely preposterous. For the traditional conservative in the United States, America could never be wrong, and those who might say otherwise are not true Americans.

Similarly, Islamists view the Islamic past as glorious and hearken back to the inspiration of the seventh century of Mohammed and the four caliphs that followed. As explained in a booklet by the Cairo Muslim Students' Association entitled, *Contemporary Reflections on Our Heritage*, Islamists argue that (Quoted in Sivan, 1985, pp.69–70)

> Any renaissance begins by going back to the heritage, any thought capable of change proceeds from a contemporary reading of the past. Any rejection of the status quo is inspired by a feeling that the present is unworthy of the past of our umma (body of believers), and by a belief that our community is capable of building a future worthy of her glorious past. ... We turn to the heritage not in order to bring back the past, for the past cannot be resuscitated, but rather to seek inspiration in its ever-living values, its eternal ideals.

The Islamist view of history, like that of their traditional conservative counterparts in the West, however, is seriously lacking in objectivity. In the Islamists' view of history, Islamic history takes on the character of a mythical epic, and the heroes involved in the epic take on a status akin to angels and superhuman beings rather than mere mortals. As a consequence, Islamists are unable to draw rational lessons from a history that is awe inspiring, but lacks any semblance of objectivity, and therefore are hindered in rational analysis of the present (Sivan, 1985, pp.71–72).

Return to a Better, Vanished Time

A major goal of the traditional conservatives in Western societies is to return society to a mythical, better, vanished time (Eatwell, 1989, p.69). To clarify, the "mythical, better, vanished time," is not mythical in the mind of the traditional conservative. To the traditional conservative, there was indeed once a time of virtue, but today's society has strayed from the original founding principles and what is needed is a return to those original principles and virtues. As a consequence, traditional conservatives in the United States can be expected to frequently call for a return to "what the founding fathers intended." In religion, traditional conservatives tend to hearken back to the original principles supposedly in place when the religion was founded (Dunn and Woodard, 1991, p.77). For traditional conservatives in fundamentalist Protestantism, for instance, this tends to mean a return to "The Bible" or the principles of the "First Century Church." For Islamists, such as the Taliban and Osama bin Laden, the call is for a return to the Koran and the original texts and the practices of Mohammed and the four orthodox caliphs in the seventh and eighth centuries (Sivan,

1985, p.70 Roy, 1994, p.31,). Even the call for jihad or Holy War is justified by a hearkening back to the historical example of Mohammed's
conquest of Mecca and caliph Abu Bakr's wars against the apostate
tribes of the Arabian Peninsula from 632–634 AD (Sivan, 1985, p.115).

Rule by the "Good People"

In order to return society to that "better, vanished time," traditional
conservatives believe that a "good government" resembling that of the
past can be reconstructed, as long as it is directed by "good people"
with the correct set of values and correct ideology. In the traditional
conservative mindset, there are indeed "those who know best," and it
is those people who must be put in place to rule (Hoover, 1994, p.49).
For the traditional conservative Christians of the Middle Ages, this
meant rule by the Pope and the Catholic Church. For the traditional
conservatives of the United States in the last several decades, this
means that "good Christian leaders" should be elected. For the traditional conservatives of Islamism, this means rule by the ulama. In the
words of noted Islamist Abdul Ala Maudoudi (Quoted in Roy, 1994,
p.62), leaders should be, "such whose sincerity, ability and loyalty are
above reproach in the eyes of the public." Similarly, Hasan al-Turabi
(Quoted in Roy, 1994, p.62) states that, "the prevailing criteria of political merit for the purposes of candidature for any political office
center on moral integrity." Islamists, however, typically do not trust
the ulama of the here and now and often view them as lackeys of the
apostate governments that they are intent on overthrowing; consequently, they argue that not just any jurist should rule, but one that is
"truly knowledgeable," meaning an Islamist (Sivan, 1985, p.69).

Purpose of Government

The purpose of government in traditional conservatism is to keep order and correct human weaknesses (Schumaker et al., 1996, pp.86,
93). For example, traditional conservatives in the United States in the
last several decades pushed for laws to end abortions and favored laws
against sodomy, pornography, prostitution, alcohol, gay marriage,
and other human "weaknesses." For justification, American traditional conservatives point to Old Testament laws in the Bible that call
for executions of those who curse their parents, commit adultery, sodomy, or have sex with animals (Leviticus 20:9–15). Similarly, traditional conservative Islamists call for the institution of Islamic law or
sharia so as to implement God's will and prevent immoral human be-

havior. In the words of Olivier Roy (1994, p. 63), the role of governmental institutions in Islamic society are,

> that of providing a permanent constraint that, on the one hand, removes
> any opportunities for sin and, on the other hand, establishes a system of
> punishment that aims to reestablish the purity of the community to elimi-
> nate sin.

Consequently, under the sharia, much like the Old Testament book of
Leviticus, families may execute other family members that have "dis-
honored" the family (in this case by becoming pregnant out of wedlock), and the sharia calls for execution of prostitutes and
homosexuals. In such a society (whether Muslim or Christian) the
state is less a mediator between individuals and more an enforcer of
God's higher moral laws. In so doing, humans mirror God's kingdom
on earth, much as the Puritans of the seventeenth century attempted
to construct God's "City on a Hill."

Moral Absolutism

The use of government to "correct human weaknesses" by traditional
conservatives is tied to their views of moral absolutes. To traditional
conservatives, there most definitely *are* moral absolutes and they can
most definitely and definitively identify and define those moral absolutes (Hoover, 1994, p.50). As a consequence, it is irresponsible to allow people the freedom to do things that are morally wrong and
therefore harmful to society. Hence, freedoms, including academic
freedoms, are limited to these "basic truths" or moral absolutes (Nash
et al., 1979, p.40).

Generally, traditional conservatives have a source for their moral
absolutes, and that source is very likely to be a religious book. In the
Middle East, the vast majority of the people are Muslims; hence, the
primary source of moral absolutes for most traditional conservatives
in that region is the Koran. In the United States, the religion of the
majority is Christianity; hence, the primary source of moral absolutes
for most American traditional conservatives is the Bible. In either
case, traditional conservatives call for governmental enforcement of
the moral absolutes found in their Holy books; hence, Osama bin
Laden and other Islamists call for governments to adopt sharia, the
Islamic religious laws, and make those Islamic laws into governmental
civil laws as well. Similarly, traditional conservatives in the United
States push for the incorporation of "Bible truths" (such as antisod-
omy laws and laws against abortions and gay marriage) into the laws
of the United States and call for federal enforcement.

Reinforce Societal Building Blocks

Furthering their goal to create a good and moral society, traditional conservatives argue that government should reinforce the main societal building blocks of church and family (Freeden, 2003, p.88). In Iran, Sudan, and Afghanistan under the Taliban, what this came to mean in practice was theocracy or rule by religious leaders. In Saudi Arabia, the government has provided millions of dollars for the construction of mosques and madrassas, many of which have been constructed by the bin Laden family. In the United States, President George W. Bush has pushed for "faith-based initiatives" or the provision of government goods and services through religious institutions. Traditional conservatives in the United States have also fought to eliminate the "marriage penalty tax" and some American States have developed new, more stringent marriage laws that eliminate "incompatibility" as a "cause" for divorce (Loconte, 1998, pp.30-34). Recent referendums in numerous states purposed to ban gay marriage are also examples of the traditional conservative impulse to defend the societal "building block" of the traditional marriage between one man and one woman.

Opposition to Social Change

In general, the adherence to moral absolutes tends to create a resistance to social change among traditional conservatives (Freeden, 2003, p.88). In the West, this has meant resistance to a plethora of societal changes including the end of segregation, women's liberation, abortion rights, gay marriage, and even resistance to the end of slavery in the nineteenth century. This pattern of resistance to social change is not unique to Western traditional conservatives, however, but also has been prevalent among Islamists. In the words of Roy, (1994, p.20), "The Islamic political imagination has endeavored to ignore or disqualify anything new." In Islamic societies, traditional conservatives currently oppose equality of the sexes, Western dress, Western music, Western movies, and other "abominations" such as women without veils and men with clean-shaven faces. In short, traditional conservatives can be expected to resist most social changes unless those changes (such as those imposed by the Taliban) are a return to a discarded dogma of the past. Hence, Islamism is a reactionary ideology and the rise of Islamism should be viewed in part as a reaction to Western globalization, but also as a reaction to the failure of the political movements of the previous generation in the Islamic world, Pan-Arabism and Socialism, that led only to corrupt military-authoritarian dictatorships and the continuation of rule by authoritarian families (Sayyid, 2003, p.19).

One of the unintended consequences of the stifling authoritarianism in the Islamic realm in places such as Iran under the Shah or Iraq under Saddam Hussein during the twentieth century was that the mosque emerged as one of the few places where people could voice political discontent that was not monopolized by the state. Given that political participation and political dissent were generally forbidden in the Islamic world, the mosques became politicized, but the politicization of the mosques has also meant that Islamism has become the most important voice of political dissent in the Islamic political world (Ajami, 1981, p.171).

Withdrawal and Revolt

Traditional conservatives in Western societies have often viewed society as so corrupt that the "good people" must withdraw from it. For example, the separatists that became known in American history as the "Pilgrims" that arrived at Plymouth on the Mayflower fit this model. Essentially, the "Pilgrims" viewed the Anglican Church and English society as so corrupt that they were forced to withdraw from it. The Mormons of the nineteenth century and the Branch Davidians of David Koresh in the 1990s similarly withdrew from society at large to form their separate societies of true believers.

For Islamists, withdrawal from a decadent society is viewed as an act of "hijra" (migration), patterned after Mohammed's withdrawal from Mecca to Medina in 622 AD. In the twenty-first century, Islamists often follow Mohammed's example and withdraw to isolated enclaves, whether they be caves in Afghanistan or Islamist enclaves within urban societies. Islamists boycott Western media and other influences that they view as corrupting true Islam and often desert the army or leave jobs, so as to avoid serving the decadent powers that prevail in society. Noted Egyptian radical Islamist Sayyid Qutb of the Egyptian Muslim Brotherhood of the 1960s, for instance, envisioned the formation of cult-like Islamist counter societies of small, self-contained groups of Islamists that would interact only with each other while living within the larger society (Sivan, 1985, pp.86–87).

Plot Mentality

The "plot mentality" is the ultimate result in the traditional conservative mindset where the traditional conservatives view the world as a cosmic struggle between the forces of good and evil (Eatwell, 1989, p.71). In this construct, the "evil" forces are always "plotting" to destroy society. The McCarthy hearings and investigations of the 1950s fit this type of traditional conservative behavior. "Liberals" in the United States argue that the Whitewater investigation of Bill Clinton by Kenneth Starr was a similar "witch-hunt" conforming to the conservative "plot mentality" pattern as well. Perhaps George W. Bush's obsession with Saddam Hussein and the other individuals in the famous "deck of cards" should be similarly categorized. In Bush's arguments for invasion, Saddam Hussein was not portrayed merely as a poor leader or a threat, but as an "evil" person (part of an "axis of evil" between Iraq, Iran, and North Korea) plotting to destroy the American way of life with Weapons of Mass Destruction (WMDs). For Saddam Hussein's now known to be fictitious WMDs to be a threat, one had to assume not only that Saddam was attempting to build them, but that he was also "evil" enough to use them against the United States for the express purpose of killing thousands of innocent Americans without provocation, and was secretly plotting to do so.

This "plot mentality," however, is not limited only to George W. Bush or the American side of the "War on Terror." In the case of Islamic terrorism, the "plot mentality" is a major driving force behind the actions of many of the terrorists. According to Berlet (1998), Islamists tend to blame all of the world's problems on a conspiracy between the United States and Zionists in Israel. In this conception, the United States is not merely trying to eliminate terrorism or terrorists, but is instead determined to stamp out Islam itself. In the words of Roy (1994),

> The worst legacy of the West was no doubt to offer the Muslim people a ready-to-wear devil: conspiracy theory is currently paralyzing Muslim political thought. For to say that every failure is the devil's work is the same as asking God, or the devil himself (which is to say, these days, the Americans), to solve one's problems. Between the miracle that doesn't happen and the pact in which one loses one's soul, there is plenty of room for discontent. (p.19)

As a consequence, religious terrorists are not necessarily seeking a "wider audience," as are other terrorists, but their primary purpose is the defense of and God's righteous religion against evil and ungodly entities; hence, their play is for God and God alone.

Apocalyptic Thinking

Indiscriminate killing by intolerant and demonizing religious traditional conservatives is aided by apocalyptic thinking (Eatwell, 1989,

p.71). In the Koran, for example, Mohammed speaks of a final judgment against evil, and a similar story is found in the Bible book of
Revelation. In this conception, the Islamic terrorists are merely "soldiers of God" aiding him in his judgment, as are the bombers of abortion clinics in the United States. All deterrents to violence are
rendered meaningless by the promise of a new age that invites terrorists to fight as holy warriors in a period of fanatic zeal, when the deity
is about to bring creation to an end. What difference does it make if a
mess is made of this world if it is going to end tomorrow anyway? Furthermore, since God rewards the faithful, if innocent people are killed
this morning, surely the dead will be in a better place in heaven this
afternoon, so what is wrong with that? Finally, if "evil" people are
killed, then this world is a better place without those evil people and
the sooner that God can be aided in casting them all into hell, the better.

Concluding Remarks

Obviously, the problems and contradictions within traditional conservatism are legion and therefore the policy prescriptions that can be
expected to arise from this ideology, whether Western or Islamist, can
be expected to be fraught with problems and contradictions as well.
After all, this is the group in American politics that believes that
witchcraft is real (hence the boycotts of Harry Potter) is seriously concerned about the sexual orientation of Tinky Winky, a fictional puppet
character on a television show for small children, and spent the 1970s
spinning rock and roll records backwards in a fruitless search for re-
versed satanic messages. The concern over gay teletubbies (Tinky
Winky), though misplaced, is probably largely benign. The same could
not be said, however, for the case of the "Godly" Pilgrims and Puritans
of the seventeenth century, who not only executed people for witchcraft and butchered the Indians, but also in 1642 put a man to death
for "buggery" after he admitted to copulating with "a mare, a cow, two
goats, five sheep, two calves and a turkey" (Bradford, 1856, 1981,
pp.355-356). Traditional conservatism in American politics should
also be credited with the Red Scare of 1919, the McCarthy witch-hunts
of the 1950s, the opposition to civil rights in the 1960s, the support for
the Vietnam War in the 1970s, the Clinton impeachment, and the invasion of Iraq in 2003.

In the Islamic world, Islamist traditional conservatism is the ideological force behind jihad and Islamic terrorism. The dangers posed to
the world by Islamic traditional conservatism are mostly different
from the Salem witch hunts, in that the Islamists now have access to
modern technology, thus allowing their ideology to be more lethal

than that of the traditional conservatives of Salem Village in 1692. It is this danger posed to the world by ideology that makes the study of ideology, and Islamism in particular, perhaps as important as any other subject in political science.

• CHAPTER THREE •
Islamism

"Islamism" refers to radical, militant, ideological versions of traditional, conservative Islam, where the practitioners typically consider Islamic jihad against infidels to be a primary duty of all Muslims. As a consequence, Islamists have often engaged in violent actions, including kidnapping, summary executions, suicide bombings, and other forms of terrorism. The horrific terrorist attacks of 9/11, the July 2005 bombings of the London transportation system, and many of the suicide attacks on Western coalition troops in Iraq were perpetrated by Islamists under the influence of the ideology of Islamism.

One does not, however, have to engage in terrorism in order to subscribe to the ideology of Islamism. In general, those who should be considered as Islamists are those who place Islam at the core of their political beliefs and practices and use the language of Islam and Islamic metaphors as a framework through which they view reality. Islamists are also those who subscribe to the ideology of Islamism and justify their radical political activities through religious terminology. It should be noted that Islamists, like those that subscribe to other ideologies, such as Marxism, for instance, are not all identical in their beliefs and motives, so the discussion of Islamism below is a discussion of the general tendencies. Selected individuals may violate some of the general tendencies listed below, yet still be considered as Islamists. In the words of S. Sayyid (2003),

> Islamism is a discourse that attempts to center Islam within the political order. Islamism can range from the assertion of a Muslim subjectivity to a full-blooded attempt to reconstruct society on Islamic principles. (p.17)

In other words, there are Islamists who simply believe that Islam should be the basis of politics and society, whereas other Islamists believe that it is necessary to intervene in the affairs of state and seize control of politics in the name of Islam, so that a global Islamic order can be imposed. Other Islamists argue that they must wage a physical war against the enemies of Islam. Islamism also includes, however, the goal of the moral reform of society according to Islamic principles. It does little good to seize control of politics in the name of Islam if the people are to remain infidels resistant to Islam (Sayyid, 2003, p.17).

Islamic Conservative Extremism

Ideologically speaking, Islamism or Islamic extremism equates to the Islamic form of extremist traditional conservative ideology in Islamic societies. The central elements of Western traditional conservatism, that is, the view that humans are depraved and society is in decay, a call to return to a better, vanished time, a premium on tradition, opposition to social change, a focus on moral absolutes, demonization of enemies, and "ends politics," are all present, along with a preference for a blend between church and state and rule by the "good people," in this case identified as the "ulama" (Islamic jurists, interpreters of the Koran, or Islamic clergy). As Olivier Roy (1994, pp.5–6) explains, Islamists have numerous characteristics in common with Western Christian fundamentalists. Perhaps first and foremost, they are obsessed with "conversion," but they also

> have in common the cult of the return to the past, of authenticity and purity; the concern with dress, food, and conviviality; the rebuilding of a "traditional" way of life in a context and by methods that presuppose that the tradition is obsolete; the shift into terrorism for the most radical fringe.

Hasan al-Banna, for instance, the founder of the Radical Islamic group, the Muslim Brotherhood in the 1930s, called for a "return" to the original Koranic texts, to the Islamic civil and criminal code (known as sharia) and to the original inspiration of the first community of believers (Roy, 1994, pp.viii–ix). The better, vanished time that al-Banna and other Islamists desire to return to is the golden age of Mohammed in the seventh century when (in their view) all was right with the world and Muslims conquered the Arabian Peninsula with God's help under Mohammed's leadership. The name al-Qaeda itself means "the base," a specific reference to the group itself as the base from which a new global Islamic society will be constructed in conformity with the pure Islamic society of Mohammed in the seventh century. All things are justified in the pursuit of this "righteous" end, including indiscriminate killing (Gunaratna, 2002, p.3). The consequence of such a religious ideology has been the production of what amounts to a global culture war between Western societies and the Islamists.

Part of the reason for the culture war is that Islamism is spread far and wide across the globe and can be found both outside and within Western countries due to the immigration of Islamists to the West. In spite of such geographic diversity and fragmentation both across the globe and within individual countries, not to mention the lack of any one true leader (although Osama bin Laden may be its greatest symbol), Islamism has proven to be a remarkably consistent ideology with amazingly similar characteristics, trends, and tendencies, regardless of geographic locations.

For Islamists, Islam is the one and only true religion, the religion of the one and only God (Allah), and Mohammed was his final Prophet who was sent by God to set all things straight (Kramer, 1993, p.38). Islamists view Islam as a complete and universal system that provides all of the correct answers for the human existence, whether they are social or economic. In the words of Roy (1994, p.39), "For Islamists, Islam is more than the simple application of the sharia (Islamic Law): it is a synthesizing, totalizing ideology that must first transform society in order that the sharia may be established, almost automatically." "Development" in this model does not necessarily mean economic development, but instead refers to how close society conforms to God's Law, wherein exists (in their view) all of the correct answers for human existence. Islamists believe that when Muslims followed the correct path, as outlined by Mohammed in the seventh century, they were blessed by God with power on earth. This power was manifested in Mohammed's conquest of Mecca and further military conquests of Mohammed's followers after his death. Currently, Islamists argue that Muslims lack political power in the world because they have fallen away from God. If they will merely return to the correct path of Islam, God will again bless Muslims, who will again rise to a position of prominent military and political power in this world (Kramer, 1993, pp.38–39).

The long-term goal of Islamists is to convert the entire world to Islam and create an Islamic political order where all humanity is subject to God's Law. Politics, religion, and all social and educational activities in the Islamist society would be intertwined, and academic inquiry would not question the preeminent place of Islam and the sharia in all societal activities. For example, Khuram Murad (1981, p.3) an Islamist and former head of the world wide Islamic Foundation, as well as adviser to the President of Pakistan, succinctly described the world Islamist movement as,

> an organized struggle to change the existing society into an Islamic society based on the Qur'an and the Sunna, and make Islam, which is a code for entire life, supreme and dominant, especially in the socio-political spheres.

In order for the entire world to be converted to Islam, the enemies of Islam must be eliminated and Muslims must seize control of the world's political machinery so as to construct a truly Islamic state under the sovereignty of God, not men. Islam cannot be simply equal to other faiths or even the dominant religion, but the only religion and the sharia the only law. In the words of Khuram Murad (Quoted in Cox and Marks, 2003),

> Islam isn't in America to be equal to any other faith, but to become dominant. The Qu'ran ... should be the highest authority in America and Islam the only accepted religion on earth. (p.57)

Islamists believe that only under such complete control of politics by Islam can God's will be truly implemented among men. Given that the "end" pursued by Islamists is willed by God, it is a just and moral end that justifies all means, including all manners of political violence. Furthermore, Muslims have no choice but to implement God's will, no matter the costs, due to the just and sacred goals (Kramer, 1993, pp.38–39). Islamists reject, however, that notion that an omnipotent God could convert the entire world to a pure Islamic society on his own. In the words of radical Islamist Said Hawwa (Quoted in Sivan, 1985)

> We should reject the negativist approach, that counsel of despair which says: 'All is lost; we can do nothing. Allah should save his religion.' Such Muslims resign themselves to the fait accompli and forget that Allah helps only those who help themselves. (p.66)

Thus, Islamism is a call to action, and its adherents believe that they have an obligation to take action to eliminate all the corrupting influences on the earth and construct the pure, Godly society as intended by God himself. Islamist Said Hawwa points to Abraham and Moses as examples, arguing that they both resisted the Godless Egyptian Pharaoh, thus proving that revolt against an illegitimate ruler is justified. In fact, Hawwa claims that for pious Muslims to shun political activity in such cases would be "the root of all evil" (Quoted in Sivan, 1985, p.105).

Islam

In order to understand Islamism fully, it is necessary to have an understanding of Islam itself since the ideology of Islamism is derived from the Islamists interpretation of the religion of Islam. In the words of Murad,

> The idea of the Islamic movement is inherent in the very nature of Islam...innumerable Qur'anic verses amply bear it out, like those laying down the concepts and objectives of jihad (Holy War). (1980, p.3).

It must be noted, however, that the Koran is interpreted by Muslims in many different ways. Often, the question of religious authority in the Islamic realm may be more important than the actual words in the religious text since the words themselves are interpreted in such a diverse manner. When the words from the religious texts appear to truly provide impetus to Islamism is when they are placed in the hands of leaders (often religious authorities) that command the obedience of the faithful, and the Holy text can be connected by Islamists to current political and socioeconomic situations (Pape, 2005, p.4).

Islamic Monotheism

Islam, like Christianity and Judaism that came before it, is monotheistic, and the one, all-powerful, rational and ethical God in Islam (Allah) is the God of Abraham of the Bible, the same God worshipped by both Christians and Jews. The name for God in Islam, Allah, is formed by joining the definite article "al," meaning "the" with "lah" (God). Allah, therefore, literally means "the God," rather than "a" god, for Muslims, like Christians and Jews, believe there is only one, Allah. When the masculine plural ending "im" is dropped from the Hebrew word for God "Elohim," the two words, the Hebrew "Eloh" and the Arabic "Allah" sound much the same and they refer to the same entity. Islam, like Christianity and Judaism, teaches that there is a final Day of Judgment as well as eternal reward for the faithful and eternal punishment for the unbelievers (Bickerton and Klausner, 2005, p.9). The word Islam is properly a verbal noun meaning surrendering self to God. The root s-l-m primarily means "peace," but in a secondary sense, "surrender," its full connotation is the peace that comes when one's life is surrendered to God. The Muslim idea that one experiences spiritual peace when one surrenders to God is a theme consistent with both Christianity and Judaism (Smith, 1991, pp.221–222).

The Koran and the Bible

The Koran, the primary Islamic religious text, is neither anti-Jewish nor anti-Christian, and generally accepts the Jewish Old Testament and the Christian Bible as inspired. The Koran supports the Genesis story in its entirety (with the exception of a different interpretation of God's promise to Abraham), and supports both Old and New Testament interpretations of Biblical prophets as true prophets of God. For example, in Cattle VI: 83–90, it is stated that,

> Those who believe, and have not confounded their belief with evildoing-to them belongs the true security; they are rightly guided. That is Our argument, which We bestowed upon Abraham as against his people. We raise up in degrees whom We will; surely they Lord is All-wise, All-knowing. And We gave to him Isaac and Jacob--each one We guided, and Noah We guided

before; and of his seed David and Solomon, Job and Joseph, Moses and Aaron--even so We recompense the good-doers--Zachariah and John, Jesus and Elias; each was of the righteous; Ishmael and Elisha, John and Lot-- each one We preferred above all beings; and of their fathers, and of their seed, and of their brethren; and We elected them, and We guided them to a straight path. That is God's guidance; He guides by it whom He will of His servants; had they been idolaters, it would have failed them, the things they did. Those are they to whom We gave the Book, the Judgment, the Prophethood; so if these disbelieve in it, We have already entrusted it to a people who do not disbelieve in it. Those are they whom God has guided; so follow their guidance. Say: I ask of you no wage for it; it is but a re-minder unto all beings.

In addition to its reverence for Bible prophets (including Jesus of Nazareth, credited with virgin birth in the Koran), the Koran itself does not necessarily declare that Muslims must be at odds with Chris-tians or Jews, instead essentially offering salvation for both if they are willing. For example, in The Table 5:70, it is stated, "We made a cove-nant of old with the Children of Israel and you have nothing of guid-ance until you observe the Torah and the Gospel." This verse essentially validates the Bible and entitles Jews and Christians to be included with Muslims as "People of the Book," meaning the Koran. Similarly, the Koran invites all people in all lands to join the "people of the book" and proclaims that they have all been sent a "messenger" extending the invitation. For example, in Jonah 10:47 it is stated that, "To every people we have sent a messenger.... Some We have men-tioned to you, and some we have not mentioned to you."

Unscientific Islamic Religious Fundamentalism

A central feature of Islamism is that it is a religious fundamentalist ideology. In other words, Islamists believe that the Koran represents the perfect, literal, inerrant word of God and it must be followed to the letter. Religion and politics must be intertwined, because God's law and human law must be the same, otherwise humans violate the per-fect laws revealed to them by God. Consequently, one cannot abandon ancient practices of beheadings, amputations, etc., because they are prescribed by God and cannot be changed. To argue against such practices is to argue against God; consequently, Islamists tend to be uncompromising and inflexible on the political positions and pre-scriptions. Women, therefore, must wear veils because God has so de-creed, and women must be subordinate to men for the same reasons. Like other religious fundamentalists, Islamists also reject pluralism, because the acceptance of pluralism means the division of the body of believers and acceptance of positions that are contrary to the will of God.

Religion by nature is unscientific since it deals with supernatural phenomena instead of the natural, which is the realm of science. Islam is no exception, but even more antithetical to science in 2005 than most sects of Christianity. Islamists, like fundamentalist Christians, accept the Bible book of Genesis and its creation story as literal in spite of any scientific evidence to the contrary. As explained by Islamist Pasha Mohamed Ali Taeharah (2005),

> Our introduction to Islamism must consider the beginning or the genesis of mankind in order to be worth the paper upon which it is written. We believe that any explanation that was written in communication with the Allah is a valid explanation even if the explanation doesn't meet the acid-test of present-day scientific analysis. Such credibility is applicable to sacred writings of the messengers of Allah (p.35)

Consequently, Ali Taeharah (2005, pp.35–36) explains that Islamists reject the big bang theory and evolution as un-Islamic, since neither are mentioned in the book of Genesis. In this conception, when scientific knowledge conflicts with the word of God, it must be rejected out of hand without question.

Meanwhile, the idea that the Koran could be fallible or in some way contradictory is foreign to Islam in general and to Islamists in particular. The Koran is viewed as timeless, ahistorical, and beyond criticism. Any suggestion that the Koran might not be divine, or might contain errors and contradictory passages, is rejected without analysis. In the words of Wansbrough (1977, p.ix), "As a document susceptible to analysis by the instruments and techniques of Biblical criticism, it is virtually unknown." Similarly, Rippin (1991) concludes,

> I have often encountered individuals who come to the study of Islam with a background in the historical study of the Hebrew Bible or early Christianity, and who express surprise at the lack of critical thought that appears in introductory textbooks on Islam. ... To students acquainted with approaches such as source criticism, oral formulae composition, literary analysis and structuralism, all quite commonly employed in the study of Judaism and Christianity, such naïve historical study seems to suggest that Islam is being approached with less than academic candour. (p.ix)

Rippin can hardly be accused of overstating his case. In the world of Islam in general, but among Islamists in particular, the questions "What is the evidence?" or "Are their witnesses to the Muslim accounts of the sayings and works of Mohammed from non-Muslim sources that corroborate or validate the Islamic writings?" or "How do we know that the Koran was compiled into its written form shortly after the death of Mohammed?" are simply absent from Islamic scholarship. That Western scholars such as Rippin (1998, p.354) have concluded that there are no non-Islamic sources testifying to the existence of the Koran until the eighth century (a full century after the death of Mohammed, when the Koran was written according to Islamic traditions) and that the full text may not have been fixed until the early ninth century, thus suggesting that much in the Koran may not be attributable to Mohammed at all, a fact that is completely ignored by Islamic scholars. Additionally, any appearance of error or contradiction is explained away through "interpretation" by Islamic scholars or by the principle of "naskh" or "abrogation" under which some Koranic verses override or abrogate others. In general, the position of Islamic scholars in such cases is that the verse last revealed to Mohammed overrides or abrogates all earlier verses. In this principle of "naskh," the Koran is perhaps unique among sacred scriptures. The importance of knowing which verses were revealed last and therefore "abrogate" others has given rise to an entire field of study among Islamic scholars known as "Naskh wa Mansukh" or "the Abrogators and the Abrogated." (Jeffrey, 1958, p.66)

A World of the Unseen and Supernatural

The world of the Islamists, as well as the world of Christian fundamentalists, is a world of unseen forces where the natural and supernatural are inextricably interlaced. To the Christian and Islamic religious fundamentalists, the world is populated not only by humans, but by an unseen but all powerful God, a powerful devil or evil entity, angels, evil demons, and perhaps even the spirits of the dead. It is a world of both Divine and demonic intervention into human affairs, where both blessings and tragedies are caused by the unseen entities. An all-loving God may intervene into human affairs at any time to perform miracles, and people are visited and rescued by angels, but also tormented and possessed by demons. For Islamists, there is also a belief in an evil variety of invisible beings known as the jinn. The jinn are evil entities that are loose in the world that intervene in human affairs for evil purposes and torment and tempt human beings to do evil, even copulating and procreating with unsuspecting humans (Sivan, 1985, pp.135–136). In such a mindset, current events are often explained not through nature or the choices of humans, but through the intervention of the unseen beings. For example, after the terrorist attacks of 9/11, the Reverend Jerry Falwell announced on the American Christian television program, The 700 Club, that he believed the terrorist attacks to be punishment from God on America for allowing abortions and allowing feminists, gays, and the American Civil Liberties Union (ACLU) to secularize America and introduce alternative lifestyles (www.religioustolerance.org_ter7.htm). In the words of Falwell,

> the American Civil Liberties Union has "to take a lot of blame for" the tragedy. And, I know that I'll hear from them for this. But, throwing God out successfully with the help of the federal court system, throwing God out of

the public square, out of the schools. The **abortionists** have got to bear
some burden for this because God will not be mocked. And when we destroy 40 million little innocent babies, we make God mad. I really believe
that the **Pagans**, and the abortionists, and the feminists, and the **gays
and the lesbians** who are actively trying to make that an alternative life-
style, the ACLU, People For the American Way ... all of them who have tried
to secularize America ... I point the finger in their face and say 'you helped
this happen.'

The Reverend Pat Robertson quickly concurred with Falwell's analysis. Later, Robertson would proclaim that the devastation from Hurricane Katrina in New Orleans in 2005 was the result of God's
punishment on America for the choice of Ellen Degeneres (a noted
.esbian native of New Orleans) as the host of the Emmy Awards
(www.datelinehollywood.com/.../2005/09/05/).

Similarly, Robertson proclaimed in January 2006, that the stroke
suffered by Israeli Prime Minister Ariel Sharon was part of God's
wrath on Sharon for "dividing God's land," a reference to Sharon's
championing of the Israeli withdrawal from the Gaza Strip in 2005
(*Amarillo Globe News*, January 7, 2006, p.4A).

The interpretation of history and world events by Islamists is similar, even in their preoccupation with events in Israel as connected to
Divine intervention. For example, an American-born Islamist Ali el-
Timmimi, who was convicted in April 2005 for inducing others to engage in terrorism, interpreted the February 1, 2003 crash of the space
shuttle *Columbia* and deaths of astronauts as God's judgment on the
infidel America for which Muslims should rejoice. In the words of el-
Timmimi (quoted in www.danielpipes.org/article/2579),

> There is no doubt that Muslims were overjoyed because of the adversity
> that befell their greatest enemy. The Columbia crash made me feel, and God
> is the only One to know, that this is a strong signal that Western supremacy
> (especially that of America) that began 500 years ago is coming to a quick
> end, God Willing, as occurred to the shuttle. God Willing, America will fall
> and disappear.

In much the same way, the Arab defeats in the Arab-Israeli wars of
1948 and 1967 are interpreted by Islamists as God's punishment upon
Muslims for not being true to Islam, while the "victories" of the Yom
Kippur War of 1973 and the jihad in Afghanistan in the 1980s are interpreted as Divine intervention by God on behalf of his people (Sivan,
1985, p.161).

In such a mindset, Islam conforms well to Marx's categorization of
religion as the "opiate of the masses" and a reactionary force against
change. Those who denounce such mythology as nonsense are denounced by the religious fundamentalists as sinful and part of the evil
plot against Islam, much like Jerry Falwell's diatribe against the People for the American Way and the ACLU. Finally, like fundamentalist

Christianity, in Islamism there is an overriding preoccupation with the afterlife that makes all activity in this world insignificant in comparison. In such a mindset, if one gives his life in holy war as a martyr for God, it is unimportant since the current life is fleeting and finite, and the afterlife is infinite and glorious.

Islamic Beginnings

From 610–613 AD, in the town of Mecca in the Jabal Mountains of the Arabian Peninsula, Muslims believe that Mohammed received the "Revelation" of the Koran and wrote down his visions on leaves (though Mohammed was illiterate, thus proving the Divinity of the Revelation). Mecca, of course, is Islam's holiest location since it is there that Mohammed received his visions. The belief is that the visions came from Allah to Mohammed and were written by the Prophet on leaves in no particular order. Consequently, there is no chronological ordering to the Koran. Instead, the books or "Surahs" in the Koran are generally arranged from longest to shortest (Smith, 1991, pp.225–227).

Mohammed was convinced that he was chosen to be a prophet and was told by an Angel to "proclaim" what God had told him. Consequently, what Mohammed began preaching is Revelation shortly after the Revelations ceased in 613 AD. His first convert was his wife, further proof to Muslims of his authenticity, because no person knows a man's character more than his wife (Smith, 1991, pp.225–227).

Mohammed never claimed to be a deity, only that he was a preacher of God's word. He taught that although there had been many prophets before him, he was their culmination; hence, Muslims refer to him as the "Seal of the Prophets" and no valid prophets or Revelation would follow him. Through the Revelation to Mohammed, God had made straight and clear his will, and there was therefore no more need to reveal his will to humans (Smith, 1991, pp.223–224).

The first three years of Mohammed's ministry were a struggle for Mohammed, and he only had about forty converts after the first three years. Between 616 and 622 AD, however, Mohammed's teachings became successful enough to attract converts in ignorant, polytheistic, and decadent seventh-century Mecca and by 622 AD Mohammed's following was sufficient to alarm the Meccan nobility. Mohammed's monotheism violated pagan beliefs, and the Meccan nobility used Mohammed's "atheism" to inflame the masses against him, although the main fear of the nobility, for valid reasons, was that he was a threat to their power. Mohammed was forced to flee Mecca to seek safe haven in Medina where he continued his preaching. This moment, known as the hijra (migration), marks the beginning date of the

Muslim era, Year One on the Islamic Calendar. In 630 AD, Mohammed and his Muslim army conquered Medina, and by the time of Mohammed's death in 632 AD, almost the entire Arabian Peninsula had
been conquered. After Mohammed's death, his followers continued
their conquests so that they had conquered Armenia, Persia, Syria,
Palestine, Iraq, North Africa, Spain, and part of France before their
defeat at the hands of Charles Martel in the Battle of Tours in 733 AD
(Smith, 1991, pp.228–231).

Politics in the Time of the Prophet

During the time of Mohammed, political authority in the Muslim
community was centered in the Prophet himself, and Mohammed
himself revealed to the people what Islam was, and how it was interpreted in any given situation. During this time, whatever Mohammed
said and did essentially was Islam, and when disputes arose, Mohammed was the final arbiter (Sayyid, 2003, pp.53–54). Upon Mohammed's death in 632AD, however, the caliphate emerged as the
center of political authority and legitimacy. The codification of the Koran also began at the time of the death of the Prophet, although there
is dispute over when the process was finished, and the collection of
the Hadiths (sayings attributed to the Prophet), and the formation of
the Sunnah (traditions of the Prophet) also began their formulation
that would not culminate into an official canon for over two hundred
years (Sayyid, 2003, p.54).

With the death of the Prophet, the unifying principle of Islam
shifted from the Prophet himself to his message and thus the need to
interpret the Prophet's message quickly developed. The successor to
Mohammed (known as the caliph) was Mohammed's father-in-law,
Abu Bakr, who quickly inherited Mohammed's authority of interpretation, and with it the executive authority previously held by the
Prophet himself (Lapidus, 1996, p.9). As a consequence, the caliph became the link between the lawgiver and the law and the point around
which Muslim identity was structured. The caliph also provided some
semblance of Muslim unity, even if all Muslims were not united under
the same political entities, and served to limit the possible interpretations of Islam, thus providing some appearance of religious stability
(Sayyid, 2003, p.57).

The power of the caliph, however, became fragmented in 929 AD,
when Emir Abdul-Rahman III of Cordoba proclaimed himself caliph
in direct challenge to the sitting caliph then residing in Baghdad. In
1258, the Baghdad caliph was sacked and trampled to death by Mon-
gols under Hulagu Khan, and the Mamluks in Egypt reestablished a
caliph three years later in the person of one of the refugees from the

Mongol sack of Baghdad. The caliph remained seated in Egypt until 1517, when the Ottomans conquered Egypt and the caliphate was moved to Turkey. By the late nineteenth century, the Ottoman Sultan had also assumed the role of caliph and the relationship remained as such until the abolition of the caliph in 1924 by Kemal Ataturk (Sayyid, 2003, pp.57–58).

Islamic Jihad or Holy War

The word "jihad" is typically interpreted as meaning Holy War against the enemies of Islam, but more literally it means "struggle" and refers to the struggle for the good Islamic life. Jihad is widely considered one of the basic commandments of the faith and an obligation imposed on all Muslims (Lewis, 1988, pp.72–73). Jihad is largely an affair between the believer and God, and is an act of faith rather than an act of politics; consequently, there is no obligation for the jihadists to obtain the desired result (defeat the enemy of God). Instead, the struggle is for God; hence, the struggle itself is successful if it demonstrates one's devotion to God and is therefore pleasing in his sight, even when a specific attack is physically unsuccessful (Roy, 1994, p.157).

Jihad is normally declared by a religious leader and consists not of a war between states, but of the struggle between Muslims and nonbelievers or infidels (Roy, 1994, p.153). For Islamists currently, the focus of global jihad is on the struggle or war against infidels, represented by Israel and the West (and the United States, in particular, as the most powerful supporter of Israel and the occupier of Muslim lands), whom they view as the enemies of Islam. The struggle is ongoing and without limits of time or space, and Islamists believe that they are obligated to continue the jihad until the entire world has either accepted Islam or submitted to the power of a global Islamic state. In the Islamists' conception, until Islam ultimately prevails, the world will remain divided into the House of Islam and the "House of War" that comprises the rest of the world (Lewis, 1988, pp.72–73). Until then, Islamists believe that enmity will permanently exist between the House of Islam and the rest of the world. In the words of Lewis (1988),

> Between the two there is a morally necessary, legally and religiously obligatory state of war, until the final and inevitable triumph of Islam over unbelief. According to the law books, this state of war could be interrupted, when expedient, by an armistice of truce of limited duration. It could not be terminated by a peace, but only by a final victory. (pp.72–73)

Jihad is not limited, however, to war against unbelievers, but is also directed against those who had once been Muslims or claimed to be

Muslims, but had either renounced the faith or failed to follow it properly. In the words of Lewis (1988),

> The Muslim who abandons his faith is not only a renegade; he is a traitor, and the law insists that he must be punished as such. The jurists agreed on the need to execute the apostate individual, and to make war against the apostate state. The rules of warfare against the apostate are very much harsher than those governing warfare against the unbeliever. He may not be given quarter or safe conduct, and no truce or agreement with him is permissible. The only options before him are recantation or death. He may choose to return to Islam, in which case his offence committed during his apostasy will be pardoned and his confiscated property—or what remains of it—be returned to him. If he refuses, he must be put to death by the sword. (pp.84–85)

For justification and example of Jihad, Islamists need look no further than the life of the Prophet himself. From the moment Mohammed arrived in Medina after the hijra in 622 AD, he taught that his new religion could be spread by the sword, if necessary, and Mohammed proceeded to engage in a Holy War or jihad in order to spread Islam. For justification from the Islamic Holy texts, the collections of Hadiths that contain the sayings and deeds of the Prophet all contain sections devoted to military jihad against the enemies of Islam (Lewis, 1988, pp.72–73). Furthermore, reference to jihad is contained in numerous passages in the Koran itself. For example, in The Cow II: 187– 188, it is stated that believers should

> fight in the way of God with those who fight with you, but aggress not: ... God loves not the aggressors. ... And slay them wherever you come upon them, and expel them from where they expelled you; persecution is more grievous than slaying. ... But fight them not by the Holy Mosque until they should fight you there; then, if they fight you, slay them—such is the recompense of unbelievers—but if they give over, surely God is All-forgiving, All-Compassionate.

Islamic extremists now use these verses to support their self-proclaimed Holy War against Jews and infidels and they compare their struggles against the present-day enemies to the struggles of Mohammed against his seventh century enemies in Mecca. In particular, the Koranic command to "slay them wherever you come upon them" is eerily similar to Osama bin Laden's famous fatwa of 1998 where he called for the killing of any American anywhere in the world (Halliday, 2002, Appendix 1). Secondly, "expel them from where they expelled you" is normally interpreted by contemporary Islamists as applying to Palestine, and the passage in their view clearly constitutes a direct command to Muslims to expel the Jews from Israel by force if necessary and indiscriminate killing is allowed. Osama bin Laden well exemplified this perspective when he declared that "there is no more important duty for Muslims than expelling the Americans from the

Holy Land," thus placing jihad against Israel on a pedestal over the traditional five pillars of Islam. (Gunaratna, 2002, p.27)

Although Muslims are clearly commanded to "aggress not," since "persecution is more grievous than slaying," the Islamists conclude that it would be far worse for Muslims to endure their continued expulsion from Palestine than it would be for them to slay Jewish infidels that have taken over land that they believe is theirs by gift of God as promised to Abraham in Genesis.

Fight to Defend Islam

Above all, however, Islamists believe that Muslims have a responsibility to fight so as to defend Islam against its enemies (Allah, though all-knowing and all-powerful, evidently being unable to do it himself). The justification for warfare and killing in this instance is that it is for God and against God's enemies; otherwise, Muslims are instructed to "aggress not." In cases where Islam is under attack, or the followers of Mohammed are under attack from infidels, however, the good Muslims need show no mercy. Islamist Pasha Mohamed Ali Taeharah of the Congress of the Sunni Sect of Islam explains his vision of Muslim obligations against those "intent to destroy Islam" thus,

> If the Congress of the Sunni Sect of Islam and all other Muslims after prayer and deliberation determine that the danger is opponents who have the ability and the intent to destroy Islam we must declare Holy War against them. We must use our combined military forces against the wrongdoers ... where Muslims have been expelled from their ancestral homes (i.e. Palestine), where many Muslim men, women, and children have been martyred; where our adversaries continuously obstruct justice and progress available to members of the mystical body of Islam, we will take appropriate military action. We will oppose aggressive military action with aggressive military action. We will direct war against those who persecute Muslims. We will direct war when any opponents of Islam are bent on the murder of helpless people. Holy War will take place when wrongdoers are engaged in the ruin of the righteous of Islam and the slaughter of innocent men, women, and children. We will direct war under those circumstances where the divine law of security demands the safeguarding of the persecuted against total destruction. It is a grave error on the part of our opponents if they imagine that because we depend upon revealed divine guidance for entry into Holy War that our forces must under no circumstances take aggressive action against our enemies. It is also grave error for our opponents to conclude that we will always demonstrate our love and mercy by way of meekness and gentleness. (2005, p.22)

Again, it is worth reiterating that within the Koranic verses sanctioning war against the enemies of God, believers are also instructed to "aggress not: God loves not aggressors." Consequently, more moderate Muslims may not necessarily agree with Taeharah, and therefore may condemn Islamic jihad and terrorism in any given circumstance, depending on the importance they give to "aggress not" and their interpretation of its application. In other words, Islam need not be a violent religion in spite of the Koranic sanction of jihad, and Muslims are likely to disagree as to what conditions are necessary to justify jihad in any given situation.

Further ambiguity is introduced into the situation in The Cow II: 212–215 where believers are instructed that fighting would be "hateful" and "heinous" to them; however, they are also instructed that there are worse things than jihad, such as unbelief, but again there is also encouragement to passivism in that it is also stated that, "persecution is more heinous than slaying." The complete passage is presented below.

> Prescribed for you is fighting, though it be hateful to you. ... Yet it may happen that you will hate a thing which is better for you; and it may happen that you will love a thing which is worse for you; ...God knows and you know not. ... They will question thee concerning the holy month, and fighting in it. Say: ... 'Fighting in it is a heinous thing, but to bar from God's way, and disbelief in Him, and the Holy Mosque, and to expel its people from it—that is more heinous in God's sight; and persecution is more heinous than slaying.' ... They will not cease to fight with you, till they turn you from your religion, if they are able; and whosoever of you turns from his religion, and dies disbelieving—their works have failed in this world and the next; those are the inhabitants of the Fire; therein they shall dwell forever. ... But the believers, and those who emigrate and struggle in God's way— those have hope of God's compassion; and God is all-forgiving, All-compassionate.

These verses from The Cow II are especially useful to the jihadists in that they teach that the goal of the enemies of God is to turn the Muslims away from their religion so that they die to an eternity of hell's fire. Against such an enemy, true believers would surely be compelled to fight even if the act itself is heinous. "Unbelief" would be a far more heinous thing. Furthermore, those who fight and "struggle" for Allah will be rewarded.

Indiscriminate Killing

Although indiscriminate killing generally has been condemned by Muslim jurists throughout history, Islamists have been able to justify indiscriminate slaughter, including the slaughter of innocent Muslims, under the Islamic principle of "proportionality." Essentially, the argument is that if the infidels indiscriminately kill innocent Muslim men, women, and children, then it is permissible for Muslims to return the indiscriminate killing in the same proportions. Islamists could therefore justify indiscriminately killing 30,000 Americans since at this writing an estimated 30,000 Iraqis have died since the American invasion. Similarly, it is estimated that up to 500,000 Iraqis died between 1991 and 2003 due to Western sanctions on Iraq; consequently, under the concept of "proportionality," jihadists would be justified in the indiscriminate killing of 500,000 Westerners. For a concrete example of this type of thinking, one need look no further than the arguments of Omar Bakri Mohammed, an Islamist Imam in London, who justified the indiscriminate killing in Beslan, Chechnya in 2004, where more than 300 innocent people were killed by Islamic terrorists, stating

> If an Iraqi Muslim carried out an attack like that in Britain, it would be justified because Britain has carried out acts of terrorism in Iraq. ... As long as the Iraqi did not deliberately kill women and children, and they were killed in the crossfire, that would be okay. (Quoted in Syal, 2004, p.1)

Similarly, Islamist Saudi Sheikh Nasir bin Hamad in 2003 justified the prospective use of nuclear weapons against the United States under the principle of proportionality. In the words of Hamad (Quoted in Benjamin and Simon, 2005, p.72), "If a bomb was dropped on them (the Americans) that would annihilate 10 million and burn their lands to the same extent that they burned the Muslim lands—this is permissible, with no need to mention any other proof."

Beheadings

Perhaps nothing else has stirred the Western conscience (not to mention curiosity) during the American war in Iraq more than a series of beheadings of Westerners by Islamists in Iraq that have been posted and played on the Internet for the world to witness. Dan Klinger of Orgish.com, a Web site that specializes in such gory images, reported that the video of the Nicholas Berg beheading has been downloaded 15 million times from his Web site alone (Quoted in Talbot, 2005, p.28). Although it is impossible to know how many of those accessing beheading web sites are Islamists (and no one is suggesting that it is a large percentage), it is clear that the videos of beheadings are popular among Islamists. One Islamist even explained on his Web site that watching beheadings improved his health. In the words of the Islamist himself (Quoted in Benjamin and Simon, 2005),

> We used to start our day by watching a slaughter (beheading) scene, for it is no secret to the knowledgeable that it stimulates and appeases the contents of the chests ... By Allah, many of those who suffer from high blood pressure and diabetes, have complained about the cease of these operations, for they were tranquilizing them. ... Someone even told me, and I believe he speaks the truth, that he does not eat his food until he has watched a beheading scene, even if it were replayed or old. (p.65)

The Koranic sanction of beheadings of infidels is found in Muhammad 47:4, where believers are commanded,

> So when you meet in battle those who disbelieve, then smite the necks until when you have overcome them, then make (them) prisoners, and afterwards either set them free as a favor or let them ransom (themselves) until the war terminates.

Further justification for beheadings is found in the writings of Ibn Ishaq, the Prophet's earliest biographer, who details that Mohammed ordered the beheading of 700 men of the Jewish Banu Qurayza tribe in Medina. As a result of these Koranic verses and Mohammed's example, beheading has been viewed as a legitimate component of Muslim warfare ever since (Benjamin and Simon, 2005, p.63).

Beheading is also viewed by Islamists as a way of making the violence a sacramental act and Holy. The Arabic word used by Islamists to refer to beheadings is the same word that is used for the cutting of a sheep's throat during the Muslim holiday of Eid al-Adha, a ritual that is a symbol of the Biblical sacrifice of Isaac by Abraham. As explained by Benjamin and Simon,

> Severing the infidel's head from his body thus becomes an act redolent with the sense of sacrifice and the literal execution of God's law, which to the jihadist means death for infidels and apostates. (2005, pp.63–64)

Benjamin and Simon (2005, p.64) also note that the 9/11 hijackers killed the members of the flight crews aboard their hijacked planes through the slitting of their throats, thus making the killings (in their view) sacramental acts.

Beheadings (and terrorism in general) are also justified by Islamists through a classic application of "ends politics" that is common among traditional conservative groups. Essentially, while the Islamists themselves in many cases may admit that beheadings and other acts of terrorism are bad, they are not as bad as allowing Western decadence to destroy Islam or allowing the infidel United States to invade and occupy an Islamic country. In the words of one Islamist, who spoke of the kidnapping and beheading of Western contractors to a French journalist (Quoted in Hashim, 2006),

> We don't kidnap to frighten those we are holding ... but to put pressure on the countries that help or are preparing to help the Americans. What are they thinking; coming to an occupied country? They come to terms with the United States in the name of their business interests, but their contracts are stained with the blood of Iraqis. Should we just sit there while we're being murdered? It's not a good thing to behead, but it is a method that works. (p.197)

Mercy for Those That Pay a Tax to the Islamic State

In the Koranic Surah of Repentence 9:29, mercy is allowed to unbelievers who pay a tax to Muslims so as to display their willing submission to their Islamic conquerors. As stated in the Koran, believers are commanded to,

> Fight those who do not believe in Allah, nor in the latter day, nor do they prohibit what Allah and His Apostle have prohibited, nor follow the religion of truth, out of those who have been given the Book, until they pay the tax in acknowledgement of superiority and they are in a state of subjection.

Bernard Lewis (1988, p.77) explains that such a person is referred to in Islam as a dhimmi, termed as an unbeliever who submits to Muslim rule and pays the special tax, but essentially accepts that he will have considerably limited legal rights compared with those of Muslims (such as the ability to own property or engage in certain occupations). Other restrictions on the dhimmi include that they are not allowed to present evidence against Muslims in Islamic Courts of Law and they often have no recourse but to pay Muslims to present their evidence in court for them (Cox and Marks, 2003, p.39). Dhimmi, however, are granted the right to worship, right to property, and security of life and limb, and are thus exempted from being targeted in jihad (Sivan, 1985, p.77). Some Islamists, such as Sudan's Hassan al-Turabi, argue that Muslims have a moral obligation to be fair and friendly to the dhimmi or they will face God's judgment (Roy, 1994, p.65). Unfortunately, victims of jihad typically have not been given the option to pay a tax in practice so as to attain dhimmi status and spare their lives from religious fanatics bent on genocide. The recent beheadings of Westerners in Iraq, Osama bin Laden's call to Muslims to "kill any American, anywhere," and the carnage that has occurred in the Southern Sudan for more than a decade at this writing are cases in point.

Finally, Mohammed's command in Women IV:78 to "fight you therefore against the friends of Satan" is interpreted by Islamic extremists to be a call to fight against the Satanic enemies of Islam, and in the view of the Islamists, there is little more Satanic than Israel. For the Islamists it logically follows, obviously, that the United States is easily interpreted by Islamists as a "friend of Satan" since the United States was instrumental in the creation of Israel and has been a major supporter of the Jewish state since its inception in 1948.

Rewards in Heaven for Martyrs

In the Koran in The Terrible Calamity 101:6–11, it is promised to Muslims that those who do good deeds in their lives on earth will receive a

pleasant life in heaven, while those who do not do good deeds in their
lives on earth will live in an abyss of burning fire. Obviously, one desires to avoid the abyss of burning fire, but if one has not engaged in
many good deeds, the burning fire may await slothful Muslims in the
afterlife. Martyrdom in Holy War, however, may provide a way to escape the imminent burning fire for those who have not spent their life
engaged in good deeds and serving Allah. Thus, martyrdom can be
seen as a sacramental act or an act of atonement where one is able to
make things right with God.

There are numerous Koranic verses that promise rewards in heaven
to those that are martyrs in Holy War. In Islam, like Christianity, the
"world to come" in the afterlife is believed to be infinitely better than
the world of the here and now in the present life on earth. For example, in Muhammad XLVII, the afterlife is referred to as "Paradise,"
and those who die fighting for Allah will be admitted there in the next
life. Specifically, in Muhammad XLVII:8–9, it is stated, "And those
who are slain in the way of God, He will not send their works astray. ...
He will guide them, and dispose their minds aright, and He will admit
them to Paradise, that He has made known to them." Hence, to end
one's own life as a martyr while killing the enemies of God makes rational sense if one is able to believe that through death in Holy War
one will be quickly admitted to Paradise and avoid hell's fire. Martyrdom can therefore be seen in some cases as atonement for sin and the
attempt by an individual to make things right with God. If one has not
been a good Muslim and is expecting to spend an eternity in hell, then
dying as a martyr can be relied upon as one's ticket to Paradise instead.

An exemplification of this mindset is offered by Anthony Shadid
(2005, p.290), an American journalist embedded in Iraq during the
American occupation, who reported reading a Koranic saying written
above the picture of a local martyr in an Iraqi barbershop that stated,
"Do not consider those killed for the sake of God dead. Rather they are
living with God." Similarly, Palestinian suicide bombers often leave
detailed statements, often on video, made to be released after their
death that they expect to be watched and honored by members of
their family and community (Pape, 2005, p.133). The prevalence of
such a practice is a strong indication that the "martyrdom" of the suicide bombers is not only accepted, but revered by the community at
large. Survey data in the West Bank and Gaza have revealed that support among Palestinians for suicide attacks against Israel is often as
high as 70% (Pape, 2005, p.191). In Lebanon in the 1980s, major
streets were named after fallen martyrs and their pictures were often
used as symbols in political rallies. No political leader in Lebanon at
the time condemned the suicide attacks (Pape, 2005, p.135).

In such a mindset, all ranges of actions for God are imaginable, obviously including flying jetliners full of innocent civilians into buildings full of more innocent civilians in an effort to strike the enemies of God. The same mindset allowed the Iranians during the Iran-Iraq war to hang keys around the necks of Iranian children and send them to detonated land mines. In order to induce the children to perform such deeds, the children were told that their "martyrdom" would "unlock the doors to paradise" (Shadid, 2005, p.26).

Muslims who might be squeamish about giving their lives for God are cautioned in the Koran not to avoid jihad so as to preserve one's own life in the present world only to lose it in the next. Perhaps the best example is in Women IV:73–78, where it is stated

> O believers, take your precautions; then move forward in companies, or move forward all together. ... Some of you there are that are dilatory; then, if an affliction visits you, he says, 'God has blessed me, in that I was not a martyr with them.' But if a bounty from God visits you, he will surely say, as if there had never been any affection between you and him, 'Would that I had been with them, to attain a mighty triumph!' ... So let them fight in the way of God who sell the present life for the world to come; and whosoever fights in the way of God and is slain, or conquers, We shall bring him a mighty wage. ... How is it with you, that you do not fight in the way of God, and for the men, women, and children who, being abased, say, 'Our Lord, bring us forth from this city whose people are evildoers, and appoint to us a protector from Thee, and appoint to us from Thee a helper'? The believers fight in the way of God, and the unbelievers fight in the idols' way. ... Fight you therefore against the friends of Satan; surely the guile of Satan is ever feeble.

Some Islamic extremists, such as Taeharah (2005), use these verses and the example of Mohammed's flight to Medina to argue that only those who fight against infidels will receive heavenly rewards. In the words of Taeharah (2005, p.22), "Only those who draw the sword in the name of the faith will be rewarded." The religious call to war does not get much more explicit. Believers must join the fight against the Satanic unbelievers or lose their place in heaven. It must be stressed, however, that the Holy Warriors that lose their life in jihad are not referred to by Muslims as "suicide bombers," since suicide is forbidden in the Koran in The Cow II:195 where it is commanded that believers should not "cast yourselves to perdition with your own hands"; hence, Muslims draw a clear distinction between martyrdom and suicide.

The Mighty Wage and Seventy Virgins

The Koran and other Islamic writings provide numerous visions of the afterlife where martyrs will eat the finest foods, occupy the most pleasant places, and indulge their most pleasurable sexual fantasies with the most desirable heavenly creatures. Such visions provide incentive to martyrdom in addition to the elimination of the fear of spending an eternity in hell. The Islamic vision of a heaven complete with "seventy virgins" became familiar in the United States the month before the 9/11 attacks when CBS aired an interview with Hamas activist Muhammad Abu Wardeh, who recruited terrorists for suicide bombings in Israel. Abu Wardeh told CBS that he recruited his suicide bombers by describing to them how God would compensate a martyr for sacrificing his life for the expulsion of the Jews from Palestine. Abu Wardeh's vision of heaven for martyrs was a vision of a place where each martyr for Allah would be given seventy virgin wives and "everlasting happiness" (www.guardian.co.uk/religion/story).

The seventy virgins to whom Abu Wardeh was referring are found in the Hadith collected by Al-Tirmidhi in the ninth century. In the Book of Sunan, Volume IV:21:72, Al-Tirmidhi states that,

> The Prophet Mohammed was heard saying: 'The smallest reward for the people of paradise is an abode where there are 80,000 servants and 72 wives, over which stands a dome decorated with pearls, aquamarine, and ruby, as wide as the distance from al-Jabiyyah (Damascus) to Sana'a (Yemen).

This passage in the Hadith clearly applies to all believers, and not just martyrs, however; consequently, from using this passage alone, one cannot conclude that martyrs are receiving anything in paradise that other Muslims will not also receive. For this, Islamists must combine the seventy-two virgins passages from the Hadith with several passages from the Koran itself. For example, in Man 76:17–22, the Prophet wrote,

> Immortal youths shall go about them; when thou seest them, thou supposest them scattered pearls, when thou seest them then thou seest bliss and a great kingdom. Upon them shall be green garments of silk and brocade; they are adorned with bracelets of silver, and their Lord shall give them to drink a pure draught. 'Behold, this is a recompense for you and your striving is thanked.'

The most important portion of this Surah for the Islamists is the last sentence where they are informed that the rewards in heaven are direct compensation and thanks for their "striving." For the Islamists, "striving" is almost the very definition of jihad, and those that carry out jihad refer to themselves as Mujahadeen, or "strugglers." To this reward are added some bonuses in the Koranic Surah, The Terror 56, where those who have "labored" will be granted some heavenly creatures known as "wide-eyed houris." Exactly what these "houris" are is not explicitly stated, but fifteenth-century Muslim theologian Al-Suyuti suggested that the "houris" are some sort of beautiful heavenly female creatures that will take care of one's sexual desires in paradise. Al-Suyuti explained that

> Each time we sleep with a houri we find her virgin. Besides, the penis of the Elected never softens. The erection is eternal; the sensation that you feel each time you make love is utterly delicious and out of this world and were you to experience it in this world you would faint. Each chosen one will marry seventy houris, besides the women he married on earth, and all will have appetizing vaginas. (www.guardian.co.uk/religion/story)

"Appetizing" or not, Islam clearly provides both push and pull factors designed to compel believers to engage in Holy War against the enemies of Islam. The push factors are the fear of falling out of God's good graces and ending up in hell, while the pull factors are clearly the pleasures of Paradise.

Islamic Culture and Martyrdom

Culture and propaganda in some areas of the Islamic world further enhance the attractiveness of martyrdom to young Islamic radicals. For example, in Palestine, radical summer camps for children between the ages of eight and twelve begin inculcating the ideas and training that lead some to eventually become suicide bombers (Podhoretz, 2001, p.23). When young Islamists choose the path of self-destruction while attempting to destroy the perceived enemies of Islam, their martyrdom is generally revered and celebrated in the Islamic community and their families are given financial support from radical Islamic groups. As explained by Nasra Hassan (2001),

> The bomber's family and the sponsoring organization celebrate his martyrdom with festivities, as if it were a wedding. Hundreds of guests congregate at the house to offer congratulations. The hosts serve the juices and sweets that the young man specified in his will. Often, the mother will ululate in joy over the honour that Allah has bestowed upon her family. (p.8)

Again, the suicide bombers are not labeled "suicide bombers" in the Islamic society since suicide is expressly forbidden in the Koran. Instead, the "suicide bombers" are viewed by Islamists as "Holy martyrs" in an Islamic jihad and their direct admission to paradise for their martyrdom is celebrated (Lewis, 2001, p.127). Other honors bestowed on such martyrs include the fact that they are buried in the clothes they died in with the wounds unwashed as a witness for all to their martyrdom. Devout Muslims also believe (contrary to overwhelming evidence) that the bodies of martyrs do not produce any foul odor because the blood of martyrs does not clot, but "stays fresh" (Shadid, 2005, pp.296, 300).

Peace with Infidels

Concerning the prospects of peace between the Muslims and the unbelievers, the Koran again offers contradictory statements that are
open to vastly differing interpretations. For example, it is stated that
the believers are not to make friends of unbelievers, but are obligated
to kill them wherever they are found; yet, if the infidels withdraw and
offer peace, God does not allow them to be slain. The full passage is
contained in the Koran in Women IV:91–93, where it is stated that,

> They wish that you should disbelieve as they disbelieve, and then you would
> be equal; therefore take not to yourselves friends of them, and slay them
> wherever you find them; take not to yourselves any one of them as a friend
> or helper except those that betake themselves to a people who are joined
> with you by a compact, or come to you with breasts constricted from fight-
> ing with you or fighting their people. Had God willed, He would have given
> them authority over you, and then certainly they would have fought you. If
> they withdraw from you, and do not fight you, and offer you peace, then
> God assigns not any way to you against them. You will find others desiring
> to be secure from you, and secure from their people, yet whenever they are
> returned to temptation, they are overthrown in it. If they withdraw not from
> you, and offer you peace, and restrain their hands, take them, and slay them
> wherever you come on them; against them We have given you clear author-
> ity.

Clearly, these Koranic verses provide room for interpretation and allow Muslims to make peace with non-Muslims if the "infidels" withdraw and offer peace; however, Islamic radicals prefer to focus on the
command to "slay them wherever you come upon them" and claim the
full authority from God to do so, arguing that Mohammed's final
command was to conquer the world in the name of Islam and that
there are no subsequent Koranic verses that contradict this final
command found in the Koran in The Spoils of War 8:39. If no subsequent command contradicts this command, Islamists argue that conquest of the world under Islam must remain the goal of Muslims in
the present. For further validation of the need for continued jihad,
Islamists point to the example of Mohammed himself, who led twen-
ty-seven battles and authorized almost fifty more during his ten years
in Medina. Furthermore, after Mohammed's death, his followers continued the jihad, capturing Jerusalem in 638 AD, and much of Spain
by 715 AD. The jihad against infidels continued even into the seventeenth century, though it was interrupted by almost 200 years of Crusades from 1096–1270. In the words of Bernard Lewis (1995),

> For roughly a thousand years, from the first irruption of the Muslim armies
> into the Christian lands of the Levant in the early seventh century until the
> second and final Turkish withdrawal from the walls of Vienna in 1683,
> European Christendom lived under the constant and imminent menace of
> Islam. (pp.11–12)

The Crusades, which Muslims so often hold up as examples of Christian cruelty, therefore more properly should be viewed in the context of more than a thousand years of Muslim expansion and aggression.

Defeating More Powerful Enemies

In Islam, anything is possible if God is on the side of the believers; hence, believing that one can attack and defeat a much more powerful enemy, such as the United States, is well within reason. In the Koran in The Spoils VIII:66–68, for instance, it is stated that believers can win battles against larger odds because God is on their side. ... Taking prisoners, however, is not permitted until there is "wide slaughter." The entire passage reads

> The Spoils VIII: 66–68: ... O Prophet, urge on the believers to fight. ... If there be twenty of you, patient men, they will overcome two hundred; if there be a hundred of you, they will overcome a thousand unbelievers, for they are a people who understand not. Now God has lightened it for you, knowing that there is weakness in you. If there be a hundred of you, patient men, they will overcome two hundred; if there be of you a thousand, they will overcome two thousand by the leave of God; God is with the patient. It is not for any Prophet to have prisoners until he makes wide slaughter in the land.

Given these verses, Islamists can believe that they can destroy the United States, a much more powerful entity, if they are patient and God is with them. The fact that Muslim armies may be technologically inferior to that of the Americans is not a cause for concern if the Muslims have God on their side. In the words of Taeharah (2005),

> It is error on the part of our opponents to believe that we can't coordinate a military offensive because we lack an industrial complex that is capable of supporting the military forces needed for modern warfare. That is, an industrial complex that has contemporary technology for the design and the production of state of the art ships, aircraft, submarines, and all other military equipment needed to sustain our forces in the field. We are certain the military people who are members of the House of Ishmael are capable of coordinating personnel activities, military logistics or supply problems and battle tactics necessary to prevent the destruction of the House of Ishmael. (p.31)

For proof, the Islamists again need look no further than the life of the prophet Mohammed himself. Mohammed's new religion (empowered by Allah) provided a powerful stimulus that mobilized Arab society almost overnight. By 630 AD, Mohammed and the Medinese would defeat the more powerful Meccan army and control almost the entire Arabian Peninsula. Mohammed's victory is proof to Muslims that God was with him and sanctioned his holy war, thus allowing him to defeat a more powerful enemy. Mohammed captured much of the Arabian

Peninsula by 629 AD and died in 632 AD, but Arab armies carrying the banner of Islam formed, invaded, and conquered, converting wherever they went. By 700 AD, Islam had reached far into North Africa, Transcaucasia, and into most of Southwest Asia. By 1000 AD, Islam had spread into Southern and Eastern Europe and as far east as China (Ochsenwald and Fisher, 2004, pp.38–62).

For more recent proof, Islamists point to the Mujahadeen victory against the Soviets in Afghanistan in the 1980s, followed by the complete collapse of the nation-state that was known as the Soviet Union just a few short years after the war. In the views of the Islamists, it is obvious that groups of impoverished tribesmen could not have defeated the Soviets without God's help, and with God's help, the greatly overmatched Mujahadeen were able to defeat the Soviet Union, one of the world's two military superpowers in the latter half of the twentieth century. By the same logic, if the Mujahadeen, with God's help, could defeat the Soviets, then they could also defeat the Americans, as long as God is with them.

Sharia

Huston Smith (1991, p.249) describes Islam as "the most socially explicit of the Semitic religions" because it requires Muslims to establish a specific social order and blend religion, politics, and society in an inseparable mix. To Islamic extremists, the Koran is not only a religious book, but also provides a set of inviolate moral, civil, and criminal codes for society from which individuals and society as a whole cannot deviate. This set of moral, civil, and criminal codes is known collectively as the sharia. Bernard Lewis (1988, p.72) translates the word "sharia" simply as "Holy Law." The sharia is derived from the Holy Koran and the Hadiths, and is a collection of statements and deeds of Mohammed that were written over the 250-some years after the death of the Prophet, that Muslims also view as divinely inspired. For Sunnis, the sharia may also include legal points derived from analogous situations (Qiyas) or local traditions and customs (Bickerton and Klausner, 2005, pp.8–9). The sharia is much more than basic moral precepts, is enormous in scope, and is directed toward keeping believers on the correct path to God in all aspects of their lives. In fact, sharia itself translates as "correct path," meaning the correct path to salvation. Given this definition, it is little stretch for Islamists to argue that deviations from sharia essentially remove Muslims from the correct path to salvation and therefore must be forbidden (Ochsenwald and Fisher, 2004, pp.85–86).

According to Lewis (1988, p.72), however, the word is tautologous. In other words, "The sharia is simply the law, and there is no other. It is Holy in that it derives from God, and is the external and unchangeable expression of God's commandments to mankind." In short, the sharia is Holy because it is derived from the Koran, and the Koran is Holy because it says so in the Koran. Such a tautology is not unique to Islam among the world's religions, but it is a tautology nonetheless. Regardless, what develops with this type of tautological thinking is the comprehensive control by religion of virtually all aspects of life, creating a religious totalitarian system that is above criticism and antithetical with Western Democracy and "rule by the people." Anything that conflicts with the sharia is "unholy" and must be prohibited.

Martin Kramer (1993, p.38) reiterates these ideas and explains the aims of the Islamists regarding the sharia thus,

> A virtuous government, they affirm, can rest only on obedience to the divinely-given law of Islam, the sharia ... which is not legislated but revealed law; as such, in the eyes of the fundamentalists it has already achieved perfection, and while it is not above some reinterpretation, neither is it infinitely elastic.

Hence, Islamists argue that the sharia must be implemented not by the popular will, but by the state as interpreted by the shura, an advisory council of learned Islamic jurists, whose knowledge of the law and piety make their judgments acceptable to God. The shura are under no obligation whatsoever to consider the will of the majority, which may be contrary to the will of God. Instead of the people governing themselves, they are governed by the set of laws imposed by God. The laws are absolute, unchanging, and can never be altered. Freedom is not viewed as freedom from restraints, expansion of choice, or rights under law, but as obedience to God's law and submission to his rule (Sivan, 1985, pp.74–75).

Contents of the Sharia

As to the contents of the sharia itself, as explained by Olivier Roy (1994, pp.9–10), the sharia is noteworthy for two characteristics: autonomy and incompletion. In terms of autonomy, Roy (1994), explains that

> The sharia does not depend on any state, on any actual, positive law, on any political decision; it thereby creates a space that is parallel to the political space, to power, which, it is true, can circumvent the sharia or manipulate it...but which cannot make it into something other than what it is: an autonomous, infinite commentary. For the sharia does not depend on any official body, church or clergy; the fatwa, formal legal opinions that decide matters not mentioned in the text, are always pronounced in the here and now and can be annulled by a subsequent authority. The sharia is never closed, for it is based not on a core of concepts, but rather on an ensemble of precepts which is at times general, at times precise, and which expands

to include the totality of human acts through induction, analogy, extension, commentary, and interpretation. While the basic precepts, as they are explicitly formulated, cannot be called into question, their extension is a matter of casuistics. The work of the judge is not to apply a principle or a concept, but to bring the case before him back to the realm of what is already known. (pp.9–10)

Given that sharia involves all of the social relations, as well as civil and criminal codes in society, it is simply too large to explain in detail in this space; however, a few tenets are perhaps worthy of mention. The focus of sharia, instead of freedom and democracy; Jefferson's life, liberty and the pursuit of happiness; or the "liberty, equality, and fraternity" of the French Revolution, is on ethics, justice, and privacy in the home and personal family space, and honor. In the Islamists' conception, freedom demanded is in the home and family space rather than in the political space (Roy, 1994, pp.10–11).

The sharia forbids smoking, alcohol, social dancing, and gambling, and acknowledges the virtues of monogamy, though it tolerates polygamy. Prostitutes, however, are publicly whipped (Packer, 2005, p.262). In Women IV:3, it is stated in the Koran that men can "marry such women as seem good to you, two and three and four," but adulterers are sentenced to death by stoning. Homosexuals are similarly executed (Packer, 2005, p.261). Conversely, "pleasure marriages" (zawaj mutea) are allowed based on the instructions from Mohammed in the Koran (The Cow II: 234) where he states

> And those of you who die and leave wives behind, they should keep themselves in waiting for four months and ten days; then when they have fully attained their term, there is no blame on you for what they do for themselves in a lawful manner.

As George Packer explains (2005, pp.272-273), Such "pleasure marriages" have many of the trappings of conventional Islamic marriage, with contracts, payment up front, consent from both parties, approval of the woman's family, and blessing by a cleric, but the pleasure marriage is temporary and could last anywhere from one hour to twenty years, though it can be indefinitely renewable. Such an arrangement is viewed by Shiites as a form of mercy for widows.

Women's rights in general in the Koran are greatly limited in numerous areas in comparison with those of men. For example, in The Cow II: 230–237, it is suggested five times that men can divorce women at their discretion, with the statements, "So if he divorces her," "And when you divorce women," "And when you have divorced women," "There is no blame on you if you divorce women," and "And if you divorce them (women) before you have touched them," but nowhere does it mention "when she divorces him," thus suggesting that only men can initiate divorce. Similarly, Islamic laws of inheritance discriminate against women based on a statement in the Koran in Women 4:11, where it is stated that "the male shall have the equal portion of two females."

It is also stipulated in the Koran in Women IV:34 that women are to be subordinate to men in the household and that "good women are therefore obedient." As for those women that have caused their husbands to fear their desertion, they are to "leave them alone in the sleeping-places and beat them." Islamists use this verse to argue that if a woman refuses sexual relations with her husband, it is permissible for the husband to physically beat her until she submits (Gabriel, 2002, pp.42–43). Women are also instructed in the Koran in The Allies 33:33 to "stay in your houses and do not display your finery," with the result that women throughout the Islamic realm have had more limited educational and occupational opportunities than men, and in some cases, such as in Afghanistan under the Taliban, are not allowed to leave the house without male escorts (Goodwin, 2002, p.75). In fact, under the Taliban, women were not even allowed to answer the door when their husbands were not home based on Mohammed's Koranic instructions in The Allies 33:53, where the Prophet instructed people who visited his home that if he were not at home, they would have to speak to his wives through a screen.

"Honor killings" are also allowed in Islamic societies in cases where single women have disgraced the family by having sex out of wedlock. Women who become pregnant, thus proving their dishonor to the family, or women who fail a medical examination of the hymen, are often drowned or burned to death by family members in order to erase the family disgrace. Husbands are known to kill their new wives on their wedding night if they find that their new bride is not a virgin; consequently, families often subject their daughters to medical examinations of the hymen prior to the marriage. An entire medical subspecialty in Islamic societies deals with the question of female virginity, and the forensic evidence from such examinations often becomes the most important piece of evidence in criminal cases involving women (Packer, 2005, pp.259–260).

In general, radical Islamists argue that the Koran teaches that the family must be patriarchal and the primary female role is for procreation and the care of children. Women are viewed as physically, intellectually, emotionally, and spiritually inferior and in need of the protection and guidance of men. Some Islamists allow women to work outside the home, but not at the expense of their maternal obligations, and preferably in professions that draw on their maternal instincts, such as teaching, nursing, and social work. Islamists prescribe sexual segregation and argue that women must be chaperoned by men in public. Furthermore, Islamists argue that women must be veiled so as to stem the tide of indecency. The basic argument is that men are not able to control their sexual desires if they see female faces and bodies; consequently, the complete covering of women is necessary for the sexual morality of society (Sivan, 1985, pp.145–146).

Among the more notorious segments of sharia, amputations are prescribed for theft according to the command of Mohammed in the Koran (The Food 5:38), "And as for the man who steals and the woman who steals, cut off their hands as a punishment for what they have earned, an exemplary punishment from Allah." Although hymen examinations, floggings, amputations, and executions are generally thought of by Westerners as harsh, in the Islamist mindset, given that these laws are handed down by God through his Prophet Mohammed, to deviate from them in any way is un-Islamic and makes one an apostate or an infidel who must change his ways or face death (Roy, 1994, p.10). No one is exempt from the Islamic limitations and Islamists have even assassinated ulamas that they believed to be remiss in implementing sharia or too close to what they viewed as illegitimate apostates in positions of governmental authority (Roy, 1994, p.36). Furthermore, Islamists argue that deviation from these ancient practices will lead to corruption of society and Western decadence. Western-style freedoms and individual rights may free persons from these practices, but also remove persons from the right relationship with God and therefore erode the foundations of society (Packer, 2005, p.263). Islamists argue that Islamic societies that have strayed from sharia have reverted to jahiliyya, a term from the Koran that refers to the condition of society prior to Mohammed that combined both ignorance of God's laws and savagery. For Islamists, Holy War or resistance against such a government is sanctified (Roy, 1994, pp.41–42).

Economic Restrictions

The sharia also places some economic restrictions on society in that Mohammed denounced "usury" or the charging of interest on a loan (The Cow II: 275), a practice that was also forbidden to the ancient Jews under Mosaic law (Ex. 22:25; Deut 23:19). Given that money and banking are essential to capitalist economies, Islamists argue for an alternative model of banking where banks may charge fees for services and bankers often become partners in the ventures for which their money is used, but they may not charge interest on loans (Smith, 1991, p.250). The Islamic economy allows the accumulation of personal property and encourages entrepreneurship, profit, and economic competition, but requires social obligation of those who accumulate capital and property in the form of alms (2.5% of one's net worth annually). Islam also forbids the practice of primogeniture and even dictates that inheritance is shared by daughters as well as sons. In this way, the harshness of social inequalities is lessened. No one, however, may use their property in a manner that is inconsistent with Islam (Ishaque, 1991, p.275).

The sharia also sanctions legal inequalities between Muslims and non-Muslims, thus placing Islamists at odds with the principles of equality embedded in Western democracies. The sharia also forbids marriage between a Muslim woman and a non-Muslim man, thus denying complete freedom to choose one's own spouse. As for freedom of religion, conversion out of Islam is a capital offense; consequently, Islamists find themselves at odds with the Universal Declaration of Human Rights (Kramer, 1993, p.38).

Sunni-Shiite Division

Islam is not monolithic, and like virtually all religions, there is great diversity in beliefs among its adherents. The most significant division, however, is between Sunnis (Traditionalists) and the Shia or Shiites (partisans of Ali, Mohammed's cousin and son-in-law). Approximately 85% of all Muslims are Sunnis, but the vast majority in Iran and approximately 60% in Iraq are Shiites. Shiites believe that only a blood relative, in particular, Ali (who eventually became the fourth caliph in 656 AD), was the rightful successor to Mohammed, but was wrongfully passed over three times before finally being assassinated near Karbala in 680 AD, the event that Shiites now commemorate with the observance of Ashura (Smith, 1991, p.258). Shiites argue that Ali was chosen by Mohammed himself and point to an event that occurred in 632 AD as Mohammed journeyed toward Medina after the final pilgrimage of his life to Mecca. Mohammed is believed by all Muslims to have stopped by a pool of stagnant water in the desert and held up the hand of his cousin and son-in-law, Ali. Mohammed then stated, "For whomever I am his mawla, Ali is his mawla." Shiites argue that the word "mawla" meant "master" and argue that Ali was therefore chosen by Mohammed to be the Prophet's chosen successor or caliph. The word "Shia" essentially means partisans of Ali and his son Hussein, and all of the imams who descended from them. The Shiites also believe in the coming of "the Hidden Mahdi," a great religious leader whose reappearance in the future will usher in the apocalypse and the end of the world (Packer, 2005, p.432). Shiism is often known as "twelver Shiism," because it also awaits the return of the "twelfth imam," a direct descendant of Mohammed who is absent (since 873 AD), but somehow not dead, but may instead reappear at any moment to establish God's perfect justice on earth (Roy, 1994, p.169). Essentially, the direct lineage of Mohammed through Ali and Hussein was ended in 873 AD when the Twelfth Imam, Muhammad al-Mahdi, went into hiding from his enemies. Shiites not only believe that he will return one day to do away with all injustice and oppression, but also believe he is the only legitimate ruler; consequently, all temporal power and political actions taken in his absence are illegitimate without the approval of the highest Shiite clerics, who act as deputies for the absent Twelfth Imam. As deputies of the Twelfth Imam, the highest Shiite clerics or Ayatollahs may issue edicts that are binding on all Muslims, including all temporal political authorities (Hashim, 2006, pp.234–235).

Sunnis, on the other hand, argue that the Muslim community as a whole is able to decide on the succession of Mohammed and that the rules of succession should follow the rules of succession as they existed prior to Islam (Sayyid, 2003, p.56). For Sunnis, any devout follower of Mohammed was qualified to be his successor, and Sunnis accept the first caliph (successor) to Mohammed to be his father-in-law, Abu Bakr, who was not a blood relative. Sunnis argue that the word "mawla" mentioned in the story did not mean "master," but instead meant "friend," and Shiites have therefore misinterpreted Mohammed's gesture toward Ali (Packer, 2005, p.432). Sunnis also typically view the intense processions of Ashura, where marchers beat themselves with chains and slice their own heads with swords, to be unseemly and excessive.

Differences between Sunnis and Shiites do not stop with the dispute over the caliph, however. Shiites consider their imams (mosque officials who lead worshipers in Friday prayers) to be infallible and the sole source of true knowledge, endowed with the vision of Mohammed. For Shiites, the Ayatollahs (the highest religious leaders, literally "sign of God") have the exclusive power to interpret the Koran, and are charged with preserving and disseminating the faith. To observant Shiites, the pronouncements of the Shiite Ayatollahs have the force of law (Shadid, 2005, pp.301–302). Sunnis, on the other hand, tend to argue that all Muslims are equally capable of interpreting the will of God and none have a more perfect vision than others. Shiites are also more adamant that the ulama have more direct input into the affairs of State, whereas Sunnis tend to see a consultation role as sufficient (De Blij and Muller, 2002, p.290). As explained by Roy (1994, p.171), under Shiism, each believer must

> follow the interpretation of an ulama, whom he chooses from among the college of grand ayatollahs, in general by intermediary of the local mullahs, who have received their investiture either directly or indirectly from a grand ayatollah. Clericalization (the formation of an autonomous body of clerics separate from the state) is a consequence. This evolution also consecrated the financial autonomy of the clergy, which is still in effect, with followers

paying the Islamic tax directly to their mjtahid's representative rather than to the state. The money is gathered by the clergy, then redistributed into pious works, many of which have a social component. Since the eighteenth century then, the Shiite clergy has played a social and educational role with no parallel among the Sunni clergy...all operated to make the clergy a political force.

Under the Shiite political structure, the Ayatollah Khomeini developed the concept of vilayat-I faqih, or government by the doctor of law. In Khomeini's conception, there can be no Islamic society without an Islamic state, and there can be no Islamic state unless the state is subservient to the Islamic doctor of law who interprets the sharia for the state to implement. This placed the supreme religious authority in Shiism in Iran as the ultimate power above all state institutions, since the Ayatollah is the representative of the hidden Twelfth Imam. Under the Iranian constitution, a Council of Guardians, consisting of six ulama, verify that all laws passed by the Iranian government are consistent with Islam (Roy, 1994, pp.173–178).

Shiism is clearly a traditional conservative religious ideology with its focus on history, millenarianism, and the devaluation of temporal power. For these reasons, Shiism is also conducive to revolution in that Shiite revolution, like Marxist revolution, is intent upon bringing about the completion of history, which in the Shiite case means the realization of the promise of the hidden Imam. The Shiites perceive of the Shiite community much in the way Marx thought of the proletariat, as a particular group that will bring about the emancipation of all humanity through global revolution. Iran's Shiites have been striving, although not particularly successfully, to export that emancipating Revolution ever since their seizure of power in 1978 (Roy, 1994, p.p.175, 184).

Islamism and Colonialism

The twentieth century was witness to tremendous economic contact between Western cultures and the realm of Islam due to the Western need for oil and the prevalence of petroleum supplies in the Islamic realm. Added to the economic contact, and the potential for conflict that accompanies that contact, was the twentieth-century history of Western colonialism of Islamic lands and what Islamists view as Western cultural imperialism. Throughout the twentieth century, and certainly through the present with the George W. Bush administration, Western governments have often accepted the position that the Muslim world would be well served through the adoption of Western cultural, political, and economic structures (Packer, 2005, pp.60–68). In the words of Ahmed Hashim (2006, p.323) when discussing British attitudes in Iraq in 1920, "the British viewed themselves as bringers of the benefits of civilization and progress to the poor benighted heathen." This attitude is labeled by Edward Said as "Orientalism," the central idea of which is that Islamic cultures are unable to produce the kinds of innovations that are necessary for modernization. In "Orientalist" thought, for Muslims to develop economically and culturally, they must essentially diminish the significance of Islam in social and political fields, and replace it with the adoption of Western culture, including everything from Western political theories and structures to Western styles of dress and habits of personal hygiene (Said, 1979). The Orientalist view of Islam was used throughout the twentieth century by Western governments to justify colonialism and subjugation of Islamic peoples, theoretically for the benefit of the Islamic people. With such attitudes, not to mention the twentieth century history of Western physical occupation and colonialism of Islamic peoples, it is little wonder that Radical Muslims view the West as waging war against their culture. The emergence of contemporary Islamism is therefore partially explained as a response to the colonization of the Islamic world after World War I, the decolonization that occurred after World War II, the creation of the Jewish State of Israel on what Muslims view as their God-given land, and the continuing influence of Western culture and economics on Muslims societies (Schumaker et al., 1996, pp.372–373).

Throughout the aforementioned period of "colonialism," Islamism has proven to be adaptable to local histories and political situations and tends to serve as a rallying cry for the indigenous peoples against colonization. For instance, in the view of the Muslim Brotherhood in Egypt, Islam is a message of social reform and the answer to Western decadence and corruption. For the Palestinians opposed to Israel, Islam is a vehicle for resistance, providing a justification and vocabulary for continued resistance, violence, and martyrdom. The same could be said for the Mujahadeen in Afghanistan in the 1980s and the same is now true for the insurgents in Iraq. In the Islamist interpretation of colonialism, Americans and Jews are seen not only as imperialists, but as infidels and enemies of God that are illegitimately in Muslim lands and it is therefore moral to kill them (Shadid, 2005, pp.288–289).

Furthermore, Islamists reject the notion that Islamic culture may somehow be flawed and in need of Westernization. Instead, Islamists argue that Orientalist thinking is "cultural imperialism" that is being carried out by Western governments and other Western entities (corporations and religious interests) that are bent on Westernizing Muslim societies. This attitude was explained by Dr. Haider Moshin, a young medical internist in Iraq in 2004, to American journalist

George Packer. In the words of Moshin (Quoted in Packer, 2005, pp.429–430),

> The Jean-Jacques Rousseau idea, the French Revolution ideas—we think that these ideas are typical ideas for the European society, but how far it is from Iraq to the European societies is the distance from Islam to the French Revolution. Cultural Imperialism is the most dangerous kind of imperialism, and Iraq needed to resist the wave of low morals and rampant individualism emanating from the West. One of the causes that made France fall down in the Second World War was the sexual freedom.

It should not be surprising that the suggestion to any group, in this case Muslims, that their culture is somehow inferior, might be rejected. Instead, Islamists predictably react to such suggestions with calls for "decolonization" of Islamic societies at all levels. Anti-imperialist Islamists argue that a "new Muslim consciousness" must be developed among all Muslims through the elimination of all contact with the West and all influences of Western culture, politics, education, and economics. In order to do so, the Islamists argue that Muslims must pursue a purer form of Islam, and ensure that the segments of sharia inconsistent with Western culture, such as bans on alcohol and the exposure of the female body, must be enforced. Through the return to a purer form of Islam, the Islamists argue that a more Godly, just, and uncorrupted society can emerge (Ingersoll et al., 2001, pp.277–278).

Islamism and Education

Bernard Lewis (1982, pp.222–223) explains that innovation, in the Muslim tradition (as could be expected from any traditional conservative ideological perspective), is generally "assumed to be bad unless it can be shown to be good." Islamists therefore reject all education and technology that they view as inconsistent with the Koran. Since the Koran is perfect, all reason and critical thinking outside the Koran is rejected. In the words of Maudoudi (Quoted in Sivan, 1985, p.67), "Instead of claiming that Islam is truly unreasonable, one should hold that the true reason is Islamic." Such thinking has caused the realm of Islam to remain in what Egyptian scholar Murad Wahbah referred to as "an age of myth" rather than an "age of reason." For example, fundamentalist religious thinking in the Islamic world has produced an outpouring of unscientific nonsense in the Islamic community, similar to Christian books in the United States disputing the validity of Darwin's theory of evolution. For instance, one booklet distributed in Egypt by a religious student association attempted to prove that the sun revolves around the earth (Sivan, 1985, p.159). In such a mindset, the only education that one needs is a strict education in Islam.

The obvious result of such thinking is the limiting of the growth of technology through shared ideas from other cultures with the long-term result that the Islamic world remains centuries behind the West in technology. The adoption of foreign technologies essentially makes Muslims appear less "Islamic" and Islamists argue that those who embrace it have taken a first step toward apostasy. As a consequence, Islamic history has been one of rejection of technologies developed in the West. The printing press, for instance, was banned for several centuries in the Islamic world after its development in the West (Huff, 2003, p.128). In the Middle Ages, the Muslims even shunned gunpowder and guns that were invented by the Chinese to the east as un-Islamic (Lewis, 1982, p.222).

Again, however, there is also great hypocrisy among Islamists since radical Islamists apparently have no problem adopting Western technology in the areas of the communications technologies, transportation, and military weaponry necessary for jihad, and many Islamists are university educated. Osama bin Laden, for example, holds a bachelor's degree in engineering. In fact, so many Islamists are university-educated that some scholars, such as Nikki Keddie (1988), argue that Islamism is partially a crisis of the petty bourgeoisie in Islamic countries who become university educated, but find that the system still provides no opportunity and no upward mobility, thus leading them to turn to radical Islam as an alternative.

Islamists do, however, believe that Islamic education is useful and some advocate that education is a path to creating the true Islamic society desired by the jihadists. Even Egyptian radical Sayyid Qutb, who viewed all contemporary Muslim societies as jahiliyya, argued that jahili society could be regained for Islam through Islamic education, and advocated a long-range Islamic education effort for that purpose. The impact of the Islamists' push to implement Islamic education perhaps cannot be understated. For example, the share of religious books sold in Egypt is approximately 20%, while it is only 2% in France. Similarly, circulation of the Islamist magazine, *Mayo,* reached approximately 700,000 in Egypt by 1980 (Sivan, 1985, p.131). It must be noted, however, that Qutb was still able to accept violence while advocating Islamic education as a route to forging the true Islamic society (Sivan, 1985, pp.89–90). Exactly what sort of mix between real technological education and Islam is advocated by the Islamists is somewhat unclear.

Islamism and the Mass Media

Similar to traditional conservatives in Western societies, traditional conservative Muslims view the mass media as a corrupting influence.

In the words of Emmanuel Sivan (1985, 63), "Hostility against the media is endemic among militants of the Muslim students' associations who quite often refuse to watch TV as a matter of moral rectitude." Music, film, television, and radio are generally condemned as un-Islamic, and Islamists have made popular television, music, and film stars the subjects of terror attacks. By the 1960s, some Islamists had come to view the new mass media as so decadent that they even blamed its corrupting influences for causing the defeat in the Six Day War (Sivan, 1985, p.61). In 1971, Islamic radical Said Hawwa stated that a principal objective of the Islamic movement was a takeover of the communications media so that no un-Islamic element could slip into society through the mass media (Sivan, 1985, p.62). Similarly, the Islamist "Egyptian Jihad Organization" in the 1980s justified their argument for seizure of control of the state through the need for Islamists to control the media.

・CHAPTER FOUR・

Islamism and Terrorism

Although the 9/11 terrorist attacks (as well as the July 2005
London bombings) were bewildering to most Westerners, they
did not come as such a shock to those who have studied
Islamist ideology. Samuel Huntington (1993, pp.22-49), for instance,
argued at the end of the cold war that the world changed after the collapse of the USSR, and the nature of conflict in the world would therefore change to reflect that new order. Huntington further argued that
the United States stood alone as the world's only superpower and that
the struggles that threaten world peace would no longer focus on nationalism or capitalist/communist ideological conflict, as they had for
the previous 200 years, but instead would result from cultural con-
frontations. One of the major cultural factors that would cause this
conflict, according to Huntington, is religion. Huntington correctly
argued that the democratic capitalist West would be targeted by religious zealots from other cultural paradigms because these zealots believe the West (especially the United States), has wrongly intervened
in their realms by violating their sacred norms.

World of Misinformation and Conspiracy

The world of the Islamic terrorists is a world of misinformation and
conspiracy theory, where the Islamists view their existence as one in
which the forces of evil are constantly plotting against Islam. The existence of the anti-Islamic plot may not be apparent to others, but the
Islamists have seen through the veils imposed by the evil ones and un-
covered their sinister designs. The Islamists then must work to ensure
that others also recognize the plot and help combat it. The Islamist
conspiracy theorists are aided by the fact that the region of Islam is an
undereducated region where rumors and myths are as likely to circu-
late and gain widespread belief as the truth. For example, according to
Anthony Shadid (2005, p.92), many Iraqis believed that Saddam Hus-

sein remained in power as long as he did because he was backed by the United States (twelve years of severe American sanctions on Iraq including no-fly zones and frequent bombings being unpersuasive evidence to the contrary). For these conspiracy theorists, the belief was not that the United States favored regime change in Iraq at all, but that the United States instead favored and supported the continuation of Saddam's regime. Evidence in support of this belief was provided not only by the massive US aid to Saddam during the Iran/Iraq war, but also by the December 1983 visit to Baghdad by Donald Rumsfeld as a special envoy of Ronald Reagan. Pictures of Rumsfeld shaking hands with Saddam Hussein were familiar to many Iraqis and suggested that the United States was fully behind Saddam Hussein.

A vivid testimony to the prevalence and importance of rumor and myth in the Islamic world is provided by the Baath Party's intelligence offices in Saddam Hussein's Iraq, which kept official government files on rumors and conspiracy theories that circulated on the streets of Baghdad. After the Americans invaded Iraq, they discovered that in Saddam's files were reports of rumors that Israeli Prime Minister Ariel Sharon was plotting to destroy Palestinian homes in Jenin, so as to weaken the Iraqi economy before the impending American invasion. Saddam Hussein himself was purported to be working with the Americans and was planning to give gifts of automobiles to foreign Arabs who had been living in Iraq since before the 1991 intifada. The King of Jordan was rumored to be plotting to support exiles from Iraq in a Bay of Pigs-style invasion of Iraq that would accompany an American invasion that was to come on September 11, 2002, the first anniversary of the attacks on the United States It was also rumored that the United States planned to attack all the mosques in Iraq under the presupposition that the Iraqi government was hiding its Weapons of Mass Destruction in the mosques. It was further supposed that the United States would hit the Iraqi population with a new type of gas that would cause people to lapse into a coma for more than eight hours. Similarly, in spite of the celebrated American photo images of the corpses of Saddam Hussein's slain sons, Uday and Qusay, rumors circulated in Iraq that the two were still alive, Uday in particular having escaped to Spain, and the reports of their deaths were merely part of President Bush's re-election campaign propaganda (Packer, 2005, pp.162–164).

Outlandish rumors have persisted in Iraq since the US invasion as well, some of which have been perpetuated by the Iraqi media. For example, an Iraqi newspaper, al-Hawza, printed side-by-side photographs of President Bush and President Clinton holding up their index and pinkie fingers and alleged that the photos were proof of a Zionist-

Masonic conspiracy (Packer, 2005, p.265). Similarly, an Iraqi secondary school teacher told American journalist George Packer that "Ninety-five percent of Iraqis knew the main purpose of this (the American invasion) was to start a religious war between Shia and Sunnis" (Quoted in Packer, 2005, p.265). Iraqi clerics, the defenders of true Islam in Iraqi society, have done their own part in contributing to rumor and misinformation. One Iraqi cleric (Sheikh Mohamed Kinani) told Packer that he thought the suicide bombers were Wahhabi (a strict Sunni Islamic sect from Saudi Arabia), members of al-Qaeda working in concert with John Kerry to make President Bush look bad before the world (Packer, 2005, pp.267–268). Muqtada al-Sadr, the upstart Shiite cleric from Najaf, blamed Jews, the Americans, the British, and the Wahhabis for the violence in Iraq. Al-Sadr told his flock that the Jews had been told to stay away from the World Trade Center on 9/11 and the Americans instigated the violence in Iraq themselves so as to justify their continued occupation (Packer, 2005, pp.268–269).

Such nonsensical rumors may appear incredulous to Westerners, but they are a reality for Islamist believers, and thus provide incentives to indulge in indiscriminate violence against the omnipresent evil. After all, if one can believe in the miracles of the Koran (or for that matter in the talking snakes of Genesis), then almost any rumor, no matter how incredible, becomes believable.

Apocalyptic Thinking

Much like American Protestant Christianity, where the apocalyptic *Left Behind* book series has sold tens of millions of copies, anticipation of the apocalypse is a major industry and preoccupation in the Islamic world, and apocalyptic-thinking Muslims look forward to a day when God will bring the world as it exists to an end. Islamic bookstore shelves are full of their own versions of Left Behind type literature. In the apocalyptic mindset, all deterrents to violence are rendered meaningless by the promise of a new age. What difference does it make if one dies in Holy War today if the world is about to end tomorrow? Apocalyptic thinking essentially encourages jihadists to fight as holy warriors in a period of fanatic zeal, with little concern for the future since all the world is soon coming to an end. In the Koran, Mohammed speaks of a final judgment against evil. The terrorists, therefore, view themselves merely as soldiers of God aiding him in his judgment (White, 2002, p.53). In this paradigm, the attacks of 9/11 were purposed by the soldiers of God to humiliate and slaughter those who had defied the hegemony of God, and to please God by reasserting his primacy. What appeared to be senseless violence to the bewildered

Americans made perfect sense to the terrorists, who viewed the mass killings as Holy acts of worship, obedience, and redemption. Furthermore, since God is just, the "innocents" who were slain would receive their just reward in heaven from God, so the mass murder only accelerated their receipt of their just rewards (Benjamin and Simon, 2002, p.40).

The Hadiths

Though all justifiable actions (including terrorism) for Muslims must be consistent with the Koran, the Koran is not the only Islamic writing that is influential in Islam or influential to Islamic extremists. There are literally thousands of "Hadiths" (meaning reports) testifying of God and Mohammed, and all Muslims do not necessarily accept all of the same Hadiths. The Hadiths touch on a myriad of topics including slavery, divorce, photographs, forgiveness, sexual activity, and jihad (Ochsenwald and Fisher, 2004, p.77). From these thousands of writings, the Islamists in general, and al-Qaeda terrorists in particular, place a premium on the passages that call for jihad or Holy War. Radical Islamists also tend to subscribe to the writings of the radical thirteenth-century Muslim philosopher, Ibn Taymiyya.

Ibn Taymiyya

Ibn Taymiyya's primary goal was the restoration of what he viewed as the pure Islam of the first four decades from the hegira through the death of Ali, the last of the four caliphs (622-661 AD). Taymiyya believed that Islam had suffered centuries of spiritual decline since the purity of its early years; consequently, Taymiyya sought to cleanse Islam of its impurities. In order to do so, Taymiyya called for jihad and the institution of strict sharia (Sivan, 1985, p.95). Although sharia is not one of the five pillars of Islam as outlined by the Koran, Taymiyya argued that one ceases to be a Muslim when he fails to keep, or in the case of a Muslim ruler, apply sharia. Furthermore, Taymiyya argued that one fails to remain a Muslim if he breaks major Islamic injunctions concerning sexual conduct, alcohol, gambling, or property (Sivan, 1985, p.97).

Taymiyya taught that anyone who did not join with God's people should be attacked, whether they fought alongside the enemies of God, or simply did business with them. Those that should be attacked include not only infidels, but Muslim apostates or those that did not practice true Islam (Benjamin and Simon, 2002, p.42). Taymiyya called for a restoration of the age of Mohammed when the religious leader (Mohammed) was also the leader of state and Islamic law was also civil law. Taymiyya essentially argued that government should be subordinate to the ulama and the ulama should share the responsibilities of government. Furthermore, any ruler who did not enforce sharia would be an apostate and Muslims were obligated to rebel against such a leader (Benjamin and Simon, 2002, p.48). As a consequence, current Islamist followers of Taymiyya oppose Islamic leaders, such as the former Shah of Iran, Hosni Mubarak of Egypt, Saddam Hussein of Iraq, and Bashar Assad of Syria, who Westernize, institute laws other than Islamic sharia, allow Western-style music and dress, do not grow beards, and allow women to advance through education. Against such leaders, Taymiyya condoned assassination (Baer, 2002, p.87). Taymiyya, however, considered the superior form of jihad to be combat against infidels.

Obviously, Taymiyya's call for the restoration of the age of Mohammed is a perfect example of a traditional, conservative ideological call for a return to a better, vanished time and his call for the overthrow of apostate rulers and approvals of assassinations are clear preferences for "ends politics." Although murder is considered an evil in all religions, including Islam, Taymiyya essentially condones the evil in the interest of preventing what he views as a greater evil, the falling away of society from true Islam. For example, in his *Treatise on Public Policy in Islamic Jurisprudence*, Taymiyya argued that any trespasser of the sharia should be fought, "provided that he had knowledge of the mission of the Prophet" (Quoted in Sivan, 1985, p.98). For Taymiyya, the knowledge of God's law makes one responsible for obeying its orders and prohibitions. If one disobeys, he should be "fought" (Sivan, 1985, p.98). Taymiyya's thinking is similar to Jesus' teaching in Luke 12:47 where he is credited with stating, "that servant who knew his master's will, and did not prepare himself or do according to his will, shall be beaten with many stripes, but he who did not know, yet committed things worthy of stripes shall be beaten with few."

Muhammad ibn Abd al-Wahhab

Similar to Taymiyya is al-Wahhab, the person essentially responsible for the rise of the Wahhabi sect of Sunni Islam in Saudi Arabia. Wahhabism has received much greater attention in the West since 9/11, due to the fact that several of the 9/11 terrorists had been members of a radical Wahhabi mosque in Khamis Mushayt, Saudi Arabia and Osama bin Laden himself is a Wahhabi (Bradley, 2005, p.66). The Saudi Arabian ruling family also claim to be Wahhabis (even if their behavior does not always conform to Wahhabi teaching) and have supported Wahhabi-style sharia and education in Saudi Arabia throughout the twentieth century. In return, the Wahhabi religious establishment has generally supported the Saudi ruling family (Bradley, 2005, pp.25–27).

Al-Wahhab was an eighteenth-century student of Islam who viewed Islam in his time as corrupted (again, a clear traditional conservative ideological perspective) and called for the reformulation of Islam into what he viewed as "true Islam," drawing on the works of Taymiyya (Baer, 2002, p.87). Al-Wahhab was outraged at the lavish and decadent lifestyles of the Egyptian and Ottoman nobility, who made the pilgrimage to Mecca each year. Al-Wahhab viewed the pilgrims as apostates, blasphemous polytheists, and worshipers of false idols. Al-Wahhab was also angered by native Arabians who honored saints with monuments or decorated gravestones and mixed Islam with animist superstitions. For Al-Wahhab, all who engaged in such practices were Allah's enemies who should be converted or destroyed. In contrast with Jesus, who is revered in Christendom for saying "let he who is without sin cast the first stone," when Al-Wahhab came across a woman accused of fornication, he ordered her stoned to death (Coll, 2005, p.75).

Al-Wahhab's teachings were essentially a form of salafism, a radical interpretation of Islam that emphasizes the emulation of the salaf (men of old) of the time of the Prophet and the earliest generation of Islam (again the traditional conservative reverence for the figures of history). The word "salaf" itself means predecessor or early generation, and refers to the companions of the Prophet and the two generations of Muslims that succeeded the Prophet. Salafis desire to restore the pure Islam as it existed in the golden age of the Prophet along with the true ancient interpretations of the Koran and Hadiths, while eradicating the corrupted more recent interpretations (Pape, 2005, p.106 Hashim, 2006, p.25).

Salafism is fundamentalist in character and insists on the inerrancy of the Koran and Hadiths, and strict interpretations of the sharia (Benjamin and Simon, 2005, pp.54–55). All more recent interpretations of the Koran or the Hadiths are considered to be suspect by the Salafis, and surely corrupted by non-Islamic influences that dilute the true message of God. Consequently, other forms of Sunni fundamentalism, such as Sufism, which accommodates more recent interpretations of the sacred texts, stresses reverence for saints, and teaches personal contact with the divine through mystical devotions, are considered heretical by the Salafis (Pape, 2005, p.106). Salafis are known as "pious pioneers if Islam" and the Salafi Daway (call of the Salafis) is Islam in its totality, applied to all humanity irrespective of ethnicity, culture, or national origin (Auster, 1998, p.49). Unfortunately, the methods of the Salafis have often included political violence and numerous scholars credit Salafism as a principal cause of al-Qaeda terrorism (Pape, 2005, p.107).

In pursuit of reconstruction of the "golden age" of Islam as it existed at the time of Mohammed, al-Wahhab discarded customs that he viewed as developing between Mohammed and the eighteenth century and condemned "innovation" in Islam as sinful, in what constitutes a clear example of traditional conservative ideological resistance to change. Al-Wahhab was exceedingly intolerant and argued that those who committed sins of "innovation" should be executed. Al-Wahhab argued that delivering any legal ruling on the basis of anything other than the Koran or Hadith was apostasy, as were heresies such as the denial of predestination, profiting from trade, interpreting the Koran figuratively rather than literally, failing to attend public prayers on Fridays, and shaving one's beard (Benjamin and Simon, 2002, pp.52–53).

The Salafist approach to Islam as espoused by Al-Wahhab restricts diet, dress, manner, and daily routine to those espoused by Mohammed in the seventh century (Benjamin and Simon, 2005, p.56). In Saudi Arabia, the Royal family continuously negotiates with the Salafist clergy to ensure their support and the support of the Salafist masses. When it appears that support for the regime from the Salafists is waning, the Saudi Royal family has typically enforced more strict Salafist limits on society. For example, after the seizure of the Grand Mosque in Mecca in 1979 by Islamists that viewed the Saudi Royal family as apostates for their modernization, the Saudi Royal Family implemented new rules to satisfy Salafist and Wahhabi radicals that banned women's hair salons, female television announcers, and prevented women from continuing their education abroad (Coll, 2005, p.35).

Wahhabis also condemn recreating or displaying the human form; consequently, they do not allow human photos, paintings, or graven images that they view as having potential to interfere with the devotion to Allah (Bradley, 2005, p.4).

In 1965 when Saudi television debuted, for instance, Wahhabis stormed the government television studio in protest and a cousin of Saudi King Faisal died in a resulted shootout (Coll, 2005, p.79). Similarly, the Taliban in Afghanistan banned images of humans and destroyed television sets (Goodwin, 2002, p.75).

Wahhabis despise "polytheism" and therefore condemn not only Trinitarian Christianity as polytheistic, but also Shiite Islam for its reverence for the Twelve Imams and reverence for shrines (Bradley, 2005, p.5). In fact, during the war in Afghanistan in the 1980s, Arab Wahhabis clashed with local Afghan Muslims (who adorn graves) when they destroyed graves decorated by local Muslims under the premise that such adornment of graves constituted the worship of false idols (Coll, 2005, p.152).

In spite of these activities that obviously stir up divisions among Muslims, the Wahhabis stress the unity of Muslims under Allah (much like the Puritans and Medieval Catholic Christians who stressed unity of Christians and purged heretics) and argue that it is the duty of Muslims to be loyal to other believers. One of the duties that accompanies the Wahhabi vision of unity is the requirement that Muslims should have nothing to do with the idolatrous and polytheistic infidel enemies of Islam. For Al-Wahhab, these enemies of Islam included Shiite Muslims. Al-Wahhab argued that practices such as invoking prophets, saints, or angels rather than Allah were not merely sins, but acts of apostasy that merited the ultimate penalty. Furthermore, anyone who stood in the way of eventual Wahhabi domination of the entire world should be killed (Bradley, 2005, pp.6–8).

Under the strict teachings of Al-Wahhab, if his instructions are to be followed to the letter, more secular Middle Eastern leaders Saddam Hussein, Bashar Assad, Hosni Mubarak, and the former Shah of Iran, would merit execution if for no other reason than the fact that they shaved their beards. The call for the execution of apostates for the transgression of shaving is clearly extreme, but it should be remembered that it is no more extreme than executing people for witchcraft in Salem Village in 1692 or shooting doctors who perform abortions through their kitchen window, as more recent traditional conservative Christians have done in the West.

The Wahhabis and Salafis (not all Salafis are Wahhabis. Shiites, for example, revere the "men of old," but are not followers of the Sunni Al-Wahhab) subscribe to the traditional conservative plot mentality and therefore view themselves and Islam as under siege from secularism, materialism, and a global anti-Muslim conspiracy led by Israel and the United States. The Wahhabis and Salafis view themselves as the select few who not only can see the plot that others cannot, but must defend Islam against the pervasive and persistent attacks (Benjamin and Simon, 2005, pp.56–57).

The impact of Wahhabism on global terror and Islamism cannot be understated, and has been intertwined with Saudi Arabia since its beginning as a modern state in the twentieth century. After World War I, the al-Sauds under Abdul Aziz conquered much of the Arabian Peninsula in the name of Wahhabism. Aziz sponsored a new vanguard of war-fighting believers who enforced bans on alcohol, tobacco, embroidered silk, gambling, fortune-telling, magic, telephones, radios, and automobiles. In fact, when the first motor-driven truck arrived on their territory, they burned it to the ground as a sinful "innovation"

(Coll, 2005, p.76). Aziz conquered Mecca, Medina, and Jeddah by 1926 and then founded the Ministry for the Propagation of Virtue and Prevention of Vice (Saudi Religious Police) to enforce Wahhabi doctrine. Aziz' Saudi Arabia became the only modern nation created by Sunni Islamic jihad (Coll, 2005, pp.76–77).

The Saudi Arabian government and Saudi philanthropists, many of whom subscribe to Wahhabism, have spent hundreds of millions of dollars over the last thirty years on missionary activity and education to spread Wahhabi Islam. The results have been impressive, since 80% of university majors in Saudi Arabia are in Wahhabi Islam. The Wahhabi connections with global Islamic jihad and terror have been even more impressive. A proverbial "who's who" of international jihadist terrorism has arisen from the Wahhabi sect. Fifteen of the nineteen 9/11 hijackers were Wahhabis from Saudi Arabia, as is Osama bin Laden. Abu Muhammad al-Maqdisi, the mentor of Abu Musab al-Zarqawi, the head of al-Qaeda in Iraq, is a radical Wahhabi teacher who denounces the Saudi ruling family as apostates. Similarly, Abu Bakr Bashir, the leader of the Indonesian terrorist organization, Jemaah Islamiyah, is a Wahhabi who studied in Saudi Arabia (Benjamin and Simon, 2005, p.99).

In recent years, radical Wahhabis have also proven themselves to be "takfiri," those who believe that it is justified to kill Muslims who commit apostasy and collaborate with the enemy. Al-Zarqawi's terror attacks against the new Iraqi government are cases in point, as are al-Qaeda's 1998 Africa bombings in Nairobi and Dar as Salaam (which killed mostly Muslims), and the bombing of a residential compound in Riyadh in 2003 that killed 17 people and wounded 120, most of whom were Muslims (Benjamin and Simon, 2005, p.101).

Wahhabism has experienced tremendous growth since the 1970s due to oil money in the hands of prominent members of the Saudi Royal Family that support Wahhabism on a global basis as a form of Islamic charity and evangelism. The last five decades have also witnessed a concerted effort by the government of Saudi Arabia to spread Wahhabism. In 1962, the Saudi government founded the Muslim World League, a nongovernmental organization created for the express purpose of spreading Wahhabism worldwide. In pursuit of its goals, the Muslim World League has dispersed missionaries and distributed the works of Ibn Taymiyya and Ibn Al-Wahhab on a global basis. The league has also distributed funds for the building of mosques and madrassas (Islamic schools) in Saudi Arabia and all over the world, and subsidized other Islamic associations and charities (Kepel, 2003, 52).

Rashid Rida

Rashid Rida was a Cairo Islamic intellectual in the early twentieth century during the time of Western colonialism that followed World War I. Rida opposed the Islamic leaders at the time that substituted Western law for sharia and, in the words of Rida,

> thus abolish supposedly distasteful penalties such as cutting off the hands of thieves or stoning adulterers and prostitutes. They replace them with man-made laws and penalties. He who does that has undeniably become an infidel. (Quoted in Sivan, 1985, p.101)

Rida, like other traditional conservative Islamists, was obviously another Muslim fundamentalist and moral absolutist whose source for his moral absolutes was the Koran. Rida used the word jahiliyya, a word from the Koran meaning "barbarity," to describe Muslims that submitted to man-made law rather than the sharia. Rida condemned secular government as a violation of the Koran and, like other traditional conservative Islamists, favored a return to the "better, vanished time" of Islam in the seventh century and hearkened back to the age of Islamic caliphs as a model for the government of the present. Rida desired to reestablish the caliphate in a new form, similar to an Islamic version of the papacy, so as to unite all Muslims under a true and pure Islam (Sayyid, 2003, p.61). Rida believed that only a return to true and pure Islam would bring Muslims political and economic power and end the rule of the colonialists (Benjamin and Simon, 2002, p.56). Rida's work helped lay the groundwork for radicals that would arrive later, such as Egyptian Islamist Sayyid Qutb, but Rida, focused primarily on the elimination of the introduction of foreign laws and stopped short of declaring jihad against Westernized Muslim rulers (Sivan, 1985, p.102). His successors in radical Islamist thought would not be so reserved.

Maulana Maudoudi

It is worth noting that at the beginning of the twentieth-first century approximately 80% of the world's Muslims are not Arabs and do not live in the Middle East. Instead, Indonesia is the world's largest Muslim country with over 250 million Muslims and Islamism is just as prevalent in South Asia as it is in the Arab World (Kepel, 2003, p.33). Although India is thought of as a Hindu country, approximately 140 million of its inhabitants are Muslim. Another approximately 140 million Muslims live in Pakistan and 130 million in Bangladesh (Bradshaw et al., 2004, pp.270–271). Representative of the large population of non-Arab Islamist thinkers is Maulana Maudoudi, also known as Abu al-Ala Mawdudi and Sayyid Abul Ala Maudoudi, who was a radical Islamist thinker in what is now Pakistan during the Great Depression and World War II.

Maudoudi was the founder of the Islamist organization Jamaat-e-Islami in the part of British India (which later became Pakistan) in the early twentieth century. Jamaat-e-Islami would eventually receive funding from Saudi Arabia and grow to become the vanguard of Islamism in South Asia (Coll, 2005, pp.25–27). Maudoudi formulated a radical Islamist ideology that eventually provided the framework for an Islamic backlash against the West and against secular Arab governments that had embraced selected aspects of Western culture. Maudoudi, like Al-Wahhab, offered a sweeping condemnation of modernity and declared it to be incompatible with Islam as jahiliyya (barbarity) (Sivan, 1985, p.22). Maudoudi opposed secularism (of course), but also opposed nationalism and democracy as un-Islamic "imported" institutions that had no legitimacy in Islam. Maudoudi believed that nationalism violated the Islamic goal of unity and was therefore illegitimate, evil, and corrupt. Similarly, Maudoudi argued that the Western conception of democracy tended to lead to factions, and was therefore also converse to the unity of the umma (Islamic people) and consequently counter to Islam itself (Sivan, 1985, p.39). For Maudoudi, the only legitimate source of laws in Islamic society was the divinely inspired sharia, from which any deviation should be considered apostasy (Murphy, 2002, p.114). Maudoudi argued that the proper Islamist state would be one in which sovereignty would belong to Allah alone, but would be exercised by a just ruler under the guidance of the sharia. In Maudoudi's conception, the ideal Islamic state therefore would be inconsistent with Western democracy. In the words of Maudoudi (Quoted in Kramer, 1996),

> In such a state, no one can regard any field of his affairs as personal and private. Considered from this aspect the Islamic state bears a kind of resemblance to the fascist and communist states ... the very antithesis of secular democracy. (p.148)

Maudoudi envisioned that the goal of Muslims should be that the entire world would eventually submit to Islam. In order to accomplish that goal, Maudoudi called for unrestrained global jihad. Maudoudi argued that the five traditional pillars of Islam were merely phases of training and preparation for jihad, which he viewed as the ultimate service to God (Kepel, 2003, p.34). Maudoudi further argued that "Islam can use every power available every way it can be used to bring worldwide revolution" (Quoted in Gabriel, 2002, p.82). Consequently, though Maudoudi viewed Islam as under attack from infidel globalization and infidel technology, Maudoudi would allow Islamists to utilize that same Western technology to enable the globalization of Islamism.

As with other traditional conservatives, for Maudoudi the righteous ends would justify the means.

Maudoudi further argued that the jihadists who would bring the global revolution were not simply normal Muslim missionaries, but were a "Party of God" established by Allah himself to

> take the truth of Islam in one hand and to take the sword in the other hand and destroy the kingdoms of evil and the kingdoms of mankind and to re-place them with the Islamic system. This group is going to destroy the false gods and make Allah the only God." (Quoted in Gabriel, 2002, p.82)

Maudoudi envisioned his organization, the Jamaat-e-Islami, as the "vanguard of Islamic Revolution" on a Leninist model and compared his organization to the earliest Muslims, whom he viewed as a "vanguard" that formed around Mohammed during the Hegira in 622 AD (Kepel, 2003, p.34).

The impact of Maudoudi's teachings since the mid-twentieth century has been immense, as his ideas have spread around the globe. In the half-century that has passed since Maudoudi called for global jihad, the basic messages of militant Islamists have changed little. Those that reflect the influence of Maudoudi in their approach to world affairs would certainly include Osama bin Laden and al-Qaeda as well as numerous other Islamist groups in the early twenty-first century. Among the first to be influenced by Maudoudi outside of South Asia, however, were the Egyptian Muslim Brotherhood of Hassan al-Banna.

Hassan al-Banna and the Muslim Brotherhood

The Muslim Brotherhood formed in Egypt amid the disarray of the colonial period in the Middle East and North Africa that followed World War I (Kepel, 2003, p.27). Prior to World War II, Islamism had generally taken a back seat to anticolonialism in the Islamic realm as the indigenous peoples struggled against their colonial masters for self-rule. After World War II, however, education expanded in Islamic countries and greater numbers of traditionalist rural, formerly illiterate Muslims, suddenly came into contact with secular knowledge and Western culture that they viewed as inconsistent with Islam. Following World War II, governments in Muslim countries introduced numerous changes that traditional conservative Muslims could have been expected to oppose. Women were educated at the Middle Eastern universities under the Baathist and Nasserist regimes in Egypt, Syria, and Iraq, and traditional social mores began to erode. Young women began to shun the veil, Western-style political structures and laws were adopted, and the radio and television age brought Western mass media to the realm of Islam, complete with its secular culture (Sivan, 1985, pp.38–61).

Following World War II, Islamic traditional conservatives also objected to what they viewed as secular and un-Islamic positions of the ulama, who out of fear of persecution, death, or losing their positions of privilege, were generally supportive of the changes introduced by the new secular Arab regimes (Sivan, 1985, pp.50–52). In the words of Egyptian Islamist Sayyid Qutb, who denounced the Egyptian ulama, "We see the ulama only in the orbit of the rulers, declaring legal whatever the latter want to permit, forbidding what they want to outlaw" (Quoted in Sivan, 1985, p.55). In such a situation where religious leaders have become lackeys of temporal authorities, one might expect a reactionary backlash from the traditional conservative religious elements in any society. That backlash would be provided after World War II in the Middle East by an Egyptian teacher from the Nile delta named Hassan al-Banna and the organization he spawned known as the Muslim Brotherhood (Kepel, 2003, p.27).

Following in the traditions of Rida, in 1928, al-Banna formed the Muslim Brotherhood to revive pure Islam and resist colonialism and secularism. Al-Banna opposed not only Western culture and colonialism, but also what he viewed as the "calamity" of 1924, where Kemal Ataturk had ended the caliphate and declared Turkey to be a secular state. Although the caliph at that time had little power and was largely only symbolic, al-Banna viewed the development as a "declaration of war against all shapes of Islam" and feared that similar events could occur in his homeland of Egypt and throughout the rest of the Islamic world (www.ummah.net/ikhwan/).

For Islamists such as al-Banna, the caliphate represents the idea of global Islamic power and their eventual goal would be the establishment of a caliph under whom all humanity would be subordinate in a world united under Islam (Sayyid, 2003, p.xviii). Consequently, al-Banna and the Muslim Brotherhood argued that Muslims could not fulfill their rightful destiny in the absence of a true caliphate. The Muslim Brotherhood's credo, again reflecting traditional conservative ideology, essentially called for the return to sharia and pure Islam, but the call was also for jihad as a means to those ends. To al-Banna and the Muslim Brotherhood, Islam could be used as a means for the people to gain political power (Kepel, 2003, p.29). In their credo, the Muslim Brotherhood proclaimed, "God is our objective; the Koran is our constitution; the Prophet is our leader; struggle is our way; and death for the sake of God is the highest of our aspirations" (Quoted in Benjamin and Simon, 2002, p.56). As such, al-Banna rejected Western culture and government and the separation of church and state that accompanied Westernization. Al-Banna and the Muslim Brotherhood instead called for what they termed "Islamic modernity" which entailed a complete blending of society, religion, state, and culture. To the Muslim Brotherhood, Islam is a complete system, and nothing else is needed (Kepel, 2003, p.28).

The Muslim Brotherhood equated Turkey's Kemal Ataturk and the abolition of the caliphate not only with secularism, but with the ultimate fragmentation of Islam and the true enemies of Islam, Jews, crusaders, and imperialists. Communism and socialism (socialism being a major component of Nasserism and Baathism) were equally condemned as corrupting influences and enemies of Islam (Sivan, 1985, pp.56–58). Hence, the Muslim Brotherhood began waging their jihad against the Egyptian government with the result that al-Banna was killed by Egyptian governmental authorities in 1949. The Muslim Brotherhood was outlawed in Egypt in 1954 and a government crackdown led to mass arrests of the Muslim Brotherhood's leadership. In spite of the death of al-Banna and the Egyptian government's backlash, the Muslim Brothers, if anything, became more radical and determined to bring down "apostate" governments, and their ideology spread throughout the Middle East over the next several decades. The ultimate result has been that the Muslim Brothers have been involved in terrorism against both "apostate" Muslim governments and the "infidel" West ever since (Sivan, 1985, pp.42–43 Baer, 2002, pp.86–91). The Muslim Brotherhood claims to have provided 10,000 warriors for the 1948 war against Israel and in the later conflicts in Afghanistan and Kashmir (www.ummah.net/ikhwan/).

The defeat of the Arab countries at the hands of the Israelis in the Six-Day War spawned a new round of radicalism in the Muslim Brotherhood and provided new recruits dedicated to ending the jahili regimes that brought about the 1967 debacle. The Muslim Brotherhood then planned further terrorist attacks against the apostate governments, leading to another round of arrests, executions, and imprisonments in the 1960s (Sivan, 1985, pp.48–49).

The Muslim Brotherhood currently has branches in over seventy countries throughout the world. Their objectives remain not only building the ideal Muslim individual, family, and society, but also building the ideal Muslim state, reinstating the caliphate and the accompanying unity among the umma, and finally "mastering the world with Islam" (www.ummah.net/ikhwan/). It must be mentioned, however, that the official mission statement of the Muslim Brotherhood at present emphasizes the goal of bringing about Salafi ideals through peaceful political change, rather than through violence (Pape, 2005, p.106). The success of any ideology largely depends on how it is able to adapt to the needs of society. For the Muslim Brotherhood, this has meant developing an elaborate system of support for itself as an "Islamic Charity" and the dispensing of goods and services throughout the globe to the Islamic community so as to gain support of Muslims everywhere in addition to radical Islamists (Kepel, 2003, p.30). The fact that the Muslim Brotherhood has been going strong for over half a century in the face of sometimes severe government oppression suggests that it is an organization that has developed the ability to adapt and is here to stay.

Sayyid Qutb

Sayyid Qutb, a member of the Egyptian Muslim Brotherhood during the reign of Nasser, studied in the United States at the University of Northern Colorado, where he came to view the West as irreparably decadent and in decay, with unbridled individualism, depravity, and moral and social decline. Qutb wrote prolifically and was eventually executed by the Egyptian government in the 1960s, but his words and "martyrdom" have been an inspiration to Islamists ever since. Qutb vehemently denounced Western culture and Western forms of government as jahiliyya. In particular, Qutb was unimpressed with Western capitalism, individualism, Christianity, and democracy, which he characterized as a failure and "bankrupt," and for that reason (among others) opposed its introduction into the Islamic world (Sivan, 1985, p.73). In the words of Qutb (Quoted in Sivan, 1985),

> During my years in America, some of my fellow Muslims would have recourse to apologetics as though they were defendants on trial. Contrariwise, I took an offensive position, excoriating the Western jahiliyya, be it in its much-acclaimed religious beliefs or in its depraved and dissolute socioeconomic and moral conditions: this Christian idolatry of the Trinity and its notions of sin and redemption which make no sense at all; this Capitalism, predicated as it is on monopoly and interest-taking, money-grubbing, and exploitation; this Individualism which lacks any sense of solidarity and social responsibility other than that laid down by law; that crass and vacuous materialistic perception of life, that animal freedom which is called permissiveness, that slave market dubbed 'women's liberation.' (p.68)

Qutb further argued that Islam and Western values were fundamentally antagonistic and that the Western world was the "land of the crusaders," bent on destroying Islam (Murphy, 2002, p.113). In fact, Qutb termed Western culture as "The most dangerous jahiliyya which has ever menaced our faith" (Quoted in Sivan, 1985, p.25). Furthermore, he argued that globalization increased the opportunities for the West to culturally poison Islamic societies (Sivan, 1985, p.24). Qutb, however, was equally condemning of communism and socialism as un-Islamic. In the words of Qutb (Quoted in Sivan, 1985, p.76), "God did not send Mohammed on a mission of socialism, but to proclaim that there is no God but Allah."

After experiencing Western society firsthand at the University of Northern Colorado and rejecting it almost in its entirety, Qutb returned to Egypt, where he joined the Muslim Brotherhood and became head of their organ of propaganda (Sivan, 1985, p.22). Qutb built on the writings of Maudoudi in formulating his Islamist religious and political philosophy that led to his opposition to the "apostate" Egyptian Government of Pan-Arabian Socialist Gamal Abdel Nasser, and then subsequent imprisonment and eventual execution by the Egyptian government in the 1960s for his anti-government activities. Qutb, like Maudoudi, was an opponent of nationalism and of Pan-Arabism in particular because in his view they supplanted Pan-Islamism as the organizing premise for society (Sivan, 1985, p.38).

Qutb authored a best-selling book in the Middle East entitled *Signposts* where he argued that human political rule outside of God is illegitimate and that Muslims must answer to God alone. Qutb further argued that human governments that claimed to be established by Islam, but were not subordinate to the clergy, were apostate governments and legitimate targets of jihad. Only by destroying these "jahiliyya" governments could a truly pure Islamic society emerge (Benjamin and Simon, 2002, p.62).

Qutb rejected the notion that Maudoudi's ideal Islamic state could be developed through persuasion, arguing that force in the form of jihad was the only alternative. Qutb also denounced the idea that jihad should be a "spiritual" battle as opposed to physical, armed conflict (Kramer, 1996, p.148). Instead, Qutb argued that the purpose of jihad is to protect the religion of Islam and sharia and to save the "Abode" of Islam, and jihad should be carried out by military means if necessary. In the words of Qutb (Quoted in Kramer, 1996, p.148), "those who have usurped the power of God on earth and made His worshippers their slaves will not be dispossessed by dint of Word alone." Qutb argued that any land that combats the faith, hampers Muslims from practicing their religion, or does not apply sharia becomes subject to jihad (Smith, 1957, p.106). In order to implement the necessary jihad, Qutb (borrowing from revolutionary Marxism) argued that a "vanguard" of believers should organize itself, retreat from the decadent society around them, denounce apostate Muslims as unbelievers, and engage in a struggle to overturn the apostate political order. Hence, Qutb's jihad is essentially a call for revolution, and in Qutb's conception, the result of that revolution will be the liberation of Muslims from human tyranny through the removal of corrupt human laws and the replacement of those laws with the laws of God. In the words of Qutb (Quoted in Cox and Marks, 2003),

> Islam is nothing but Allah declaring his liberation to the human race on earth from slavery. Allah declares his lordship over the entire earth. This

means that Allah greatly protests all man-made government and authorities. Absolute rebellion is a must against anything on earth that conflicts with Islam. We should eliminate and destroy with great power anything that stops Allah's Revolution. (p.53)

From this succinct statement, one can easily deduce that Qutb's religious ideology is inconsistent with Western democracy. For Qutb and his followers, "freedom" has nothing to do with Western-style political freedoms, elections, and civil liberties, and everything to do with imposing the sharia and pure Islam, from which God's true freedom for humanity will be deduced. Western-style democracy is "man-made" government that is opposed by God and therefore must be opposed by all Muslims. For Qutb, only Allah is sovereign and if sovereignty is vested elsewhere, as in the people in a democracy, then the people follow an idol (Kepel, 2003, p.26). Given that Western-style democracy vests sovereignty in an idol instead of Allah, democracy hinders the development of Qutb's pure Islamic world; consequently, there must be "absolute rebellion" against it and it must be destroyed.

Like other Islamic traditional conservatives, Qutb viewed current Islamic society as in decay and called for a return to the purity of the better, vanished time of Mohammed. Qutb also expanded on Maudoudi's concept of jahiliyya, declaring that (Quoted in Sivan, 1985),

Jahiliyya signifies the domination of man over man, or rather the subservience to man rather than to Allah. It denotes rejection of the divinity of God and the adulation of mortals. In this sense, jahiliyya is not just a specific historical period (referring to the time before Mohammed), but a state of affairs. Such a state of human affairs existed in the past, exists today, and may exist in the future, taking the form of jahiliyya, that mirror-image and sworn enemy of Islam. In any time and place human beings fact that clear-cut choice: either to observe the Law of Allah in its entirety, or to apply laws laid down by man of one sort or another. In the latter case, they are in a state of jahiliyya. Man is at the crossroads and that is the choice: Islam or jahiliyya. Modern-style jahiliyya in the industrialized societies of Europe and America is essentially similar to the old-time jahiliyya in pagan and nomadic Arabia. For in both systems, man is under the dominion of man rather than of Allah. (pp.23–24)

In other words, Qutb essentially rejected all political systems designed by humans in the time that he lived (including those in Islamic countries) and viewed all as outside of the liberating system of law designed by God, since all deviated from the sharia. In the words of Qutb, "Everything around us is Jahiliyya ... people's perceptions and beliefs, habits and customs, the sources of their culture, arts and literature, and their laws and legislations" (Armstrong, 2000, p.240). Consequently, everything that is of human construct, including human-developed cultural mores, must be razed and replaced with the cultural constructs of God. It follows then that a society built on science alone, separate from God, or a society constructed on philosophical explanatory models, such as Western liberalism or Marxist-Leninism were also jahiliyya to Qutb (although he noted the unquestionable instrumental value of technology and admitted a need for scientific research). Qutb, like his traditional conservative Christian coalition counterparts in the United States, also denounced the mass media as decadent and anti-God, arguing that "radio, and television, and the kind of arts they foster and broadcast, conduct an anti-Islamic campaign" (Sivan, 1985, p.61).

Similar to Western moral absolutists, Qutb's version of Islamism views the world in black and white, "with us or against us," terms with little room for compromise, empathy, or flexibility. Qutb divided the Islamic world into what he termed as the Order of Islam, which correctly followed true Islamic teachings, and the Order of Jahiliyya, where he placed most Arab regimes of his time, including that of his own Egypt (Murphy, 2002, p.113). Qutb further argued that Islam could not survive coterminous with jahiliyya. The idea that more traditional and "correct" or "pure" Islam could survive while simultaneously allowing other less traditional Muslims to worship Allah as they saw fit was simply impossible to Qutb. In the words of Qutb,

> Islam cannot accept any compromise with Jahiliyya...Either Islam will remain, or Jahiliyya; Islam cannot accept or agree to a situation which is half Islam and half Jahiliyya. In this respect, Islam's stand is very clear. It says that truth is one and cannot be divided; if it is not the truth, then it must be falsehood. The mixing and coexistence of truth and falsehood is impossible. Command belongs to Allah or else to Jahiliyya. The Sharia of Allah will prevail, or else people's desires. (Quoted in Benjamin and Simon, 2002, p.65)

Consequently, Qutb argued that the true Muslims must remove themselves from the influence of infidels and jahiliyya and form a community of true Muslims based on the Koran. Qutb called for an all-out jihad against modernity so that the true community of Muslims could be constructed and the sharia could be fully implemented (Sivan, 1985, p.24). Once the community of true Muslims was strong enough, it could be used as a base from which jihad could be waged against infidels and Jahili rulers. It is therefore from Qutb that al-Qaeda essentially gets its name and purpose. Three decades after Qutb, Osama bin Laden would declare al-Qaeda to be that pure Islamic base from which jihad could be waged against infidels and the world would be converted to Islam (Benjamin and Simon, 2002, p.65).

Hassan al-Turabi

Hassan al-Turabi was the Islamist head of state in Sudan who attempted to implement the goals outlined by Qutb. Al-Turabi is a graduate of the Khartoum University School of Law and of the Sorbonne, but became a leader in the Sudanese Muslim Brotherhood in the early 1960s that later became known as the National Islamic Front (NIF) in the 1980s. Al-Turabi's group participated in Parliamentary elections in the 1980s, a tactic that appears to be inconsistent with Qutb's condemnation of everything that is un-Islamic, and Al-Turabi himself condemned party politics as

> a form of factionalism that can be very oppressive of individual freedom and divisive of the community, and it is, therefore, antithetical to a Muslim's ultimate responsibility to God." (Quoted in Kramer, 1993, pp.38–39)

Al-Turabi reconciled his participation in Parliamentary elections with his condemnation of party politics by calling for one-party rule from the NIF, thus justifying Islamists' participation in democratic party politics under the premise that it can be used as a means to the eventual righteous end of Islamic rule. Al-Turabi's dabbling in democracy then well fits the traditional conservative preference for "Ends Politics." Al-Turabi's party came in third in the 1986 Sudanese elections, but he proved that his commitment to Islam was much greater than his commitment to the democratic process when his party effectively seized power in a military coup in 1989. From behind the scenes, the NIF then imposed an Islamic police state dedicated to imposing sharia in the Sudan, complete with amputations, summary executions, and wholesale slaughter of their political opposition. In 1991, Al-Turabi established the Popular Arab Islamic conference for the purpose of opposing the American involvement in the 1991 Persian Gulf War (www.hrw.org/press/2002/03/turbabi-bio.htm).

Khomeini and the Iranian Revolution

Although the Muslim Brotherhood had existed since the 1920s, scholars often point to the Iranian Revolution of 1979 as a more important springboard for the rise of radical Islamism that occurred in the late twentieth century. In one sense, the Iranian Revolution represents the most successful Islamist movement to date, since the Shiite revolutionary movement of Ayatollah Khomeini not only proved that Islam could be used as a means to mobilize the masses and take control of the state, but the Islamists in Iran have retained control of state power in Iran ever since (Bickerton and Klausner, 2005, p.187). Khomeini was able to mobilize the Iranian Shiite population (90% of Iranians) against the government of Mohammed Reza Shah Pahlavi in part due to the Shah's Kemalist Westernization programs that alienated Shiite traditional conservatives. Specifically, Shiite traditional conservatives were appalled by the Shah's efforts to improve the status of women in Iran, including the women's right to vote, and the presence of 50,000 Americans in Iran who trained the Iranian military and conducted all forms of capitalist enterprise. The Shah favored Western-style education with the result that by 1977 more students from Iran attended American universities than did students from any other foreign country. Western styles of clothing and music, Western views on sex and gender relations, and Western habits with regard to gambling and alcohol became prevalent, offending the traditional conservative religious Shiite community. The Shah also helped the revolutionary cause by eliminating all opposition political parties, imposing martial law, and using his State Police, the SAVAK, to violently put down militant protests (Jones, 1996, pp.666–667 Ochsenwald and Fisher, 2004, p.515).

Khomeini had been exiled from Iran since the early 1960s and spent sixteen years attempting to direct revolution in Iran from exile, first from Baathist Iraq, and then from Paris after the Baathists expelled him from Iraq so as to relieve themselves of the incessant troublemaker. Khomeini directed his followers to use any means to take down the Shah, and the combination of religious fervor, economic instability, and outrage against the Shah's excesses, led to the Shiite coup in 1979 and the elevation of Khomeini to the controls of the Iranian government (Jones, 1996, p.667).

Though Khomeini's movement is different than those of most other Islamists because it was Shiite based rather than Sunni and it was successful in seizing power in a major Islamic country, Khomeini's political and religious views were generally similar to those of other Islamists. Like other Islamists, Khomeini rejected Western decadence and Westernization in Islamic societies and viewed Islam as a vehicle for resistance to Westernization in Islamic societies (Sayyid, 2003, p.151). Khomeini introduced an innovation into Islamism, however, in that he viewed "the people" as a political force that could bring about regime change and Islamic revolution (Sayyid, 2003, p.96). Khomeini's revolution was not led by an Islamic vanguard, as prescribed by Qutb, but by the masses who spontaneously took to the streets to overthrow the government. After the masses had accomplished his work for him, the 85-year-old religious leader returned from exile in Paris to head a new Islamist government (Jones, 1996, p.667).

Khomeini's Islamism is also different than that of Islamists who had come before him in that he, unlike Qutb and Maudoudi, was a high-ranking Shiite cleric who could use his clout as a doctor of Islamic law behind Islamism. In contrast with Maudoudi and Qutb, who had criticized Muslim clerics, Khomeini was in a position to lead the rest of Iran's Shiite clerics to Islamism with him and preached the outright seizure of power by the clergy (Kepel, 2003, pp.37, 40).

Khomeini was aided in his Islamist revolutionary arguments by the Shiite intellectual Ali Shariati (1933–1977) who drew correlations between the Shiite revolution against the Shah and the eighth century Muslim struggle against state injustice begun by the martyrs, Ali and Hussein. Shariati argued that Muslims should follow the examples of the martyrs and take up arms against the Shah, much like Mohammed himself had destroyed idolatrous Mecca. Shariati went a step further, however, and adapted the Marxist class struggle approach to Islam so as to motivate the masses for revolt (Kepel, 2003, pp.38–39). Khomeini then utilized Shariati's class struggle approach to essentially designate himself the unofficial vanguard of the disinherited masses (Kepel, 2003, 41).

Once he seized power, Khomeini also borrowed from Shariati and the Leninists in that he believed that it was necessary to eliminate all opposition if the Islamic Revolution were to succeed, and his starting point was to attack all things Western. In his first address, Khomeini said it was time to launch a holy war against the West and the traitors to Islam. Khomeini denounced the United States as an infidel and the "Great Satan" for its support of the Shah (Ochsenwald and Fisher, 2004, p.517). Khomeini did not, however, limit his venom only to the United States or the West. Islamic Revolutionary Courts were quickly established to try the enemies of Islam, torture was widely employed, and a new version of the State Police was constructed. The armed forces were purged of those associated with the Shah, the media was censored, and the Revolutionary Courts executed hundreds of "enemies of Islam" (Ochsenwald and Fisher, 2004, p.517).

Khomeini believed that the Iranian Revolution was only the first step in purifying the world. In furtherance of the ultimate goal of global Islamic purification, Khomeini argued that Israel must be eliminated and returned to Islamic rule, and that the West had become the handmaiden of the Jews. Western influence was denounced not only as un-Islamic, but as "Satanic" and therefore was completely banned. Bahais (a minority sect in Iran) were forbidden government jobs or attendance in public schools because they were declared to be apostates. Universities were closed due to the corrupting Western influences that permeated the universities (Ochsenwald and Fisher, 2004, p.517).

Khomeini assigned political power to a Revolutionary Council, which was composed of six ulama and six laymen, and a new Constitution was written that recognized the guardianship of the chief Shiite theologian (Khomeini) and declared that legitimate power could be held only by the ulama. A Presidency and Parliament were created, but they were subservient to the Council of Guardians, who scrutinized all laws to see if they were consistent with Islam. Local prayer leaders became the official political leaders in each town, and the sharia was instituted as civil law, complete with executions for adultery and homosexuality, stonings, and amputations. The legal age for women to marry was lowered to 13 years. Abortion was prohibited, but contraception was allowed and encouraged as an alternative (Ochsenwald and Fisher, 2004, p.519).

New school curriculum was introduced that emphasized Islamic values and university faculty who were viewed as un-Islamic were fired. The government sponsored books and films that supported Islamic values and about half the books published in Iran suddenly dealt with religious themes (Ochsenwald and Fisher, 2004, p.520).

Khomeini differed from most Islamists, however, in that he allowed the inclusion of the idea of the "popular will" as a source of law in addition to the sharia, an idea that is outright rejected by Qutb and most other Islamists. Furthermore, it was the Iranian Constitution, not the sharia, that in actuality organized power and legitimacy in Iran (Roy, 1994, pp.176–177). In January 1989, Khomeini even went so far as to publicly affirm the supremacy of the Islamic State to sharia, a position that is unacceptable to most Sunni Islamists and would clearly be condemned by Qutb as jahiliyya (Roy, 1994, p.177). Khomeini also declared that the authority of fatwas would survive the death of their authors. Prior to Khomeini, fatwas were only considered valid as long as the authors of the fatwas were living and declaring them to remain in force. Khomeini's purpose in doing so evidently was to ensure that Islamists would carry out his death warrant against Salman Rushdie, a Western-based author who had denounced Islam in a book entitled, *Satanic Verses*. In declaring that the fatwa would be binding after the death of its author, Khomeini violated centuries of Islamic tradition (Roy, 1994, p.179).

Hezbollah

The new Islamic Republic of Iran quickly became the primary terrorist concern of the United States due to its goal of global Islamic revolution through any means necessary, the taking of Americans hostage at the US Embassy in Tehran and holding them for over a year (444 days), and its support of the Shiite radical Islamist group, Hezbollah. Hezbollah literally means "the Party of God," their purpose is global Shiite Revolution (with backing from the Iranian government), and the means is often through terrorism. Like other Islamist groups, Hezbollah attacks all forms of Westernization and opposes Israel and the Western presence in Islamic lands. During the Lebanese civil war of the 1970s and 1980s, the Iranian Islamic Republic attempted to export its Islamic revolution to Lebanon through the support of Hezbollah and Lebanese Shiites in the Lebanese civil war. Hezbollah was responsible for the truck bombing of the US marine compound in Lebanon in 1983 that killed 241 Americans, as well as the Khobar Towers bombing in Dharan, Saudi Arabia in 1996, when Hezbollah militants blew up a fuel truck packed with explosives outside the fence surrounding a building housing US military personnel. Nineteen Americans were killed in the Khobar Towers blast that sheared off the front of the eight-story building and left a crater thirty-five feet deep and eighty-five feet across (White, 2002, pp.154–156). Hezbollah also embarked on a hostage-taking campaign in an attempt to gain leverage over the Western enemies of Iran (Kepel, 2003, p.129). Hezbollah is also credited with carrying the jihad to Europe in the 1980s with bombings in France in 1985 and 1986. Most recently, in July 2006, Hezbollah was credited with the kidnapping of two Israeli soldiers and the firing of rocket attacks into Israel from southern Lebanon. Israel retaliated with a military invasion of Lebanon resulting in hundreds of deaths, thousands of refugees, and millions of dollars in economic damage, and another full scale Arab-Israeli war breaking out at any moment remains a distinct possibility.

CHAPTER FIVE

Islam, The Promise, and Zionism

I slamic extremism contains within it a serious degree of anti-Semitism due to the political history of Palestine since the late nineteenth century, the ideological influence of anti-Semitic Islamic extremists, and differing interpretations between Jews and Islamists over God's promise to Abraham in the Biblical book of Genesis. The prevalence and depth of anti-Semitism in Islamic societies is perhaps well reflected by the fact that a former Egyptian laundryman and part-time wedding organizer named Shaaban Abdel-Rahim became a famous pop star in the Middle East/North Africa region in 2001 with the release of a song entitled, "I Hate Israel" (Shadid, 2005, pp.15–16).

The revered Egyptian Islamist Sayyid Qutb provided intellectual stimulus to anti-Semitism with his contention that Jews had conspired against Muslims since the time of Mohammed. Qutb went even further to contend that "anyone who leads this community away from its religion and its Koran can only be a Jewish agent" (Quoted in Benjamin and Simon, 2002, p.68). In other words, Qutb evidently believed that anyone who causes a Muslim to go astray is by definition a Jew and the Jews are thus the incarnation of all that is un-Islamic. Qutb further warned that the Jews' "satanic usurious activity will deliver the proceeds of all human toil into the hands of the great usurious Jewish financial institutions. They will rob the believers and kill them" (Quoted in Benjamin and Simon, 2002, p.68).

This anti-Semitism is in spite of the fact that the Koran repeatedly refers to the Jews as "people of the book" who may be saved through belief in Islam. It is also repeatedly stated in the Koran that Mohammed did not come to "cancel out" or destroy the revelations from God delivered by the previous prophets of God, including the Jewish prophets Abraham, Moses, and Jesus, and it is even stated in the Koran that Jewish and Christian believers will have their "reward," meaning salvation. For example, the passage in the Koran in The Cow II:62, contains the statement,

> Surely those who believe, and those who are Jews, and the Christians, and the Sabians, whoever believes in Allah and the Last day and does good, they shall have their reward from their Lord, and there is no fear for them, nor shall they grieve.

Similarly, in the Koranic passage in The Food V:69, the passage from The Cow II:62 is repeated almost word for word, suggesting that there is little reason that Muslims must necessarily be at odds with Jews on the basis of religion. Conversely, however, there are numerous verses in the Koran that Islamists point to, so as to justify anti-Semitism, essentially using the same religious text that praises the Jewish prophets and declares that the Jews "shall have their reward from the Lord" to further their hatred. For example, in The Food V:82, it is stated that

> Certainly you will find the most violent of people in enmity for those who believe (to be) the Jews and those who are polytheists, and you will certainly find the nearest in friendship to those who believe (to be) those who say: We are Christians: this is because there are priests and monks among them and because they do not behave proudly.

Reinforcing this demonization of the Jews, in The Food V:62, it is stated that, "And the Jews say: The hand of Allah is tied up! Their hands shall be shackled and they shall be cursed for what they say." In addition to these, there are numerous other verses that Islamists interpret so as to suggest that the Jews are the enemies of Allah; consequently, their anti-Semitism is driven and justified by their religion, although other Muslims who interpret the Koran differently or stress different passages may beg to disagree.

Hamas

One decidedly anti-Semitic Muslim group in the tradition of Qutb is the Palestinian Islamic resistance group known as Hamas, the spiritual founder of which, Abdullah Azzam, would eventually become the teacher and mentor of Osama bin Laden and a jihadist in Afghanistan (Coll, 2005, p.85). In 1978, Hamas registered as a religious organization with the Israeli government and its stated purpose was to be evangelical (White, 2002, p.159). Hamas, however, has proven to be much more than an evangelical organization. The word Hamas means "zeal" in Arabic, but HAMAS is also an acronym for the Islamic Resistance Movement (Harakat Al-Muqawama Al-Islamia). Hamas grew out of the Muslim Brotherhood in the 1980s as its armed wing for the purpose of unification of the entire Arab realm under Islam (Bickerton and Klausner, 2005, pp.227–228). The Hamas Charter of 1988 itself delineates Hamas as a jihadist organization, stating that "If an enemy invades Muslim territories, then jihad and fighting the enemy becomes an individual duty on every Muslim" (Quoted in Pape, 2005, p.31). In short, the Hamas Charter essentially declares that the liberation of Palestine is an obligation of all Muslims.

Ideology alone, however, is often insufficient for the building of any significant organization, Islamist or otherwise, and Hamas is no exception. Hamas grew in the 1990s at least partially because the autonomy granted to Palestinians in the Gaza and West Bank by Israel created little improvement in quality of life for most Palestinians (Kepel, 2003, p.330). Hamas has also benefited greatly from the benevolence of the Saudi Royal Family, who aided the Muslim Brotherhood in the West Bank after the Six-Day War, allowing Hamas not only to arm itself, but to develop their own informal welfare system among the Palestinians and thus gain popular support (Bickerton and Klausner, 2005, p.228). In 1997, for instance, an estimated 22,615 families in Palestine received assistance from Hamas (Pape, 2005, pp.191–192). Hamas was also aided by Syria, which houses a Hamas headquarters outside of Palestine, and Iran, which by 1993 was contributing an estimated $20 to $30 million annually to the organization (Bickerton and Klausner, 2005, pp.258, 294). The massive foreign aid has allowed Hamas not only to provide vital social services to Palestinians and thus help them gain popular support, but has also allowed Hamas (with an estimated budget of $70 million in 1995) to pay lifetime annuities to the families of suicide bombers (Bickerton and Klausner, 2005, p.289).

The informal leader of Hamas was a quadriplegic Palestinian cleric known as Sheikh Ahmad Yassin. Yassin altered the ideology of the Muslim Brotherhood to conform to the goals of the Palestinians in the occupied territories for the end of Israeli rule. Yassin argued that instead of first forging a pan-Islamic state as a prerequisite for waging a holy war against infidels (and Israel in particular), the war could be waged against Israel as the first stage toward the ultimate goal of a pan-Islamic state (Bickerton and Klausner, 2005, p.228). When Yassir Arafat of the Palestine Liberation Organization (PLO) gravitated toward moderation in the 1980s, Hamas held to the position that the State of Israel and anyone who supports it are abominations to Islam. In its own literature, Hamas states that it is in a war with the Jewish people as well as with the State of Israel. The Hamas literature is unreservedly hostile and militant and declares that "the purpose of every operation is to kill Jews and by killing Jews, all Zionist settlers and their allies will be driven from Palestine." Furthermore, the leaders of Hamas argue that "good" Muslims will kill anyone who accepts peace with the Jews or who speaks of an independent Palestine. Hamas also enforces vigilante sharia among the Palestinians, complete with amputations, beatings, and the execution of sex offenders (White, 2002, pp.159–161). The military wing of Hamas, known as the Qassam Brigades, named after Sheikh Izz ad-Din al-Qassam, an Islamic revolutionary who was killed by the British in Palestine in 1935, executes Muslims who are suspected collaborators with the Israelis in addition to regularly kidnapping and killing Israelis (Bickerton and Klausner, 2005, p.228). In February 2005, Hamas won control of the governing authority in Palestine in democratic elections, giving the world perhaps its first democratically elected Islamist state.

Dispute Over "The Promise"

In spite of the fact that the majority of Arabs and Jews are not strictly observant religiously, religion has been and continues to be a major component of the Arab-Israeli and Arab-Western conflict (Bickerton and Klausner, 2005, p.6). Among the most contentious areas of religious disagreement between Muslims and Jews is the general disagreement between Jews and Muslims over the proper interpretation of God's promise to Abraham in the Biblical book of Genesis. Both Jews and Muslims claim to worship the same God of Abraham found in Genesis and he and his story is viewed by both Jews and Muslims as a man of God and the patriarch and father of their respective peoples through the lineage of his sons, Ishmael and Isaac. Both Muslims and Jews essentially accept the Biblical Genesis story as Holy Scripture, and both agree that God blessed the descendants of Abraham and promised them land in the Middle East, but there is stark disagreement over which son of Abraham, Ishmael or Isaac, was to receive the benefit of God's blessings.

"The Promise" itself can be found in Genesis 15:1–6, where God promises Abraham a son from whom descendants would eventually become "as numerous as the stars in the skies." This promise is followed a few verses later with the promise of Genesis 15:18, where it is stated that, "On that day the Lord made a covenant with Abram and said, To your descendants I give this land, from the river of Egypt to the great river, the Euphrates." Geographically, God's promise to Abram in Genesis 15:18 provides that his descendants will inhabit everything from the Nile River in Egypt to the Euphrates River in present-day Iraq, and the promise apparently includes all of the land between the two rivers. If taken literally, this promise would include not only the narrow 40-by-120-mile strip of land known as Palestine or present-day Israel, but also all of Jordan, Syria, Lebanon, and the entire Arabian Peninsula, along with much of present-day Iraq and Egypt.

The Arab Muslims' interpretation of the Genesis promise is that they, not the Jews, are the recipients of God's promise to Abraham, and the rightful heirs to all of the land promised to the descendants of Abraham by God. For proof, Arab Muslims point out that most of the land between the Nile and the Euphrates has been in Arab hands for hundreds (if not thousands) of years and that the Jews, in contrast, have never possessed all of the land (or even a large fraction of it) even in the glory days of the Biblical Jewish Kings David and Solomon. In fact, the Jews were expelled from the land almost completely by the Babylonians in the sixth century BC and again by the Romans in 70 AD thus suggesting that the land was not promised to them or God surely would not have allowed them to be expelled from it. Furthermore, it has been more than 4000 years since God's promise to Abraham and since the Jews have never had most of the land, it suggests that either God has been very slow in fulfilling his promise, an unlikely proposition to devout Muslims, or it was instead the Arab Muslims, who have inhabited the vast majority of that land for centuries, who were the proper recipients of God's promise to Abraham.

For further proof, Muslims correctly point out that ancient societies of the Middle East, including the Jews, generally practiced primogeniture, meaning that the eldest son would receive the lion's share of the father's inheritance. It follows then that the eldest son of Abraham, Ishmael, traditionally recognized by both Jews and Arabs as the father of the Arab race as outlined in the Genesis story, is the true heir to Abraham's inheritance, rather than Isaac, Abraham's second son, traditionally recognized by both Arabs and Jews as the father of the Jewish race.

Muslims also point to God's promises to Hagar, the mother of Ishmael in the book of Genesis, for further proof that Ishmael was the son of the promise. In Genesis 16:10, for example, God directly promised to Hagar after she had slept with Abraham (Genesis 16:4) and conceived his child, "I will so increase your descendants that they will be too numerous to count." The wording of God's promise to Hagar (Genesis 16:10) is almost a mirror image of God's promise to Abraham in Genesis 15:1–6, thus suggesting that God's promise to Abraham and Hagar (recognized by both Jews and Muslims as the mother of the Arab peoples) are the same.

Religious Jews acknowledge that Hagar, like Abraham, received a promise from God, but they argue that she and her descendants are not the recipients of "the" promise of the land between the Nile and Euphrates. In support of their position, the Jews point to Genesis 17:15–22 where God promises that he will make of Ishmael a great nation, but then explicitly states that his covenant is with Isaac. In specific, the God of Genesis states

> And as for Ishmael, I have heard you: I will surely bless him; I will make
> him fruitful and will greatly increase his numbers. He will be the father of
> twelve rulers, and I will make him into a great nation. But my covenant I
> will establish with Isaac.

In other words, religious Jews argue that God made promises to both
Abraham and Hagar, but the important child with whom God made
his covenant and to whom all of the land between the Nile and Euphrates belongs, is Isaac. Furthermore, the Jews point to Genesis
16:11–12, which states that Hagar's son, to be named Ishmael, "will be
a wild donkey of a man; his hand will be against everyone and everyone's hand against him, and he will live in hostility toward all his
brothers." The Jewish religious interpretation of these verses is that
God promised that the sons of Ishmael would be a numerous, but hostile nation; consequently, the sons of Ishmael (Arabs) and the sons of
Isaac (Jews) have lived in hostility toward one another ever since.

Although Muslims generally accept Genesis as a valid Holy Book,
and it is undeniable that Isaac is designated as the son of the Covenant in the text, Muslims argue that the text has either been altered by
the deceptive Jews, or "confused in transmission" and part of what the
Prophet Mohammed was later sent to make straight (Smith, 1991,
pp.221–228). Proof to Muslims that the Jews have altered the text
concerning Ishmael is found in Genesis 21:8–21, where Hagar and
Ishmael are expelled from Abraham's camp due to the jealousy of
Abraham's wife, Sarah. According to Genesis, fourteen years passed
between the birth of Ishmael and Isaac since Genesis 16:16 states that
Abraham was 86 years old when Ishmael was born, and Genesis 21:5
states that he was 100 years old when Isaac was born. Further confir-
mation that Ishmael is 14 years older than Isaac is found in Genesis
17:25 where it is stated prior to the birth of Isaac that Ishmael was cir-
cumcised when he was 13 years old. According to the Genesis story,
several years then passed between Ishmael's circumcision and the expulsion of Ishmael and Hagar from the camp of Abraham, since in
Genesis 21:8 it is stated that Isaac (who was born when Ishmael was
14 years old) was "weaned" prior to Ishmael's expulsion, and thus
probably 1 to 3 years old.

If that is the case, then Ishmael must have been approximately 15 to
17 years old when he and his mother were forced to leave Abraham's
entourage, since he was 14 when Isaac was born and the child would
not have been "weaned" for 1–3 years. In spite of the fact that Ishmael
must have been essentially an adult at the time, the verses surrounding Hagar and Ishmael's expulsion from the camp of Abraham appear
to indicate that Ishmael was still an infant or small child at the time,
and are therefore inconsistent with the sections of Genesis indicating
that Ishmael must have been in his mid-teens at the time.

For example, it is mentioned in Genesis 21:14 (at the time of the expulsion of Ishmael and Hagar) that Abraham handed bread, a skin of water, and "the boy" to Hagar, the wording thus suggesting that Ishmael was at that time small enough for adults to carry in their arms, since he was "handed" from one person to the other, an inconsistent description of someone in his mid-teens. In the next verse (Genesis 21:15), Hagar then places "the boy" under a shrub, again suggesting that Ishmael is little more than an infant at the time, though he had to have been well over 14 years, to be consistent with the rest of Genesis. Obviously, an infant might be placed "under a shrub" so as to protect him from the sun, but not a 15-year-old adolescent. Furthermore, God commands Hagar in Genesis 21:18 to "Arise, lift up the lad and hold him with your hand, for I will make him a great nation," again suggesting that a "lad" that can be held "with your hand" must be very young indeed, rather than the 15 to 17 years old that he had to be at the time. Finally, in Genesis 21:20 it is stated that "God was with the lad; and he grew and dwelt in the wilderness, and became an archer." Again, the reference that "the lad grew" is inconsistent with a description of a person who was already 15 to 17 years old at the time, and appears to refer to a much younger child. For Muslims, the answer is clear enough. Not only are there inconsistencies in Genesis between the stated date of Ishmael's birth and the clear references to him as a small child at a time that must have been 15 to 17 years later (thus suggesting that human hands have altered God's Word), the Jews must have made further alterations to original passages, specifically those designating Ishmael as the son of the promise, otherwise Jews, not Arabs, would have occupied the bulk of the land in the Middle East for the last 4000 years.

The Jewish and Islamic interpretations of "the promise" become extremely important for explaining the conflict in Palestine between Jews and Muslims. Since both orthodox Jews and devout Muslims view the land of Palestine as rightfully theirs due to the "promise" from God in Genesis, neither are predisposed to compromise on the issue. Instead, compromise on the issue is viewed by Muslims and orthodox Jews alike as "blasphemy" since it would be ungodly to give away land that had been given to the people by God. For example, in Hezbollah's "Open Letter" of February 1985 that was the official mission statement for the group, Hezbollah made clear references to the "promised land" from Genesis while condemning Israeli expansion. In the words of Hezbollah,

> Israel ... poses a great danger to our future generations and to the destiny of our nation, especially since it embraces a settlement-oriented and expansionist idea ... to build Greater Israel, from the Euphrates to the Nile ... We view the recently voiced Jewish call for settlement in South Lebanon ... as part of the expansionist scheme. (Quoted in Pape, 2005, p.136)

As a consequence of this kind of thinking, Egyptian President Anwar Sadat, who recognized Israel's right to exist, was assassinated by Muslim extremists, and Israeli Prime Minister Yitzak Rabin, who favored the return to the Arabs of some of the occupied territories, was assassinated by Jewish religious extremists (Ochsenwald and Fisher, 2004, pp.575–576).

Zionism and Its Impact on Islamism

As of the late nineteenth century, the vast majority of the world's Jews did not live in Palestine, but were instead scattered throughout both the Middle East and Europe as they had been since the fall of Jerusalem to the Romans in 70 AD. Between 1882 and 1900, however, a global Zionist (the return of Jews to their "homeland" in Palestine) movement began to develop and Jewish migrations to Palestine increased greatly as a reaction to anti-Semitic persecutions in Europe, but especially in Russia. Approximately 20,000 Jews migrated to Palestine during these years with financial backing from international Jewish charities. All across Europe, a political party known as "Mizrahi" (spiritual center) arose. Mizrahi was a party of religious Jews who favored Zionism and argued that the return of Jews to Palestine was part of God's plan, and as such, would serve as the only way that Jews could escape persecution (Ochsenwald and Fisher, 2004, p.446–447).

Other adherents of Zionism, however, had little or nothing to do with religion or anti-Semitic persecution. By the 1930s, a strong socialist faction developed within the Zionist movement that favored the establishment of a Proletarian Socialist State in Israel. Consequently, socialist Jews immigrated to Israel to embark on the great socialist experiment. Still, at the close of World War I, the population of Palestine was estimated to be 620,000 Muslims, 70,000 Christians, and only 60,000 Jews. Most of the Christians were Arabic in ethnicity and most of the Jews spoke Arabic, and some of the Jews were even adherents of Islam (Ochsenwald and Fisher, 2004, p.447).

During World War I, the British assured the Arab residents of Palestine an independent State in Palestine out of the remains of the Ottoman Empire that had controlled the area prior to their defeat at the hands of the Allies in World War I. At the same time, in 1917, the British issued the Balfour Declaration, which offered new hope to the Zionist movement by guaranteeing "the establishment in Palestine of a National Home for the Jewish People." The two British promises, one to Arabs and one to the Jews, both guaranteeing an independent state for each group, were obviously in conflict. After World War I, Britain was granted a mandate by the League of Nations to rule Palestine until it could be nurtured to independence. The British tried to keep their promises to both the Arabs and Jews and between 1919 and 1922 turned away several ships full of Jewish refugees from Europe due to Arab unrest. In 1922, however, the League of Nations instructed the British to facilitate Jewish immigration without prejudicing the rights and position of other sections or the population (Ochsenwald and Fisher, 2004, pp.447–459).

Massive immigration of Jews followed so that the population of Palestine by 1939 consisted of 460,000 Jews along with 950,000 Muslims and 120,000 Christians (Ochsenwald and Fisher, 2004, p.450). Between 1890 and 1939, the Jewish population had grown by some 400,000 people and had risen from less than 10% of the population to more than 40%. Even without differences in ethnicity, religion, language, and income, one could perhaps expect political conflict to develop in a case where so many immigrants arrived in such a short amount of time in a place so geographically small. With religious, linguistic, ethnic, and economic differences between the new immigrants and the natives compounding the problems inherent in absorbing so many new immigrants in such a brief time period, however, political conflict was perhaps unavoidable.

The immigration and economic disparity between the Jews and Arabs quickly created land pressures and economic conflict between Jews and Arabs. Jewish immigrants, aided by funding from the Jewish National Fund, purchased land from absentee Arab landlords at inflated prices, paying sometimes two to three times the market rate. Arab landowners would then happily sell their land and take their profits while Jewish immigrants would move on to the land to work it in communal farms (Kibbutz), with the result that Arab tenant farmers who had been working the land were displaced and subsequently unemployed, a clear formula for political unrest. To exacerbate the situation even further, the Jews generally purchased the best agricultural land and left the Hill Country land that could not be farmed by mechanized equipment to the Muslim Arabs (Ochsenwald and Fisher, 2004, pp.447–449).

By 1939, the Jewish farmers, heavily subsidized by the Jewish National Fund, exported 10 million cases of citrus. Nevertheless, the cost of development in Palestine between 1919 and 1939 was $400 million, while annual exports were only $4 million by 1939. Palestine never approached a self-supporting status, and only foreign gifts stabilized Jewish society at a standard of living above that of the Arab Palestinians. By 1939, 75% of Jews lived in towns or cities, most working in the service sector, while only 25% of Arabs in Palestine were urban. Jewish income by 1939 was 2.5 times that of the Arabs in Palestine. Immigration literally created new major Jewish cities. Tel Aviv, for example, was a small town of 2000 persons in 1918, but had a population of 150,000 in 1939. The Jews immigrated to Palestine from all over the world and spoke dozens of languages, so Hebrew was revived as an everyday, spoken language in Palestine so as to forge commonality and national identity, but that language and national identity was separate from that of the native Arab Palestinians, thus contributing to political conflict. By the 1930s, Palestine suffered from frequent political violence and riots (Ochsenwald and Fisher, 2004, pp.447–459).

Independent Israel and Islamism

The establishment of the state of Israel in 1948 is viewed by both religious Jews and Islamists as a pivotal event in the history of the Middle East; hence, no discussion of Islamism is complete without its inclusion (Bickerton and Klausner, 2005, p.3). By 1942, the Holocaust had begun in Europe and Zionists reacted by drawing up a plan for a Jewish State in Palestine at the Biltmore Hotel in New York City. The Zionists were outraged by British policies in 1942 that would not allow Jews fleeing Nazi persecution to come to Palestine. Ships carrying Jewish immigrants from Europe to Palestine had been turned back by the Allied navies and the Jewish passengers were interned in the Mediterranean on the Island of Cyprus. In one incident in 1942, 769 Russian Jews died in the Black Sea when their overloaded ship, the Struma, was ordered back to Russia by the British (Bickerton and Klausner, 2005, p.73).

As a consequence of the Holocaust and the immigration tragedies that afflicted the Jews during the War, many religious Jews (not the Orthodox) who had opposed Zionism prior to World War II softened their stance after the war. In general, it was believed that large numbers of European Jews surely would have left Europe and therefore survived the war (as opposed to suffering extermination at the hands of the Nazis), had Zionism been sanctioned by Jewish religious leaders. As international Jewish groups pushed for the establishment of a Jewish State in Palestine in 1947, Britain announced an end to its Palestinian mandate, and the Palestine question was left to the UN (Jones, 2001, p.242). In November 1947, the UN General Assembly decided to partition Palestine into two States; one Arab (Lebanon) and one Jewish (Israel). The city of Jerusalem, desired by both Arabs and Jews, was to be governed under international supervision. Although the Jewish Lobby was happy that they finally had their Jewish State, the Arab delegation in the UN stalked out in protest because there were more Arabs on the land in Israel than Jews, and the land set aside for the Jews contained the area's best roads, railroads, and farmland (Jones, 2001, p.242).

On May 14, 1948, the British mandate came to an end and the Jews declared the independent State of Israel. Fifteen minutes later, President Truman extended recognition, as did the USSR some three days later. Independence, however, proved to be no panacea as Israel was almost immediately invaded by its Arab neighbors. The Israeli army was greatly outnumbered, but better equipped by the United States and Britain, and therefore was able to quickly defeat the Arab invaders in the first of what would eventually become five Arab-Israeli wars in the twentieth century. An armistice in February of 1949 temporarily wound down the hostilities only because the Arab states were essentially defeated on the battlefield. International supervision of Jerusalem never materialized, and the city was divided between the states of Israel and Jordan. Arab states boycotted Israel and cut off its land access to the outside, and Egypt closed the Suez Canal to Israeli shipping. The 1948 war also had a tremendous impact on the migration of people in the Middle East, as up to a million Palestinian refugees fled the Jewish State, most to neighboring Jordan, a poor country without oil that lacked the means to feed and absorb them. The Israelis destroyed the homes of the fleeing Arab refugees so as to discourage any thought of return. The homeless Palestinians, stripped of hope and means of support, began terrorist raids into Israel that have continued intermittently through the present (Jones, 2001, p.242).

Although threatened and its future uncertain, the new Jewish State had been established and survived its first major challenge from its Arab Muslim neighbors, though the armistice between Israel and Jordan left the Holy City of Jerusalem divided by a barbed wire fence. The eastern part of the City and most of the Old City containing the shrines holy to both Islam and Judaism were left in Jordan, who refused to permit Jews access to the Holy places. In spite of this contentious and uncertain status of the City, Israel announced the movement of its capital to Jerusalem, thus exacerbating the already tense political atmosphere between Muslims and Jews (Sachar, 1996, p.592).

In 1950, the new state of Israel officially sanctioned and attempted to boost Zionism when the Israeli Parliament passed the Law of Return, declaring that every Jew in every country has the right to return to Israel, and citizenship for any Jewish person would only be withheld in cases of "Acts against the Jewish Nation." Jews in other countries became formally recognized as part of the Jewish nation served by the State of Israel (Ochsenwald and Fisher, 2004, pp.533–553).

Meanwhile, Islamists denounced the UN for violating the international legal principle of self-determination that had been one of the primary principles of International Law under Woodrow Wilson's Fourteen Points and the Versailles Treaty following World War I. Islamists argued that under the principle of self-determination, only the people living upon the land at the time of the partitioning of Palestine had the right to partition the lands of Palestine; therefore, the action taken by any outside authority, including the UN, was illegal under international law, and null and void. The United States, Britain, and the rest of the West became vilified in radical Islamic thought for its role in allowing the UN to create the Jewish state (Taeharah, 2005, pp.19–20).

Six-Day War

The Israelis and their Arab neighbors would fight five wars between 1948 and 1982, the most important of which was the Six-Day War in 1967. Beginning in 1964, Yasser Arafat and other Arab leaders sought to establish a Palestinian Organization dedicated to liberating Palestine from Israel. The Arab heads of state at the first Arab summit meeting at the Arab League headquarters in Cairo in 1964 opposed direct military confrontation with Israel at the time, given that they had been defeated on the battlefield by Israel in 1948 and 1956 (although Israel received significant help from France and the United Kingdom in 1956); consequently, they informed the Palestinian leaders that the Palestinians themselves would be responsible for their own liberation. In May 1964, King Hussein of Jordan then convened a Palestinian National Council in Jerusalem and the PLO was formed (Bickerton and Klausner, 2005, p.145).

Before the Six-Day War in 1967, however, it was not the PLO, but Yassir Arafat's al-Fatah that had been the primary Palestinian organization pushing for "liberation" of the Palestinian people. The name "Fatah" itself was an acronym whose letters in reverse stand for "Harakat al-Tahrir al-Falastini" which translates as the "Movement for the Liberation of Palestine." Al-Fatah was aided in its efforts by the Syrians, and began raids into Israel from Syria in 1965. In 1966, Al-Fatah and the PLO then began to cooperate in working toward their mutual goals (Bickerton and Klausner, 2005, pp.145–146). Other than opposition to the state of Israel, however, al-Fatah did not espouse a specific Islamist ideology and instead gave the struggle against Israel priority over any ideological thinking, although it attracted religious Muslims that blended the Islamist religious cause with Palestinian nationalism (Bickerton and Klausner, 2005, pp.163–164).

In furtherance of their goals of liberating Palestine from the Zionists, the PLO demanded withdrawal of the UN peacekeeping forces from the Egyptian-Israeli border. The UN buckled under the pressure and withdrew in 1967, thus providing the PLO and their allies with an opportunity. Egypt quickly took advantage of the situation to move its army into the Sinai and seize Sharm el-Sheikh, an Israeli port on the

Gulf of Aqaba. Meanwhile, PLO terrorists from Syria and Jordan began a series of guerrilla raids on Israel, who in turn retaliated. Egypt, Syria, and Jordan mobilized their armies along Israel's borders, and the Israelis, sensing an impending invasion, attacked first on June 5, 1967. The Israeli Air Force, using American-made planes, destroyed virtually the entire Egyptian, Iraqi, Syrian, and Jordanian air forces while they were still on the ground. With total control of the air, the Israeli ground forces and tanks crossed the borders of their enemies, and within six days had taken Jerusalem and the West Bank from Jordan, the Suez Canal, the Sinai, and the Gaza Strip from Egypt, and the Golan Heights from Syria. On June 11, with the Arabs defeated, the Israelis accepted a UN cease-fire. The Israeli death ratio in the war was 16:1 (Jones, 2001, pp.371–372).

The victory in the Six-Day War had a profound long-term effect on both Jewish and Muslim politics. The capture of the Arab lands (mentioned earlier) that became known as the "occupied territories" was viewed by many religious Jews as a sign that the messianic age had begun. Just as God had created the heavens and the earth in six days, and on the seventh day he rested, in 1967, God had delivered Israel from the hands of its enemies in six days, and on the seventh day he rested. The religious symbolism could not be more obvious. Additionally, the capture of the Temple Mount in East Jerusalem was viewed by religious Jews as a sign that the war was part of God's plan to return Israel to the Jewish people. The top Orthodox Rabbi, Zvi Yehada Kook, declared that the State of Israel was "Heaven on Earth" and "every living Jew in Israel was Holy." Many religious Jews, such as the right-wing Land of Israel movement, which referred to the occupied territories by their Biblical names, Judea and Samaria, viewed the "occupied territories" as gifts from God that could not be given back. Even a discussion of such a return was viewed by many religious Jews as blasphemy. By 1974, a conservative religious group known as Gush Emunim (The Bloc of the Faithful) was calling for the permanent absorption by Israel of some of the occupied territories, but specifically the West Bank (Sachar, 1996, pp.740–746 Bickerton and Klausner, 2005, pp.170, 191).

Jewish religious conservatives are a major component of the conservative Likud party in Israel that has held power in the Israeli Parliament for much of the time since the Six-Day War. The religious influence is evident in the speech of prominent Likud Party politicians, such as former Prime Minister Yitzhak Shamar, who denounced the Oslo Accords in 1993 (providing for Israeli withdrawal from the Gaza Strip and Jericho) with a religious reference, stating, "The Old Testament prophets said it then: 'Neither Babylon nor Persia present the danger, but you, the sons of Israel'" (Quoted in Bickerton and

Klausner, 2005, p.263). Later, the Israeli Prime Minister who signed the Oslo Accords, Yitzhak Rabin, was assassinated by Yigal Amir, a Jewish religious zealot who said that he was acting on God's orders to prevent the land of Israel from being turned over to the Palestinians (Bickerton and Klausner, 2005, p.286).

The occupied territories created other political ramifications for the Jewish state as well. It was not only religious Jews who favored keeping the occupied territories, but also security-minded secular Jews, who argued that retaining the territories would provide necessary security buffers against their enemies. In furtherance of this security goal, between 1967 and 2005, hundreds of thousands of new Jewish immigrants were settled in the West Bank, thus creating a further logistical problem, since giving the land back to the Arabs would later require the relinquishing of the homes of hundreds of thousands of resettled Jews.

The addition of the occupied territories also added a further problem in that the new areas were home to large Arab Muslim populations, and the State of Israel suddenly would have a population with more Arab Muslims than Jews if the occupied territories were included in the state. Consequently, if Arab Muslims in the occupied territories were to be considered citizens and allowed to vote in Israeli Parliamentary elections, Israel would surely become an Islamic state rather than Jewish. Instead, the Jewish authorities made the decision to deny the right to vote to Arab Muslims in the occupied territories, thus creating an apartheid-type situation based on religion and ethnicity of the type that is typically condemned by the international community (Sachar, 1996, p.748).

A further problem created by the annexation of the occupied territories is the fact that the predominantly Arab Muslim areas of the occupied territories tend to have a much lower GNP per capita than Israel as a whole. For example, the GNP per capita of Israel as a whole is approximately $20,000 annually, whereas the average income of the Arab population in the Gaza strip, an area only 4 miles by 26 miles, with a population of over 1 million, is only approximately $1000. This type of income disparity could perhaps be expected to lead to political problems, even if religion and ethnicity were not factors (*Economist*, November 1, 2003). Finally, in a water-short region with a growing population, the occupied territories provided the advantage of additional water supplies needed by the Jewish state. Currently, over 10% of Israel's water comes from sources in the Golan Heights and almost one third of its water comes from aquifers in the occupied territories. To relinquish control of the territories would therefore mean relinquishing control of over 40% of Israel's water supply (Bickerton and Klausner, 2005, p.193).

Islamists and the Six-Day War

Religious Jews were not the only persons or groups that viewed the Six-Day War as being religiously symbolic. Islamists, who tend to interpret all current events through religious filters, viewed the loss in the Six-Day War as a sign from God as well. Since it is written in the Koran that Allah's followers can defeat more powerful enemies if they are faithful to Allah, devout Muslims could only interpret the Six-Day War defeat as proof that Muslims had not been faithful to Islam; otherwise, Allah would not have allowed them to lose in a battle to their enemies. Islamists argued that the defeat could only be explained by the political situation in the Islamic realm where Muslims allowed themselves to be governed by apostate rulers. In the words of one Egyptian Islamist (Quoted in Sivan, 1985, p.17), "This was no surprise to us, for how can a ruler governing his people with a whip triumph on the battlefield? Dignity is trampled under foot, hypocrisy and cowardice reign supreme." Similarly, the Syrian Muslim Brotherhood specifically blamed President Assad of Syria, whom they denounced as an apostate, for the defeat at the hands of the Jewish infidels. In order to remedy the situation, Islamists predictably called for an end to secularization and the return to religious purification and a purer form of Islam (Sachar, 1996, p.786).

In order to accomplish religious purity, however, the Islamists argued that it was necessary to depose the apostate rulers. In the words of Husni Abbu, the military commander of the Muslim Brotherhood at Aleppo, Syria in the late 1970s (Quoted in Sivan, 1985, p.19), "Only when we shall have finished purging our country of Godlessness shall we turn against Israel." Similarly, Abd al-Salam Faraj, an Islamist member of the group that assassinated Egyptian President Anwar Sadat argued that (Quoted in Sivan, 1985)

> There are some who say that the jihad effort should concentrate nowadays upon the liberation of Jerusalem. It is true that the liberation of the Holy Land is a legal precept binding upon every Muslim ... but let us emphasize that the fight against the enemy nearest to you has precedence over the fight against the enemy farther away ... In all Muslim countries the enemy has the reins of power. The enemy is the present rulers. It is hence, a most imperative obligation to fight these rulers. This Islamic jihad requires today the blood and sweat of each Muslim.

In short, the destruction of Jewish Israel remained the Islamists' goal, but the 1967 debacle taught them that their enemy could not be defeated by apostate Muslims; hence, the apostates must first be overthrown.

CHAPTER SIX

Islamism, Afghanistan, and Osama

I n 1979, the USSR invaded Afghanistan to protect a leftist pro-Soviet Government that was under siege from Islamic extremists. Numerous Islamist militia groups, calling themselves Holy Warriors or "Mujahadeen" quickly formed to resist the Soviets. The United States misinterpreted the Soviet invasion as Soviet communist expansion and quickly joined the fray with arms and economic support under the long-standing American policy of "containment" of communism and Soviet expansion. Mujahadeen leaders made trips to the United States denouncing the Soviets as "foreign devils" and "infidels" while raising support for their cause from American anti-communists and humanitarians. President Jimmy Carter and later Ronald Reagan supported the Mujahadeen due to what they viewed as the anti-communism of the Mujahadeen "freedom fighters," but neither Carter nor Reagan nor their top advisers apparently noticed that the Mujahadeen used the same terms that they used to denounce the Soviets when making reference to Americans (Jones, 2001, pp.441–442). Instead, the devoutly Catholic American CIA Director, William Casey, viewed the Islamists as natural allies with the United States as a community of God's faithful against Godless Communism (Coll, 2005, p.97). As a consequence, billions of American dollars would go to support anti-American Islamists in the name of anticommunism. For instance, Hamas founder and mentor to Osama bin Laden, Abdullah Azzam, who stridently denounced the United States, was allowed to set up a jihadist recruiting office in Tucson, Arizona in 1986 (Coll, 2005, pp.155-157). Similarly, according to Steven Coll, Gulbuddin Hekmatyar, a Mujahadeen commander who received several hundred million dollars in American aid, was invited as an anticommunist "freedom fighter" to New York to meet President Reagan, but Hekmatyar refused because he opposed shaking hands with an infidel. In spite of this overt anti-Americanism, American aid to Hekmatyar continued (Coll, 2005, p.165).

In more than a decade of anti-communist crusading, the CIA sent billions of dollars to the Mujahadeen, most of which was funneled through America's ally in South Asia, Pakistan. In fact, Pakistan, which dispersed the aid to the Mujahadeen, received $3.2 billion in aid from the Reagan administration, plus permission to purchase F-16 fighter jets, previously available only to NATO allies and Japan. In 1987 alone, the United States funneled over $650 million in aid to the Mujahadeen. To compound the American financial support for the Islamic jihad, aid given by the United States to the Mujahadeen was matched by Saudi Arabia (Coll, 2005, pp.62, 63).

Although the Saudis did consider themselves anticommunist (communism being un-Islamic), the Saudi's motivations were somewhat different than those of the United States. The Saudis, a predominantly Wahhabist Sunni State, essentially view themselves as in a struggle for global Islamic leadership with Shiite Iran. While the Saudi aid to the Mujahadeen can be viewed as the Saudi attempt to aid fellow Muslims against Godless communists, the Saudi efforts were also linked to the Saudis' struggle to ensure a pro-Saudi Arabian Sunni Islamic government in Afghanistan, as opposed to one that is dominated by Shiites and linked to Iran (Coll, 2005, p.217).

In the decade of American aid to the Mujahadeen, the CIA trained and outfitted Mujahadeen guerrilla units, taught them how to use weapons (including the handheld Stinger missile), and in some cases even planned operations against the Soviet Union with them. By the late 1980s, some CIA aid even bypassed Pakistan completely and went directly to the Mujahadeen. By 1987, the Mujahadeen were even launching raids from Afghanistan into the central Asian Republics of the Soviet Union itself (Coll, 2005, p.161). American aid also contributed to a Pakistani Intelligence (known as the Inter-Services Intelligence or ISI) plan to recruit radical Muslims from all over the world for jihad in Afghanistan. The Pakistanis used the foreign jihadists for their own purposes against Hindu India in the disputed border region of Kashmir (Coll, 2005, p.221). The Americans and other supporters of the Mujahadeen conveniently overlooked the fact that the jihadists had their own agenda and might later turn their holy wrath against the United States, which they typically viewed as just as "infidel" as the Soviet Union, or the Saudi Royal family, whom they tended to view as apostates, in spite of their support for the Afghan jihad and Wahhabism in Saudi Arabia (Rashid, 2001, p.129).

Pakistan was exceedingly aggressive in their recruiting efforts for the Afghan jihad and had standing instructions to all of its embassies across the globe to grant visas, with no questions asked, to anyone interested in joining the struggle in Afghanistan. As a result, between 1982 and 1992 more than 35,000 Muslims from 43 Islamic countries, many of whom were radically Islamist and anti-Western in their thinking, would go to Afghanistan to wage Islamic jihad. The end of the war would leave a standing army of thousands of radical fighters eager to continue their jihad against all infidels, along with an elaborate global Islamic organizational support system and a vast military arsenal that had been supplied with American and Saudi money (Rashid, 2001, p.130).

The Mujahadeen turned out to be more effective in the war against the Soviet Union in Afghanistan than anyone (other than perhaps the holy warriors themselves) had envisioned. By January 1984, the CIA estimated that the Mujahadeen controlled almost two thirds of Afghanistan and had destroyed 350 to 400 Soviet aircraft, 2750 Soviet tanks and armored carriers, 8000 jeeps, trucks, and other vehicles, and cost the Soviet government an estimated $12 billion in expenses (Coll, 2005, p.90).

As a consequence, in 1989 the USSR pulled out of Afghanistan after a decade of bloody conflict and had not only lost the war, but had totally collapsed within two years. The Mujahadeen gave credit to God for defeating their enemy and viewed the Soviet defeat and collapse as proof that God was on their side. After all, how else could the under-manned and under equipped Islamic tribesmen defeat the Red Army? If, however, the Mujahadeen could bring down one of the world's great superpowers as warriors for God (which they did), then any other nation that faced God's Holy warriors would be equally doomed to destruction (Rashid, 2001, pp.130, 131). In their "thrill of victory," the Mujahadeen began searching for more infidels against God to destroy, and the primary targets of the Mujahadeen's Holy War then shifted from the USSR to the standard Islamist targets: "apostate" Islamic governments in the Middle East, and Israel and the United States. One of the Mujahadeen leaders who fervently believed in the continuation of the Holy War against the Muslim apostates and American and Israeli infidels was Osama bin Laden (Gunaratna, 2002, pp.18-22).

The Taliban

Meanwhile, fighting continued in Afghanistan after the Soviet withdrawal between the Mujahadeen and the Soviet-supported Afghan communist government. The Mujahadeen took Kabul and ousted the government in 1989 with aid from the United States, Pakistan, and Saudi Arabia, but civil war in Afghanistan continued to rage after the demise of communism, as the country devolved into tribal factionalism, civil war, and warlordism (Coll, 2005, p.190). Amid this chaos, the Taliban (a Persian word meaning Islamic students) formed under the leadership of Mullah Mohammad Omar. With backing from the government of Pakistan, which sought to end the chaotic situation on their northern border and ensure the installation of a friendly Sunni-led regime in neighboring Afghanistan, the Taliban seized Kabul and assumed control of Afghan political power in 1996 (Bearden, 2001 p.45).

While it is clear that the primary supporter of the Taliban was Pakistan, according to French scholar Gilles Kepel (2002, p.11), the United States joined Pakistan in supporting the rise of the Taliban in the interest of restoring order in Afghanistan, in spite of the fact that it was obvious that the Taliban would install a strict form of Islam that was destructive to human rights. Although the success of the Taliban in seizing power undoubtedly should be credited to the outside funding, the Taliban were also successful in winning the hearts of millions of Afghans with their traditional conservative call for a return to rural Islamic values and appeals to forms of Afghan patriotism and symbolism. The Taliban roamed the countryside leading prayers and teaching the wonders of Islam to the masses; consequently, the Taliban were viewed by the masses as the defenders of the faith against the enemies of Islam. The Taliban were so revered that they were even memorialized by rural Afghans with traditional folk songs singing their praises (Coll, 2005, pp.284-285).

In terms of their politics and theology, many of the Taliban were schooled at the Haqqania madrassa east of Peshawar in Pakistan, where they received free education and boarding. The curriculum at Haqqania blended Islamist politics with Deobandi theology, an Islamic perspective that argued that Muslims were required to live exactly as the earliest followers of the Prophet had lived in the seventh century.

The Deobandis, like Wahhabis, disdain decoration, adornment, and music, and followed the principles of lex talionis (eye for eye and tooth for tooth) in crime and punishment. The Deobandis also compile a long list of banned activities and a minutia of rules designed to prevent any intrusion of modernism into Islamic life (Coll, 2005, p.284).

After the Taliban took control in Afghanistan, they exhibited the most extreme form of Deobandism, as they banned photographs and paintings of people and animals, movies, television, radio, magazines, newspapers, most books, cigarettes, alcohol, marbles, card and board games, applause, walking or talking loudly in public, toothpaste, dancing, music, singing, wedding parties, New Year's celebrations, homing pigeons, kite flying, children's toys, pet parakeets, nail polish, jewelry, makeup, sheer stockings, high-heel shoes, white socks and shoes, and all stylish clothing. Women were forbidden from leaving their residences unescorted by men, and were forced to wear a full burqa that kept them completely covered from head to toe. Women were prevented from attending schools and universities and working women were fired from their jobs (Goodwin, 2002, pp.74-76 Coll, 2005, pp.333-334). The denial of educational and employment opportunities to women in Afghanistan was especially harsh since it is estimated that there were 50,000 widows in Afghanistan with some 400,000 children to support at the time, and they were suddenly left with no legal means of doing so (Coll, 2005, p.350).

On crime and punishment, the Taliban famously instituted capital and corporal punishment, including amputations for theft, 100 lashes for women who walked in public with men who were not relatives, stonings for adultery, hangings, and a unique practice whereby men accused of "buggery" were buried partially in the ground and then had stone walls pushed over onto them by bulldozers. One man was hanged by a crane and then driven around Kabul swinging from the mechanism. Others were castrated and then hanged on the traffic lights of a busy Kabul street (Goodwin, 2002, pp.73-74).

In another seemingly senseless campaign, the Taliban sent Militiamen armed with rockets and assault rifles to destroy 1500-year-old sandstone statues of Buddha carved into the side of mountains in central Afghanistan. One statue was 175 feet high and the other was 120. When Mullah Omar became aware of international criticism of his destruction of such ancient art works, his response was, "We do not understand why everyone is so worried ... All we are breaking are stones" (Quoted in Coll, 2005, p.554).

The leader of the Taliban, Muhammad Omar, was a one-eyed jihadist from Kandahar who had most likely never flown in a plane, watched a movie, slept in a hotel, or ventured any significant distance from Kandahar in his life. As an Islamic scholar, Omar was not really even a Mullah since he had not completed his Islamic studies. In this state of blissful ignorance, Omar believed in the prophecy of dreams, discussed his dreams in military meetings, and relied on his dreams to make important decisions. Omar even claimed that he had been called to jihad in a dream by Allah himself. Concerning the Taliban's goals, Omar stated that the Taliban were "determined to establish the laws of God on Earth and prepared to sacrifice everything in support of that goal" (Quoted in Coll, 2005, p.288). Omar added that "The Taliban will fight until there is no blood in Afghanistan left to be shed and Islam becomes a way of life for our people" (Quoted in Coll, 2005, pp.288-289). These goals of establishing the laws of God on earth were shared by Osama bin Laden, whose welcome had been outlived in the Sudan in 1996, but was quickly welcomed back to Afghanistan by the Taliban, who stood to benefit from bin Laden's funding (Bearden, 2001, p.45).

Osama bin Laden

Osama bin Laden was one of over fifty children born to a wealthy Saudi Arabian construction magnate in 1957. Bin Laden was university educated at Jeddah, where he was taught Islamic studies by Muhammad Qutb, the brother of Sayyid Qutb of *Signposts* fame and the Muslim Brotherhood; consequently, bin Laden developed a strict view of Islam at an early age and opposed the imposition of non-Islamic rule on Muslims (*The Sunday Times*, January 2002, p.1). Drawing from Qutb and Taymiyya, bin Laden essentially viewed history as a continuing conflict between Islam and infidels. Furthermore, bin Laden believed that waging jihad against the infidels is the highest duty in Islam (in spite of the fact that it is not one of the "five pillars"), and that the call to jihad is a return to the original faith of the Prophet, who also waged a purifying jihad in the seventh century that gave Islam its beginnings. In bin Laden's conception, jihad is therefore the sacramental center of Muslim life and jihad against all innovations that threaten the faith must be waged until all have been eliminated, and the entire world is subservient to Islam. Furthermore, bin Laden argues that instead of merely waging jihad on apostate regimes (the near enemy), Muslims must also wage jihad against the "far enemy," the United States, since it is support from the United States that allows the apostate governments, such as that in bin Laden's native Saudi Arabia, to stay in power (Benjamin and Simon, 2005, p.18).

With such an Islamist mindset, when the Soviets invaded Afghanistan in the 1980s, bin Laden was compelled to leave the lucrative family construction business in Saudi Arabia to join the Mujahadeen in Afghanistan and aid in their effort to oust the Soviet infidels (*The Sunday Times*, January 2002, p.1). Bin Laden's wealthy construction magnate father also believed in the struggle of the Afghan Mujahadeen and helped fund Osama's activities in Afghanistan and those of the Mujahadeen. Osama made numerous trips from Saudi Arabia to Afghanistan from 1980 to 1982 to provide Saudi support for the Mujahadeen before finally setting up a base in Peshawar in 1982. From Peshawar, bin Laden brought in Saudi construction engineers and equipment to build roads and storage depots for the Mujahadeen (Rashid, 2001, p.132). In 1986, bin Laden helped construct the Khost tunnel complex, which served as an important arms storage depot, training facility, and medical center for the Mujahadeen in Afghanistan. Without bin Laden's road building, it would not have been possible to get many of the weapons to the Mujahadeen (Coll, 2005, p.88). Bin Laden also acted as a liaison between the Saudi Arabian General Intelligence Department (GID) and various international Islamist organizations and the Saudi-backed commanders of jihad in Afghanistan (Coll, 2005, p.87). In 1986, bin Laden opened his own training camp for jihadist volunteers at Jaji, Afghanistan. Later, bin Laden even participated in military operations against Soviet troops, apparently even being wounded in the foot at the battle of Jaji in 1987 (Rashid, 2002, p.53 Coll, 2005, pp.157, 162-163).

While in Afghanistan, bin Laden adopted the teachings of Sheik Abdullah Azzam (the spiritual founder of Hamas), who had been expelled from Egypt in 1979 for Islamic activism (Bergen, 2001, pp.55-61). It was Azzam who originally conceptualized al-Qaeda, perhaps the world's most notorious terrorist organization, for the purpose of providing direction and purpose for the Mujahadeen. Azzam argued that the Soviet war in Afghanistan was just the beginning, and it was time for Muslims to rise up and strike Satan all over the world, with the ultimate goal of converting the entire world into a pure Islamic society under a new caliphate. Azzam envisioned al-Qaeda as an organization that would channel the ideology and direction of the Mujahadeen into fighting against infidels worldwide on behalf of God and oppressed Muslims. Any time a Muslim country might be invaded by infidels, the Mujahadeen would arrive as a ready and able rapid action force to expel the invaders (Bergen, 2001, pp.55-61).

It was also in Afghanistan that bin Laden became acquainted with an Egyptian doctor Ayman al-Zawahiri, who had been imprisoned in Cairo in the 1980s for involvement in the plot to assassinate Egyptian President Anwar Sadat. Al-Zawahiri had been directing jihad throughout the Middle East for over two decades and had even been imprisoned in Russia from some months, but was released because Russian authorities were unaware of who they had in captivity due to al-Zawahiri's use of a false identity and passport (Coll, 2005, p.382). Being pursued by Egyptian authorities, al-Zawahiri volunteered as a doctor for the jihad in Afghanistan in 1997, but also became a major strategist for the global Islamist struggle and shared Azzam's ideas that eventually became al-Qaeda. Al-Zawahiri argued that the international jihadist movement needed a "base" or an arena that would "act like an incubator, where its seeds would grow and where it can acquire practical experience in combat, politics, and organizational matters" (Quoted in Coll, 2005, p.154). Al-Zawahiri also argued that the principal strategy of the Islamists should be to inflict "maximum casualties" against the West and to carry the fight against the "distant enemy" to their home soil. Al-Zawahiri understood that once provoked, the United States would retaliate with revenge attacks and wage war on the jihadists, thus provoking a global Islamist war of retaliation against the United States (Coll, 2005, pp.381-382).

The actions of the Pakistani intelligence service in Afghanistan at the close of the jihad against the Soviet Union had earlier provoked Azzam and al-Zawahiri against the United States. When the Soviets were preparing to withdraw from Afghanistan in the late 1980s, the Pakistani Intelligence Service created its own Afghan guerrilla force and used it to take control of major areas of Afghanistan, thus "robbing" the Mujahadeen of their victory in the eyes of Azzam. Azzam believed and taught that the United States was behind this Pakistani action. Bin Laden evidently agreed with Azzam's analysis and erroneously believed the United States to be in opposition to his Mujahadeen. In particular, bin Laden was angered by what he viewed as an "ungrateful" United States that had taken credit that should have gone to the Mujahadeen and Allah himself, for defeating the Soviets in Afghanistan (Auster, 1998, p. 49).

Azzam and bin Laden supported opposing warlords in the Afghan civil war following the withdrawal of the Soviet Union, with Azzam supporting Ahmed Shah Massoud, and bin Laden supporting the radical Islamist Gulbuddin Hekmatyar. Both Massoud and Hekmatyar considered both communist and capitalist systems to be jahiliyya, although both took hundreds of millions of dollars in aid from the United States. Both Hekmatyar and Massoud also believed that Islam was the proper basis for politics and government and that the goal of jihad was to establish Islamic government in Afghanistan. Both Massoud and Hekmatyar endorsed Qutb's arguments of takfir, under which true believers could identify apostate Muslims who had strayed from Islam and proclaim them to be kafir, or outside the Islamic community. For Qutb, as well as Massoud and Hekmatyar, such apostates had to be overthrown no matter how much they claimed to be following Islam, and the communist ruler of Afghanistan, Najibullah, was one of those apostate Muslims (Coll, 2005, p.203).

Bin Laden and Azzam also differed over the long-term strategy of jihad. Azzam argued that the focus should be on Afghanistan first, but bin Laden favored a broader war and began denouncing other Muslim leaders, such as Hosni Mubarak in Egypt, Benazir Bhutto in Pakistan, King Hussein of Jordan, and Assad of Syria as apostates who should be overthrown. Azzam agreed that global jihad was the eventual goal, but argued that the jihadists should finish the job in Afghanistan before taking the battle elsewhere (Coll, 2005, p.203). Azzam was killed in a 1989 car bombing (a crime that was never solved), but the ideological void left by Azzam's death was quickly filled by Egyptian Dr.

Ayman Muhammad Rabi' al-Zawahiri, a member of a well-respected medical family in Egypt. Al-Zawahiri had also been a member of radical Islamic organizations in Egypt and engaged in covert terrorism for thirty years at the time that he went to Afghanistan to aid the Mujahadeen in the 1980s. With similar ideology and goals, al-Zawahiri quickly became bin Laden's personal physician and close associate. Al-Zawahiri is a follower of the Salafi strand of Islam, and argues for the Salafi goal of Islam in its totality, applied to all humanity irrespective of ethnicity, culture, or national origin (Auster, 1998, p.49).

The global outlook of Salafism allowed bin Laden to reach across the aisle to Shiite Muslims in a mutual effort to forge a new world based on the principles of strict adherence to the Koran, where all persons of the world are strictly subject to God's laws outlined in the Koran. Bin Laden and his followers believe that Mohammed named the Salafis as the "best generation of Muslims" and that those who are Salafis are guaranteed success, victory, and salvation (Auster, 1998, p.49).

Bin Laden and the Persian Gulf War

After the Soviet withdrawal from Afghanistan, bin Laden returned to Saudi Arabia to resume work in the family construction business and brought several of his Mujahadeen Afghans with him. In 1991, when Iraq under Saddam Hussein invaded Kuwait, however, the call of jihad again reached bin Laden, who offered the services of his Mujahadeen to the Saudi government for the purpose of ousting the Iraqis from Kuwait. After all, if the Mujahadeen could destroy the Soviet Union (with the help of Allah), they certainly could oust the much-less-formidable Iraqi army from Kuwait (Gunaratna, 2002, pp.28-30).

The Saudi Royal family essentially rejected bin Laden's offer of help and turned to the Americans instead, thus humiliating Allah's hero of the Afghan war (Coll, 2005, p.223). Then when the non-Muslim US military showed up to help liberate Kuwait in the Persian Gulf War, bin Laden and other Islamists were appalled to see Muslims fighting and killing other Muslims under infidel American leadership. Islamists in Saudi Arabia denounced the arrival of the Americans as a violation of Islamic law. Two Saudi Imams known as the "Awakening Sheikhs" distributed anti-American sermons on tape to millions throughout Saudi Arabia. Sheikh Safar al-Hawali declared that "If Iraq has occupied Kuwait, then America has occupied Saudi Arabia. The real enemy is not Iraq. It is the West" (Quoted in Coll, 2005, p.229). Al-Hawali also wrote a book entitled *Kissinger's Promise* where he argued that the Americans were occupying Saudi Arabia for the purpose of seizing its oil reserves (Coll, 2005, p.229). Another

Islamist circulated a tape entitled, "America as I Saw It" in which he explained to Saudis that the United States was a "nation of beasts who fornicate and eat rotten food, a land where men marry men and parents are abandoned as they age" (Coll, 2005, p.229). Outside of Saudi Arabia, Afghan Mujahadeen warlords Gulbuddin Hekmatyar and Abdurrab Rasul Sayyaf, joined Saudi Islamists in denouncing the Saudi Royal family for accepting American assistance in the war against Iraq, in spite of the fact that they had received hundreds of millions of dollars in aid from the United States (Coll, 2005, p.223).

The Saudi Royal family assured bin Laden that the Americans would depart from the Holy Land as soon as their mission was accomplished, but after the war, the Saudi government continued to allow thousands of American troops to be stationed in Saudi Arabia and police the Persian Gulf region from Saudi soil. In reaction to what he viewed as an abomination against Islam (infidels in the form of the US military residing in the Holy Land of Saudi Arabia), bin Laden began training and financing terrorist groups and calling for the overthrow of unsympathetic apostate governments, including the government of his own Saudi Arabia. The Saudi Government, however, cracked down on dissidents, and bin Laden was forced to flee first to Afghanistan and then to the Sudan, where he began building his terrorist network. Bin Laden would eventually be expelled from Sudan as well, and return to Afghanistan where he was sheltered by the Islamist government of the Taliban that seized power in Afghanistan in 1996 (Gunaratna, 2002, pp.28-30).

Bin Laden's War on America

Bin Laden waged war against what he viewed as apostate or Jahili governments in the Middle East with a series of terrorist bombings in the 1990s. None of the governments targeted by bin Laden and al-Qaeda, including Egypt and Saudi Arabia, were overthrown; consequently, bin Laden became convinced that their ability to survive his jihadi onslaught was due to US support, thus necessitating a change in strategy away from the attacks on the apostate governments themselves and toward the United States, the infidel nation that supported the Jahiliyya governments. Bin Laden's hatred of America, however, was fueled not as much by American "decadence" or the "infidel" status of Americans, but because he viewed the United States as the power that propped up the rule by apostate or jahiliyya Muslim governments, and because of his belief that rule by jahiliyya governments was an abomination to God, and detrimental to both Islam and Muslim people (Quoted in Gunaratna, 2002, p.45).

In August 1996, bin Laden officially declared war on the United States with a religious fatwa (decree). In Islam, an attack on an enemy must be preceded by an Islamic decree or "fatwa" that can only be issued by an Islamic cleric (which bin Laden is not). Many Muslims therefore would not recognize the legitimacy of the 1996 bin Laden fatwa since bin Laden is not a cleric. Taliban leaders in particular expressed to Americans that they were "puzzled" as to how bin Laden could issue any fatwas since he was not an Islamic scholar; however, a group of forty Afghan clerics followed bin Laden's fatwa by issuing a fatwa of their own calling for jihad against the United States on March 12, 1998, and another similar fatwa was issued by Pakistani clerics and signed by Sheikh Ahmed Azzam in April 1998, thus, after the fact, legitimizing bin Laden's war on America (Bergen, 2001, pp.108-109 Coll, 2005, p.386).

In bin Laden's "Declaration of War" fatwa in 1996, bin Laden essentially provided three reasons for war with the United States. First, bin Laden argued that the United States had been occupying the Holy Land for seven years and

> plundering its riches, dictating to its rulers, humiliating its people, terrorizing its neighbours, and turning its bases in the Peninsula into a spearhead through which to fight the neighboring peoples...The best proof of this is the Americans' continuing aggression against Iraqi people using the Peninsula as a staging post, even though all its rulers are against their territories being used to that end, but they are helpless (Quoted in Gunaratna, 2002, p.44).

Second, bin Laden argued that the United States was planning to go to war with Iraq and annihilate the Muslims living there a second time. In the words of bin Laden,

> Second, despite the great devastation inflicted on the Iraqi people by the Crusader-Zionist alliance, and despite the huge number of those killed, which has exceeded one million...despite all this, the Americans are once again trying to repeat the horrific massacres, as though they are not content with the protracted blockade imposed after the ferocious war or the fragmentation and devastation. So here they come to annihilate what is left of this people and to humiliate their Muslim neighbours. (Quoted in Gunaratna, 2002, p.44)

Unfortunately, in the minds of many Muslims, George W. Bush has proven Osama bin Laden to be correct on this particular item; hence, the 2003 American invasion of Iraq lent credibility to bin Laden as a prophet in the minds of many Muslims and it appears that the Iraqi insurgents have had little trouble in recruiting jihadis from throughout the Muslim world for the purpose of ousting the infidel American invaders from Iraq.

Finally, bin Laden argued in 1996 that America's aims behind their wars against Muslims are both "religious and economic and the aim is also to serve the Jews' petty state and divert attention from its occupa-

tion of Jerusalem and murder of Muslims there" (Quoted in Gunaratna, 2002, p.44). Bin Laden goes on to argue that the proof of all he
is saying is the Americans'

> eagerness to destroy Iraq, the strongest neighbouring Arab state, and their
> endeavour to fragment all the states of the region such as Iraq, Saudi Ara-
> bia, Egypt, and Sudan into paper statelets and through their disunion and
> weakness to guarantee Israel's survival and the continuation of the brutal
> Crusade occupation of the Peninsula. (Quoted in Gunaratna, 2002, p.44)

Bin Laden concluded his "Declaration of War" fatwa of 1996 by arguing that these "crimes and sins committed by the Americans are a
clear declaration of war on God, his messenger, and Muslims" and
reminding Muslims that in such cases, ulama (Islamic scholars)
throughout history "unanimously agreed that the jihad is an individual duty if the enemy destroys Muslim countries." Bin Laden then finally ends the fatwa with the statement that "Nothing is more sacred
than belief except repulsing an enemy who is attacking religion and
life," thus suggesting that jihad against those that would destroy Islam
is the highest duty of Muslims (Quoted in Gunaratna, 2002, p.44).
Shortly thereafter, bin Laden told a British journalist in Afghanistan
that the Americans were the "main enemy" of Muslims worldwide and
the Saudi Arabian authorities were only "secondary enemies," thus
shifting his focus from a jihad against apostates as advocated by Qutb,
to a jihad against the United States, essentially the infidel friends of
the apostates (Coll, 2005, p.326).

Bin Laden followed his Declaration of War on America by issuing
two more religious fatwas in 1998 expanding his jihad to the Muslim
world. In these fatwas, bin Laden repeated the complaints of his
Islamist predecessors and condemned the Saudi government for ig-
noring sharia and replacing it with man-made civil law, with the
added condemnation for allowing the Americans to occupy the Holy
Land, a reference to US military bases in Saudi Arabia. Bin Laden declared that the use of man-made law instead of sharia and support of
"infidels" (Americans) against Muslims effectively strips the persons
who do so of their Islamic status (thus making it much easier to kill
them under Islamic law). In other words, bin Laden was declaring that
it was legitimate to kill the Royal family in Saudi Arabia whom he no
longer viewed as Muslims. Bin Laden further declared (again) that
"there is no more important duty for Muslims than expelling the
Americans from the Holy Land," again shifting the primary target of
jihad from a war against apostates to a war against the United States
(Gunaratna, 2002, p.27). In the fatwa of February 1998, bin Laden
went even further and called for the killing of any American anywhere
in the world (Halliday, 2002, Appendix 1).

Bin Laden's Islamist ideology is well exemplified by his statement of February 23, 1998, that included the charge to Muslims to kill all Americans. That statement (presented below) conforms very well to the radical Islamist ideology of Qutb and Maudoodi.

> Ulema have throughout Islamic history unanimously agreed that the jihad is an individual duty if the enemy destroys the Muslim countries. On that basis, and in compliance with God's order, we issue the following fatwa to all Muslims. The ruling to kill the Americans and their allies—civilians and military—is an individual duty for every Muslim who can do it in any country in which it is possible to do it, in order to liberate the al-Aqsa Mosque and the Holy Mosque from their grip, and in order for their armies to move out of all the lands of Islam, defeated and unable to threaten any Muslim. This is in accordance with the words of Almighty God, 'and fight the pagans all together as they fight you all together,' and 'fight them until there is no more tumult or oppression, and there prevail justice and faith in God.' We—with God's help—call on every Muslim who believes in God and wishes to be rewarded to comply with God's order to kill the Americans and plunder their money wherever and whenever they find it. We also call on Muslim 'ulema,' leaders, youths, and soldiers to launch the raid on Satan's US troops and the devil's supporters allying with them, and to displace those who are behind them so that they may learn a lesson. (Quoted in Halliday, 2002, Appendix 1)

Bin Laden's credibility has been enhanced by his ability to make predictions and proclamations that other Muslims can interpret as coming true. In 1998, for example, bin Laden announced that there was a US plan to divide Iraq into three sectors, essentially one for Kurds, one for Sunnis, and one for Shiites, and that the United States also planned to divide Saudi Arabia into two kingdoms: one for oil and one for the "two mosques" (Pape, 2005, p.121). Unfortunately, President George W. Bush's invasion of Iraq in 2003 and the subsequent chaos and sectarian violence in Iraq that followed clearly validated bin Laden's predictions of a divided Iraq in the minds of many Muslims, although Saudi Arabia remains intact.

Bin Laden's Use of Symbolism

In any traditional conservative ideology, the use of symbols and symbolism takes on enhanced importance. Close observers of Osama bin Laden will note that bin Laden is a master of using cultural and religious symbolism to enhance his legitimacy among his followers. For example, although bin Laden has frequently lived in large, luxurious houses and driven expensive luxury vehicles during his years leading jihad, his media interviews and taped conversations are always from caves, thus projecting an image of a common man who has piously foregone riches in the interest of Allah's service. On posters throughout the Middle East, bin Laden is depicted as a saint riding on a white

horse, thus evoking images among viewers of the prophet Mohammed, who also fought on a white horse. Bin Laden, unlike the jahili
leaders Saddam Hussein, Hosni Mubarak, and King Hussein of Jordan, never wears a western suit, and is always seen wearing traditional Islamic clothing. In particular, bin Laden wears a headdress
that relates to Jerusalem's al Aqsa mosque, one of Islam's holiest sites.
At other times, bin Laden wears a plain white turban, signifying that
he has near-clerical status. Bin Laden ordinarily carries a knife typical
of the design of those for rulers on the Arabian Peninsula, and he
wears a ring containing a black stone set in silver that symbolizes
Mecca, the most Holy place of Islam (Gunaratna, 2002, pp.41-42).

Bin Laden also uses symbolism recognizable to Muslims in his writings and proclamations. For example, in his "Declaration of Jihad on
the Americans Occupying the Two Sacred Places," he referred to his
haven in Afghanistan as Khorasan, a symbolic reference to a long-lost
Islamic empire that had once encompassed Central Asia (Coll, 2005,
p.332).

Hero and Leader of Jihad

With the successful terrorist attacks of 9/11/01 for which he received
credit, Osama bin Laden became the undisputed most important
leader and symbol of global Islamism. According to the Pew Research
Center in 2003, survey data from Indonesia, Jordan, Morocco, Pakistan, and the Palestinian Authority suggested that bin Laden was considered in those areas to be one of the three world figures that was in
their opinion the most likely to "do the right thing" (http://people-
press.org/reports/display.php3?ReportID=175). Similarly, according
to a Nigerian newspaper shortly after the 9/11 attacks, the most popular name for babies in Nigeria was 'Osama,' and 70% of the babies in
one particular location were given that name (Borisov, 2002, p.1). Bin
Laden's status has also been enhanced by the fact that at the time of
this writing, he remains free in spite of an American invasion and occupation of his safe haven, Afghanistan. It is noteworthy that bin
Laden and his top aid, Ayman al-Zawahiri, have eluded capture for a
period longer than it took for the United States to destroy the Nazi regime of Adolph Hitler in World War II. To Islamists, this can be
viewed merely as proof that Allah is with him and protecting him.

Bin Laden justified the 9/11 terrorist attacks as revenge for all of the
deaths of Muslims worldwide at the hands of the of the United States
in the decades since the fall of the caliphate in 1924. In the words of
bin Laden himself (Quoted from the BBC News Service online at
http://news.bbc.co.uk/1/low/world/south_asia?1585636.stm)

> What the United States tastes today is a very small thing compared to what
> we have tasted for tens of years. Our nation has been tasting this humilia-
> tion and contempt for more than eighty years. Its sons are being killed, its
> blood is being shed, its holy places are being attacked, and it is not being
> ruled according to what God has decreed.

In spite of the fact that bin Laden could only have expected an American military retaliation to his attacks, he denounced the subsequent
American invasion of Afghanistan not as American justice, revenge, or
retaliation, but as a "Crusader grudge against Muslims" by the United
States and the West (Cook, 2003, p.31). In doing so, bin Laden essentially ignored the fact that the United States and the West were not
"crusading" in Afghanistan prior to the 9/11 terror attacks, but supporting Mujahadeen warriors throughout the 1980s; hence, the deaths
of Muslims in Afghanistan could be termed as directly related to *his*
actions.

The American invasion of Afghanistan also presented bin Laden
and the jihadists with another problem in that Allah did not save all of
the faithful Muslim jihadists from the American military onslaught,
thus requiring bin Laden to explain why God had abandoned his children in their time of need. The Islamists' answer was that the defeat of
the Taliban and their supporters in Afghanistan was one of the "trials"
designed by God for the faithful. Islamists argued that such sufferings
were preludes to God's ultimate triumph and the ultimate triumph of
Islam over the infidels (Cook, 2003, pp.52-53).

In 2003, the United States provided bin Laden with another boost
when it invaded Iraq. The invasion not only altered American priori-
ties and diverted resources from the hunt for bin Laden in Afghanistan, but it also provided bin Laden and his followers with the
opportunity to confirm their "crusader" arguments. In February 2003,
bin Laden (Quoted in Benjamin and Simon, 2005, p.33) released the
statement that

> We are following up with great interest and extreme concern the crusaders'
> preparations for war to occupy a former capital of Islam, loot Muslims'
> wealth, and install an agent government, which would be a satellite for its
> masters in Washington and Tel Aviv...Needless to say, this crusade war is
> primarily targeted against the people of Islam

President Bush had already confirmed bin Laden's argument for him
during the week after the 9/11 terrorist attacks when he ignorantly described the invasion of Iraq as a "crusade," evidently not understanding the importance of the term to Islamists and Muslims in general
(Ford, 2001). Similarly, bin Laden's deputy, Ayman al-Zawahiri
(Quoted in Benjamin and Simon, 2005, p.33) issued a radio message
on the eve of the American invasion of Iraq arguing that

> After dividing Iraq, Saudi Arabia, Iran, Syria, and Pakistan will come next. They would leave around Israel only dismembered semi-states that are subservient to the United States and Israel. O Muslims, these are the facts that have been made clear to you.

Again, President Bush unknowingly helped confirm the Islamists argument for them during his State of the Union Address in January 2002 by characterizing Iraq, Iran, and North Korea as an "Axis of Evil," thus at least inferring that after toppling the regime of Saddam Hussein, the United States had ambitions to attack other regimes as well, including that of the Islamic Republic of Iran.

At the time of this writing, bin Laden, the world's most famous and infamous Islamist, remains at large and his "hero" status in the Islamic world continues. Although it is anybody's guess whether the American terrorist-hunters will ever catch up to bin Laden, what is certain is that even if they do, the ideology of Islamism will continue, and bin Laden's status as an icon for oppressed Islamists will continue in the Islamic world. Meanwhile, Afghanistan remains a basket case of a country almost four years after the American invasion to get bin Laden, oust the Taliban, and install "democracy" in Afghanistan, and democracy thus far remains more a farce than reality. For instance, the *Economist* (October 9, 2004, p.21) described an Afghan democracy event thus,

> Poorer candidates outlined their visions in the four live TV slots that each candidate was allotted. Lengthy pauses and meticulous nose-picking were common-place. Mr. Karazai, the solid favourite, recited most of his inaugural speech twice. Massouda Jalal, the only female contender, offered her air time to the President.

To make matters worse, displaying complete ignorance as to the meaning of Western-style freedom and democracy, a Pushtun tribe in the Khost province decreed that anyone who did not vote for Mr. Karazai would have his house burned down. Many voters apparently registered multiple times, and children and foreigners were apparently registered to vote. Voter registration in the Northeastern Paktia province reached 170%, whereas female registration in the Zabul province in the Southeast where Taliban influence is strong was only 7% (*Economist*, October 9, 2004, p.21).

As if the electoral problems were not enough, in 2004, Afghanistan's opium crop was estimated to be the largest in its history, making up two thirds of the national income. The security situation remains so precarious that international aid organizations and international corporations generally stay out. In 2004 on one of the only two occasions when Afghan President Hamid Karazai tried to hold a rally outside Kabul, his helicopter was repelled by ground fire. The Afghan-Pakistani border is still replete with followers of the Taliban and foreign jihadists and remains a no-go zone for anyone concerned with their own security (*Economist*, October 9, 2004, p.22). For instance, a Danish agency in September 2004 had one of its houses in Kabul destroyed by a suicide bomber and its compound in southeastern Laghman Province near the Pakistani border was bombarded with rockets, and its staff were forced to flee. Then, as if to add insult to injury, an American plane mistakenly bombed another Danish agency camp in the Kunar province, killing six people (*Economist*, October 9, 2004, p.22). It is perhaps a bit of a stretch of the imagination to conclude that the situation in Afghanistan four years after the American invasion is a vindication of American policies of regime change and installation of Western democracy through military means. Instead, much of Afghanistan still mirrors the conditions that spawned the Taliban. The government still controls little of the country outside Kabul and the border area in the south near Pakistan remains replete with opium production, warlordism, terrorism, and corruption. The Taliban forces have regrouped, and at this writing have several thousand armed fighters. Afghan President Hamid Karzai generally relies on local warlords to enforce security. In May-June 2006 alone, 1000 people died in fighting in southern Afghanistan (*Economist*, June 24, 2006, p.13). In the words of one Afghan to an aid worker, "We are so desperate, we would take help from the Devil" (Quoted in the *Economist*, October 9, 2004, p.23). If that is the case, then the door remains very much open for the "Devil" to return.

• CHAPTER SEVEN •

Islamism in Iraq

Although the ideology of Islamism was most certainly present in Iraq prior to the Persian Gulf War of 1991, Iraq was not typically known as one of the most important breeding grounds for Islamism and Islamic terrorism until after the American invasion of Iraq in 2003. Instead, Iraq had been widely viewed as one of the most secular countries in the Islamic world prior to the calamities of the Iran/Iraq war of the 1980s, the Persian Gulf War of 1991, the twelve years of economic sanctions that followed, and the American invasion of 2003, that finally unleashed the fury of Islamist ideology in Iraq. From Saddam Hussein's invasion of Iran to the present, Iraq has been catapulted from its position among the most secular countries in the Islamic realm to the center of the world's Islamist activity.

Prior to the war with Iran, Iraq was known as a land where Western music, movies, and alcohol sales flourished along with other aspects of Western culture. Even though much has changed in the last quarter century, it is still common to find people in Iraq that are well versed in "Hollywood vulgarities" they have picked up from American movies and as a consequence, some Iraqis are as likely as Americans to refer to others as "f*cking assholes" (Shadid, 2005, p.66). Iraq was known to be so "progressive" before the wars that many women in Iraq wore Western clothing (including miniskirts), worked outside the home, and sought progressive education along with men. Men could wear Western clothing and were not required to grow full beards as in Wahhabi-dominated Saudi Arabia and Afghanistan under the Taliban (Packer, 2005, p.256). Some Iraqis still enjoy watching the American Fox News channel on satellite television and regard it as Americans regard Al-Jazeera (as a propaganda machine), but Fox News is also viewed by Iraqis as a medium that provides insight into what Americans (especially the conservative Americans in charge of the American occupation) are thinking (Shadid, 2005, p.66). In any case, the Iraqi people were not completely isolated from Western influence under the regime of Saddam Hussein and were in many respects much closer to the Western model of separation of church and state than most other countries in the Islamic realm.

Impetus to Re-Islamization

The evaporation of the secular Iraq and its transformation into a hotbed of Islamism did not occur overnight with the American invasion of 2003, but was decades in the making, due to decades of calamity that were the undoing of Iraqi society. Meanwhile, extremist Islamist tendencies were always present on the fringes of Iraqi society, even while the country was undergoing overt secularization under the Baathists. For instance, Iraq, like most other Islamic countries, had its own chapter of the Muslim Brotherhood, founded in 1947 by the radical Sunni cleric, Sheikh Muhammad Mahmud al-Sawwaf. The center of Muslim Brotherhood strength was Mosul in the Kurdish area of northern Iraq, but the organization spread in the 1950s to predominantly Arab areas and major Iraqi cities in the Sunni Triangle including Baghdad, Kirkuk, Basra, Tikrit, and Samarra (Sankari, 2005, pp.67–69). Although it is true that the Iraqi version of the Muslim Brotherhood remained fairly timid during the reign of the Baathists due to Baathist oppression, the Islamist ideology that drives the Muslim Brotherhood remained intact nonetheless (Hashim, 2006, pp.109–110).

A Sunni Iraqi Islamic Party was founded in 1960, but was promptly banned by Iraq's secularizing military regime. In spite of its illegal status, the Islamic Party worked largely underground for four decades until the fall of Saddam's regime at the hands of the US military allowed them to emerge into the open in 2003 and take advantage of their newfound freedom brought to them by their Western nemesis (Hashim, 2006, p.21). Similarly, in reaction to the Marxist-Leninist and secularist leanings of the Baathists, Shiite Islamist Parties arose in the predominantly Shiite areas in the 1960s and played prominent roles within the Shiite communities. After the Iranian Revolution of 1979, the Shiite Parties actively opposed the regime of Saddam Hussein (with American encouragement), only to find themselves again repressed by the Baathist regime and forced underground. Like the Muslim Brotherhood, the fall of Saddam Hussein allowed the Shiite Parties to emerge from the underground and assume leadership roles in the Iraqi efforts to reformulate the Iraqi political landscape (Hashim, 2006, pp.238–239).

War and Sanctions

There is plenty of blame to go around for the "unleashing" of Islamism in Iraq, but Saddam Hussein, though not an Islamist himself, must shoulder his fair share of the blame for numerous reasons, most importantly for the damage caused to secular Iraq by the eight year war with Iran in the 1980s. In September 1980, Saddam Hussein's Iraq invaded Iran and began a disastrous eight-year war that resulted in almost 250,000 Iraqi deaths at a cost of approximately $100 billion (Hiro, 2002, p.32). As if that were not enough, two years after the conclusion of that war, Iraq under Saddam invaded Kuwait, only to be expelled the next year by an international coalition force led by the United States. In a six-week air campaign and 100-hour ground war that followed, 110,000 air sorties were flown against Iraqi targets in the Persian Gulf War of 1991, dropping a total of 140,000 tons of explosives on Iraq, an explosive power equivalent to seven Hiroshima bombs. Iraqi deaths in the war were approximately 60,000 people (Hiro, 2002, p.39). After the war was over, Shiites rose up to overthrow Saddam Hussein, believing that they would be supported by the United States and the Western coalition. No assistance to the Shiites was forthcoming, however, and another 200,000 people would die in Iraq during the Shiite uprising in March 1991, as Saddam Hussein brutally suppressed insurrections against his government (Phillips, 2005, p.24).

The first Bush administration exacerbated the already deplorable situation for the Iraqi people when the United States and Western powers imposed severe economic sanctions on Iraq after Saddam invaded Kuwait, but the sanctions were not lifted after the war and instead remained in force until the American invasion of 2003. Through the sanctions, the United States and its allies were trying to punish Saddam Hussein and hopefully create conditions that would lead to his demise, but it was the Iraqi people who were the ones that suffered from the sanctions, as they were cut off from water, electricity, and other basic amenities. During the twelve years of severe UN and American sanctions, basic economic goods such as seeds, pesticides, fertilizer, spare parts for farm machinery, paper, spare parts for copiers, spare parts for the sewage system, and even serums for medical vaccinations, were banned due to the fear that such commodities could be transformed from their original purposes into chemical and biological Weapons of Mass Destruction. As a result of the sanctions, children all over Iraq had no paper for school and the literacy rate fell from 90% to 66%. The child mortality rate tripled to 9%, the rate of malnutrition among children rose to one third, sewage spilled onto the streets due to broken pumps, and half of Iraq's livestock died due to the ban on vaccines for foot and mouth disease (Hiro, 2002, pp.6–18). As of 2003, Iraqi income was only 20% of what it had been prior to the Persian Gulf War, infant mortality had doubled, and most of Iraqis lacked access to clean water. One third of Iraqi six-year-old children no longer attended school (Shadid, 2005, p.38). Even worse, it is estimated that up to 500,000 Iraqi children died over a twelve-year period as a direct result of the UN sanctions (Hiro, 2002, p.6–18).

Although the sanctions did not enable the Iraqi people to rise up and overthrow Saddam Hussein, they did enable Saddam to shift the blame for the suffering from his own regime to the UN and the United States. The deplorable conditions also apparently induced thousands of Iraqi people to seek refuge in Islam, which was essentially the only entity left in Iraq to which desperate people could turn for help (Hiro, 2002, p.16). In the words of Ahmed Hashim of the US Naval War College

> The sanctions regime that existed between 1991 and 2003 promoted the return to religion among the Iraqi population. The destruction of the Iraqi middle class, the decline of the secular educational system and the rise of illiteracy, and the growth of despair and anomie have resulted in large numbers of Iraqis seeking succor in religion. (2006, p.111)

As if to add insult to injury, after the Persian Gulf War ended in 1991, the Allies mercilessly harassed Saddam Hussein in efforts to get him to capitulate. American fighter jets flew over Baghdad 24 hours a day causing 20 to 30 sonic booms daily for months, in an effort to get the Iraqi people to oppose Saddam Hussein. Such activity, however, only turned the Iraqi people against the United States, which had obviously become an annoying pest (Radi, 1998, p.59). The Americans also drew two "no-fly zones" over Iraq after the Persian Gulf War, a measure that Iraqis found humiliating. Essentially, within their own country, Iraqis could not fly north of 36 degrees (just south of Mosul) or south of 32 degrees (just north of Najaf). Later, the southern "no-fly zone" was extended north to 33 degrees, just South of Baghdad itself. The United States then spent twelve years pummeling Iraq with air sorties wherever Saddam Hussein had ground-to-air missile sites, radar sites, and telecommunications systems. In a single hundred-hour barrage in December 1998, intended by the Clinton administration to oust the Iraqi dictator, the United States fired 415 cruise missiles (90 more than in the entire Persian Gulf War) and dropped 600 laser-guided bombs, hitting 75 targets, including Iraqi military intelligence (Hiro, 2002, pp.130–131).

Such activity was clearly likely to kill civilians along with the destruction of military targets and, therefore, was perhaps more likely to unite the Iraqi people against the American "fire from the sky" than to unite them against Saddam Hussein. In the wake of such devastation from over twenty years of wars, bombings, and sanctions, the predictable reaction of many Iraqis to the hardships was a rededication to Islam, with the result that a majority of women donned the veil by the time of the American invasion of 2003. Furthermore, the number of Muslim worshipers at Friday prayers may have doubled between the early 1990s and 2003 and the number of Pilgrims to the Imam Kadhim shrine tripled to approximately 50,000 per day. Clearly, the time between the wars was a time of Islamic revival in Iraq (Shadid, 2005, p.36). In the words of one professor of sociology at Baghdad University, "When a society is in crisis like we are, with the embargo and all, religion plays a greater part in soothing the psyche of the people and giving the people greater strength to face the crisis" (Quoted in *Los Angeles Times*, November 4, 2001, p.1).

It is also true, however, that in the end, even among those that did not subscribe to radical Islam, most Iraqi people placed the blame for their hardships not on Saddam Hussein, but on the Americans (Shadid, 2005, p.90). In the minds of most Iraqis, the logic was that at least Saddam Hussein was an Iraqi Muslim instead of a foreign infidel invader. In that sense, the current Iraqi insurgency and rise in Islamism can be understood at least in part as little more than people defending their home against an invader who has stated no timetable for departure (Shadid, 2005, p.98).

Saddam's Re-Islamization

Until the 1990s, Saddam Hussein had been among the staunchest supporters of separation of state and religion in the Middle East, largely due to what he viewed as threats to his power from the Shiite clergy. In the words of Saddam himself prior to the War with Iran, "We have to resist the politicization of religion whether by the state or by others in society" (Quoted in Hashim, 2006, p.239). Changing political situations, however, caused Saddam to change his political stance so that some of Iraq's re-Islamization may be less the result of war and sanctions and instead the direct result of the policies of Saddam Hussein after the first Gulf War. In the words of one professor at the Saddam University for Islamic Studies (Quoted in Hashim, 2006, p.111), "Iraq is witnessing a religious renaissance. There was religious stagnation and a tendency toward materialism here. Nightclubs, bars, and pubs were spreading. Saddam has helped correct that." Since the Shiite clergy were Saddam Hussein's most important internal opposition, Saddam adopted a similar strategy to that of the Saudi Royal family and attempted to counter the Shiite threat with a campaign of Sunni Islamization designed to shore up his own support among religious Sunnis and provide legitimacy for his regime. In furtherance of these goals, Saddam embarked on a vigorous mosque construction program, including the Umm al-Ma'arik mosque in Baghdad at a cost of $7.5 million. Islamic studies were added to secondary school curriculum, and a men-only Islamic university, the Saddam University for Islamic Studies, was opened (Hashim, 2006, p.111). Saddam even added the words "Allahu Akbar" to the Iraqi flag in his own handwriting, and commissioned a copy of the Koran written in his own blood (Packer, 2005, p.257).

In 1999, Saddam began what was labeled as the "Enhancement of Islamic Faith" campaign that amounted to government-implemented re-Islamization. The campaign restricted drinking and gambling establishments and promoted religious education and religious programming in the Iraqi media. Radical clerics were allowed to give political sermons as long as they focused their political attacks on the Western powers that imposed sanctions on Iraq (Hashim, 2006, p.110). In response, in 1999, Islamists followed Saddam's lead and bombed Baghdad music stores and movie theaters and publicly destroyed television sets (Hashim, 2006, p.23). In Fallujah, Islamists threatened the owners of beauty parlors and bombed the only movie theater in the city (Hashim, 2006, p.41).

The American Invasion and Occupation

If there is any one factor over any other that has contributed to the re-Islamization of Iraq, it is undoubtedly the American invasion followed by unending occupation. The Iraqi insurgency is not, as has been claimed by the Bush administration, primarily "elements loyal to Saddam," but is instead a convergence of ideological forces that surely include Saddam loyalists as a minor element, but also include Islamism, anti-Americanism, Sunni dispossession, Iraqi nationalism, sectarian hatred, the Iraqis' sense of revenge and loss for the death and destruction inflicted by the Americans, and the American incompetence in restoring order and providing goods and services.

Although it should be stated that the Iraqi people were generally happy to see the end of Saddam Hussein, whom they generally reviled due to his brutality; the Iraqi people were also apparently as offended by the American invasion and occupation as they were by Saddam Hussein. In general, Iraqis have viewed the American invasion and occupation as simply replacing one evil with another. In the words of one Iraqi citizen who had suffered arrest four times under the regime of Saddam Hussein, "If you fight for Saddam and he wins, you are not winning. If America wins, you are not winning. They freed us from evil but they brought more evil to the country" (Quoted in www.salon.com/news/feature/2004/12/16/iraqi_insurgents/print.html). By the fall of 2003, polling data in Iraq suggested that less than 15% of Iraqis viewed the Americans as "liberators" (Phillips, 2005, p.176). In essence, the Iraqi people generally viewed the American invasion as an insult, and they questioned the right of Americans to intervene in order to change a political system that did not belong to them. In the words of one Iraqi quoted by American journalist Anthony Shadid (2005),

> What gives them the right to change something that's not theirs in the first place? I don't like your house, so I'm going to bomb it and you can rebuild it again the way I want it, with your money? I feel like it's an insult, really. What they're doing to us, they deserve to have done to them ... their families, their children. (p.87)

Although this complaint is not religious in character, it has certainly been made worse by the fact that the invaders that have taken control of their country are of a different religion (Pape, 2005, p.6).

Revenge and Loss

Iraqi culture is one that awards a significant place to revenge, replete with personal and group vendettas that often last for decades. As explained by Anthony Shadid (2005, p.281), "the Americans were unable to come to grips with a culture where vendettas spanned decades over things as seemingly miniscule as 'someone who killed my goat one hundred years ago.'" Similarly, American journalist George Packer, who was in Iraq during the American invasion (2005, p.308), quotes a tribal sheikh from Ramadi named Zaydan Halef al-Awad, who explains the Iraqi conception of revenge thus,

> We Iraqis have a nature, which is revenge. If my cousin kills my brother, I have to kill him. If the Americans come from thousands of miles away and dishonor our women and hurt our children, how can I spare them?

American Failure in the Shiite Rebellion

Imbedded in an already vengeful culture, Iraqis generally harbored anti-American feelings left over from the first Persian Gulf War in 1991, especially in the Shiite South. After the 1991 Persian Gulf War, the Shiites believe they were encouraged to revolt against Saddam Hussein when American planes dropped leaflets over Southern Iraq urging people to revolt against Saddam Hussein. With good reason to believe that the United States was on their side and was ready to provide assistance, the Shiites revolted, but President George H.W. Bush desired the United States remain on the sidelines in the event of an Iraqi civil war, so as to avoid any Vietnam-style quagmires, and out of fear that the Shiite uprising (which also received backing from Iran) might lead to an Iranian-style Shiite theocracy in Iraq. Instead, the Bush administration allowed Saddam to send his Republican Guard troops into the south and indiscriminately massacre Shiites with helicopter gunships that Bush allowed to fly in what was otherwise the no-fly zone (Hiro, 2002, pp.41–44).

The Shiite uprising quickly escalated into an orgy of looting and destruction of property that included summary executions of Baathists and military officers of Saddam's regime by Shiites. Fearing chaos, the United States allowed Saddam Hussein to brutally put down the Shiite uprising, resulting in Shiite deaths in excess of 200,000 and inducing 70,000 more Iraqi Shiites to flee to Iran in order to avoid Saddam's wrath (Hiro, 2002, pp.41–44). Almost simultaneously, the United States stood by idly while Saddam Hussein crushed uprisings in Kurdistan in the north, with the result that approximately 1.5 million Kurds were forced to the borders of Iran and Turkey in order to avoid slaughter. The inaction by the Bush administration could only contribute to beliefs among Iraqis in both north and south that Saddam Hussein remained in power because he was wanted there by the United States (Hiro, 2002, pp.44–45). The official policy of the Bush administration is perhaps summarized in a statement issued by the administration on March 27, 1991 announcing that it had "made no promises to the Shias or Kurds" and that "The American people have no stomach for a military operation to dictate the outcome of a political struggle in Iraq" (Quoted in Hiro, 2002, p.44). Bush's National Security Adviser, Brent Scowcroft, later explained to ABC News that

> I frankly wished (the uprising) hadn't happened. I envisioned a post-war government being a military government. ... It's the colonel with the brigade patrolling his palace that's going to get him (Saddam) if someone gets him. (Quoted in Wurmser, 1999, 142)

Similarly, Richard Haas, Bush's Director for Near East Affairs on the National Security Council, stated that "Our policy is to get rid of Saddam, not his regime" (Quoted in Cockburn and Cockburn, 1999, p.37). After the terror attacks of 9/11, the policies of the next Bush administration would not be so reserved.

Death and Destruction in the 2003 American Invasion

After the 2003 American invasion began, thousands of Iraqis gained new reasons to oppose, attack, and kill Americans after their family members were killed by American weapons, their property destroyed, and their water supply and electricity ceased to function in a land where summertime temperatures top 130 degrees Fahrenheit. Five days before the American ground invasion, the United States launched a massive air campaign against 437 Iraqi targets that included 22 sites that were considered "high CD" (civilian death) sites, meaning that the US military estimated that hitting the sites would result in the death of over 30 civilians. American General Tommy Franks favored hitting all 22 sites as a message to the regime that "the gloves were off" and President George W. Bush approved Franks' heavy-handed strategy (Gordon and Trainor, 2006, p.110). Under the best of circumstances, such an approach should perhaps be expected to turn the Iraqi people against the American occupiers. It is apparent from reports on the ground that this is indeed what has happened.

Anthony Shadid, a Lebanese-American journalist embedded in Iraq during the American invasion, describes numerous instances where death and suffering directly caused by the American invasion created anti-Americanism among Iraqis. In particular, Shadid describes one morbid scene on April 7, 2003 when an American bunker-buster bomb landed in a residential neighborhood. Shadid stood amidst a small crowd that gathered around the destruction and witnessed a group of Iraqi civilians pulling out the bodies of thirteen civilians who had been buried by the blast. During the rescue efforts, a young student turned to Shadid and exclaimed, "F*ck all Americans" (Quoted in Shadid, 2005, p.111). Later, Shadid watched as a man pulled his six-year-old nephew's body out of the rubble. The man looked at Shadid after holding his nephew's body while rocking back and forth and wailing and then inquired of Shadid, "Is he a military leader? Are all these people military leaders" (Quoted in Shadid, 2005, p.112)? It is probably accurate to conclude that the dead boy's uncle, regardless of whether he had been pro-American in the past, would be unlikely to be pro-American in the future. Given that tens of thousands of Iraqis have similar stories in a culture that is already noted for revenge, it is little wonder that the US army has incurred resistance. Colonel Douglas McGregor explained the problems thusly (Quoted in the *Saint Louis Post-Dispatch*, December 19, 2004)

> We arrested people in front of their families, dragging them away in handcuffs with bags over their heads, and then provided no information to the families of those we incarcerated. In the end, our soldiers killed, maimed, and incarcerated thousands of Arabs, 90 percent of whom were not the enemy. But they are now. (p.A1)

The revenge and loss motivation would only grow throughout the period of the American occupation as clashes between the US military and insurgents produced inevitable civilian casualties. For example, on April 28 2003, American soldiers fired into a crowd of protestors in Fallujah, killing fifteen and wounding sixty-five (Shadid, 2005, p.233). Two days later, the US troops killed two more people. Fallujah was a town where anti-Western sentiment was already high due to an accidental bombing by the British during the first Persian Gulf War in 1991 that killed 130 civilians in a Fallujah market (Hashim, 2006, p.27). The Americans claimed self-defense in the incidents, but the residents of Fallujah blamed the Americans, and the families and friends of seventeen slain individuals (in a land where families are large), suddenly had reasons to hate the United States (Shadid, 2005, p.233).

That the killings produced a religious response is testified to by the presence of leaflets that were distributed at radical Salafist mosques in Fallujah exhorting residents to

> In the name of God, kill them wherever they are and never take them as friends or allies. For those who have no honor and who prefer Jews to Muslims, it is just to spill their blood. You will suffer mighty and punishing blows. (Quoted in Hashim, 2006, p.42)

The leaflets included the names of Falluja natives who had "collaborated" with the "infidel occupier," thus discouraging citizens from helping the Americans under the threat of death. As a consequence, Fallujah became an Islamist enclave within the Iraqi state with sharia supplanting any authority of the new Iraqi government. In June 2004, Abu Musab al-Zarqawi, the leader of al-Qaeda in Iraq until his death in 2006, attended a ceremony in Fallujah where the insurgents in Fallujah swore their loyalty to al-Zarqawi (Hashim, 2006, pp.42–43).

Humiliation and Honor

Isaiah Berlin (1972, p.17) once argued in *Foreign Affairs* that "Nationalism is an inflamed condition of national consciousness which ... usually seems to be caused by wounds, some form of collective humiliation." It appears that Iraqis in general (especially Sunnis) have viewed the American invasion as such a wound. It is also clear that the Iraqi people view the American occupation as such a collective humiliation and insult to their honor that an intense sense of nationalism has arisen (especially among Sunnis) and outrage has developed against those that caused the collective humiliation. Repeatedly during the invasion and during the occupation that has followed, Americans have either completely misunderstood or disregarded the Iraqis' sense of pride. For example, after the Americans helped Iraqis pull down the statue of Saddam Hussein in Firdaus Square with a tank recovery vehicle, a source of great pride and rejoicing in the United States, the Iraqis on the scene also cheered at first, but ceased cheering when American marines draped an American flag over Saddam's visage (Shadid, 2005, p.125). In the words of one Iraqi

I felt as if a heavy burden was lifted off my back when I saw the toppling of the statue. But the minute somebody went up with the American flag, the whole thing changed. I started saying, 'No, no, no, shoot the bastard.' (Quoted in Shadid, 2005, p.326)

The humiliation would only grow worse in the months to come, as Americans stormed private homes in the middle of the night searching for insurgents. Iraqis suddenly found their homes invaded at any time, including raids at times when women in the home might be dressed immodestly, and entire families were subjected to interrogations, arrests, and stormtrooper-type tactics that included the kicking in of doors, pointing of guns at Iraqi men in front of their wives and children, and binding, blindfolding, and gagging the inhabitants. In a culture that reveres the sanctity of the home, these were major infractions. George Packer relates the story of one Iraqi man who had favored the American invasion, but then turned against the Americans after the Americans raided his house. In the words of Packer (2005)

But that night they humiliated him by mockingly spreading his secret girlie magazines across his bed next to his qur'an. Twenty minutes later the soldiers were gone, and the young man began to slap his mother, screaming that Americans were devils. He spent the night in the mosque, and when he came home the next day he threw out all the foreign-made cheese in the refrigerator, burned all the Western images in the house, and forbade his mother to watch Western news or movies. When she brought home anti-anxiety medication for her troubled son, he refused the pills: The yellow ones were from Jews and the red ones from evil foreigners. (p.309)

In general, the Americans did not respect the Iraqis' cultural mores in the simple things, such as the Iraqi aversion to the wearing of sunglasses when directly speaking to people, and behaved in generally threatening manners. Americans entered homes where women were home alone, and no men were present. American soldiers spoke directly to Iraqi women rather than to their husbands, and entered and searched their bedrooms, thus violating the Iraqis' sense of dignity. The US soldiers often made men bow their heads to the ground, an act in Islam that should only be performed before God (Shadid, 2005, pp.230, 298). In one instance, an Iraqi laborer named Abdul Razak al-Muaimi explained to Western journalists his outrage and humiliation by stating,

train my son to kill Americans. ... (U.S. soldiers) searched my house. They kicked my Koran. They speak to me so poorly in front of my children. It's not that I encourage my son to hate Americans. It's not that I make him want to join the resistance. Americans do that for me. (Quoted in *New York Times*. April 10, 2004).

Other items over which American soldiers had no control also tended to offend Iraqis. For example, the pyramid and eye on the back of an American dollar bill are considered to be Zionist symbols by Muslims, and Iraqis viewed a famous picture of an American tank positioned next to the ancient Babylon gate as a symbol of Zionist revenge for the Babylonian captivity that occurred centuries before Christ (Packer, 2005, p.153). Even American efforts to help the Iraqis by tossing military rations and bottles of water into crowds were viewed as humiliating. In the words of one Iraqi man, "They treated us like monkeys—who's the first one who can jump up and catch the food" (Shadid, 2005, pp.221, 225). In such an environment, it should not be surprising that radicals would argue that Iraqis should defend Muslim honor by killing Americans.

Nowhere was the humiliation greater than in the Sunni triangle. The Sunnis, who had ruled Iraq since the British mandate of the 1920s, suddenly found themselves dispossessed and blamed for all of the wrongs of Saddam Hussein. Instead of rulers, the Sunnis suddenly became shaad biduun, or "a people without." Iraqi businessman Talal al-Gaaod, who earned a Master's degree in construction management from the University of Southern California, explained to journalist George Packer that

> The whole guerrilla war was a terrible misfortune that needn't have happened if only the Americans had listened to people like them instead of invading their houses and dishonoring their women and compelling the Iraqis to seek Revenge. (Quoted in Packer, 2005, p. 416)

The dissolution of the Iraqi army and dismissal of Baathist Party members by Paul Bremer was another factor that appears to have contributed to Sunni humiliation and thus fed the insurgency. For example, one former army officer told Western journalist Christian Parenti that he had joined the insurgency due to the shame and humiliation he felt at the dissolution of the army and that the goal of his group was to expel the Americans and restore Iraqi sovereignty (Hashim, 2006, p.98).

Disingenuous American Motives

Another reason for the Iraqi insurgency and re-Islamization was the apparent (to the Iraqis) disingenuous nature of the American invasion and occupation of the country in the first place. It appears that very few Iraqis believe that the United States came to free them from Saddam Hussein and bring democracy. Instead, numerous other theories dominate the thinking of the Iraqi people. For example, one Iraqi insurgent explained to Canadian journalist Patrick Graham that he believed the American invasion to be a strategic war that had nothing to do with liberating Iraq, but was instead purposed to threaten Syria and Iran and protect Israel (Hashim, 2006, p.102). This is just one theory of many, but few consider American motives to be noble. The sentiments of most Iraqis (as well as those of other Muslims) toward the American invasion are well explained by Benjamin and Simon (2005), who state that

> In Muslim eyes, America is a nation of hypocrites. Roughly two-thirds of Turks and Moroccans and almost as many Pakistanis believe we are using the campaign against terror to mask other objectives. Majorities of those polled in Morocco, Turkey, Jordan, and Pakistan say that the United States wants less democracy in the world, not more. More than 60 percent of Moroccan respondents think that the United States aims to control Middle East oil, or simply to "dominate the world." In 2003, about half of those surveyed in Morocco, Kuwait, Jordan, and Lebanon said they were worried about a potential U.S. military threat to their countries; in Turkey, Nigeria, Pakistan, and Indonesia, threat perceptions ran higher still, peaking at 74%. (p.53)

Americans may find it incredible that Muslims across the world so misunderstand American motives, but these numbers suggest that the Islamists are clearly winning the propaganda war. As to why they are winning, and why Muslims believe the American invasion of Iraq was disingenuous, one need look no further than the inability of the Americans to provide the necessary utilities and goods and services to the Iraqi people after the invasion. In the words of one Iraqi man,

> People are hungry, starving. They don't believe they got rid of Saddam. If they got rid of Saddam, give me something to eat. That's why people hate Americans. We don't hate them because they are Americans. It is because they are the superpower, but where is the super power? Show it to us. (Quoted in Packer, 2005, p.225)

After the Persian Gulf War of 1991, the Iraqi people remembered that Saddam Hussein's government had the electrical power grid up and running in two weeks, a success story the Americans were unable to repeat. After the American invasion, the electricity output didn't reach prewar levels until a year after the Americans arrived, thus giving the impression that the superpower did not care about the Iraqi people (Packer, 2005, p.200). If the Americans could bring thousands of tanks in transport planes, why could they not bring electric generators? To the Iraqis, the obvious answer was that the Americans chose not to do so. Furthermore, the Iraqi people were generally aware of President Bush's speech at the American Enterprise Institute one month before the invasion where he declared that Iraq would become a democratic model for the Middle East. As a consequence, many Iraqis expected the Americans to arrive with a reconstruction plan reminiscent of the Marshall Plan that would not only provide security, but advance Iraq to an equal economic status with Europe almost overnight (Packer, 2005, p.166 Shadid, 2005, pp.148–151). Unfortunately for the Iraqis, no such plan would be forthcoming. In 2004, the

United States earmarked $51 billion for reconstruction in Iraq, but almost $4 billion per month went to maintain the American military in Iraq; hence, the American "Marshall Plan" for Iraq for all practical purposes did not exist (*Economist*, September 13, 2003, p.23).

For example, the first American loan to an Iraqi business did not come until October 2004, a year and a half after the American invasion (Packer, 2005, p.319). In other words, by the time any American reconstruction money could be flowing into Iraq, it would be too little and too late, and the insurgency already would be in full swing. In 2004, the UN Development Program and the Iraqi Ministry of Planning and Development Cooperation conducted an Iraq Living Conditions Survey of 21,000 households between April and August. More than a year after the US invasion, electricity to 85% of households was unreliable, 46% lacked access to clean water, and only 37% had sewage. Unemployment remained approximately 20% and the median household income had fallen from $255 before the invasion to $144. Obviously, for most Iraqis, their lives were not improved by the American invasion in terms of basic services and economic well-being (Hashim, 2006, p.297). Again, many Iraqis concluded that the only way these situations could not be corrected by a "superpower" was that the United States chose not to, thus suggesting motives other than building a better Iraq.

It was also not lost on the Iraqis that the United Stated targeted Al-Jazeera, the pan-Arab television network that essentially took an anti-American approach to the coverage of the American invasion of Iraq. When an Al-Jazeera correspondent was killed in a US air strike on Al-Jazeera's Baghdad bureau (the first foreign journalist to die during the US invasion), subsequent Al-Jazeera reports suggested that the American attack was deliberate. When this was combined with the fact that the Al-Jazeera bureau in Kabul, Afghanistan had been hit the previous year during the American campaign against the Taliban, many Iraqis viewed the attack on the media outlet as part of a premeditated pattern and inconsistent with the ideas of free speech and press that the Americans were preaching (Shadid, 2005, p.114).

Failure of Security

To make matters even worse in the minds of many Iraqis, the disingenuous American intentions were exposed clearly when the Americans moved into Saddam's palace and protected the oil fields and themselves, but allowed chaos and looting to go on unabated in Iraq for weeks (Phillips, 2005, p.134). The action was a clear statement to Iraqis that Americans cared very much only about themselves. This is in spite of the fact that a British pamphlet written by British experts on postwar planning, but in the possession of the head American administrator in Iraq, Paul Bremer, which stated that "In the immediate postwar period, security and the rule of law are essential" (Quoted in Packer, 2005, p.197). Unfortunately, the postwar order and security referenced by the British experts were exactly the things that the Americans were unable to provide in postwar Iraq in 2003. Although the Americans claimed to be coming to free the Iraqis from Saddam Hussein and to be bringing democracy to Iraq, the American military failed to provide the security necessary for that freedom, a failure that Iraqis believed could only be by design. The thinking of the Iraqi people concerning security was similar to their thinking concerning infrastructure and utilities. After all, if Saddam Hussein could bring order to Iraq, how could it be that the most powerful country in the world could not (Phillips, 2005, p.134)? In the words of one Iraqi man, "Why wasn't a curfew imposed as it was done in every change of government, at least five of them over the last fifty years?" (Quoted in Shadid, 2005, p.326).

After the American invasion and occupation, the number of murder victims arriving at the Baghdad morgue every night increased from one to between fifteen and twenty-five. Furthermore, it is estimated that the murder rate in Baghdad was about ten times that of Washington, DC, one of the most violent cities in the United States (Diamond, 2005, p.47). Honor killings, which before the war were normally concealed by burning or drowning the victims, were suddenly performed in the open and perpetrated with firearms that remove all question of whether or not the killings were "accidents" (Packer, 2005, pp.258–259). A September 2003 Gallup poll of the Iraqi people revealed that a full 94% of Iraqis believed that Baghdad was a more dangerous place than before the invasion and 86% responded that they or a family member had recently feared going out at night for safety reasons (*Washington Post*, November 12, 2003). While the chaos and looting raged, the Americans stayed hunkered down behind concrete barriers in the "Green Zone" rather than combating the chaos. In the words of George Packer (2005)

> For officials to leave the Green Zone required a two-vehicle military escort, which had to be arranged forty-eight hours in advance, assuming the soldiers and Humvees were available. In order to get their jobs done, some officials broke the rules and went in ordinary cars with no security out into the "Red Zone," that is to say, Iraq. Others—and over time their numbers increased—hardly ever ventured out. I met a British coalition official working on human rights that had left the Green Zone three times in five weeks. Though it was in the geographical heart of Baghdad, the CPA sat in deep isolation. (p.181)

The damage from the violence and looting in Iraq was so extensive that damaged buildings from looting outnumbered the number of buildings that had been damaged from bombing during the war (Packer, 2005, p.157). Furthermore, it was not lost on the Iraqis that the Americans protected the "Christian" St. Rafael Hospital in Bagh-dad, but not the "Muslim" Alwiya Maternity Hospital (Shadid, 2005, pp.140, 210).

The actual mistakes of the invading Americans were compounded, however, by rumors and misinformation. In a land where conspiracy theories run rampant, rumors quickly spread through Iraq that the Americans were cutting Iraqi electrical lines in retaliation for insur-gent attacks; hence, the real reason for the lack of electricity was American reprisal. Furthermore, rumors spread that the looting and chaos was instigated by the Americans who had brought Kuwaitis into Iraq with the invasion force for the purpose of instigating the looting as a form of payback for Iraq's 1990 invasion of Kuwait (Packer, 2005, p.166). The truth, that the Americans were simply incompetent and had not planned for looting and insurgents, was to the Iraqis simply not credible. The conclusions of most Iraqis ended up being similar to that of Iraqi psychiatrist, Dr. Baher Butti, who explained to American journalist George Packer that the Americans were less dangerous to him than Saddam's police, but in the end they were no better because in his view, "they had come to steal the oil" (Quoted in Packer, 2005, p.152). In September 2003, a Gallup poll of the Iraqi people revealed that almost half of Iraq's people believed that the primary US motive for invasion was to seize Iraqi oil, and only 1% believed that it was to establish democracy (*Washington Post*, November 12, 2003, p.A3).

Failure of American Propaganda

The American image was further tainted by American efforts to spread propaganda through the Iraqi media. For this purpose, the new Iraqi provisional government established by the Americans after the invasion, the Coalition Provisional Authority (CPA) awarded an $82 million contract for the Iraq Media Network to the Science Appli-cations International Corporation, an American company with ties to the Department of Defense, but with no experience in media. The re-sult was poor quality programming and American propaganda that reminded Iraqis more of the government propaganda under Saddam Hussein than of freedom and democracy. As a result, most Iraqis in-stead turned to the anti-American al-Jazeera network or to other Arab-dominated media outlets for their primary sources of informa-tion. Rumors circulating the streets continued to be as believable to many Iraqis as the new American-controlled media (Packer, 2005, p.201).

Rejection of Iraqi Exiles and Neoconservatives

The Americans also attempted to return Iraqi exiles, such as Ahmed Chalabi, to power in Iraq against the will of the majority of the Iraqi people. Although Colin Powell's State Department viewed Chalabi as little more than a scoundrel and "master manipulator," Paul Wolfowitz in the Defense Department along with aids to Vice President Dick Cheney believed Chalabi capable of successfully leading Iraq (Gordon and Trainor, 2006, p.18). Wolfowitz even argued that Chalabi and a group of Iraqi exiles could be armed to overthrow Saddam themselves, a plan discounted by Generals Tommy Franks and Anthony Zinni as nonsensical (Gordon and Trainor, 2006, pp.26, 106).

For most Iraqis, the exiles championed by the Americans were unrepresentative of the true Iraq, and they were disrespected for living comfortably in America while the "real" Iraqis suffered under Saddam Hussein, the horrendous war with Iran, and suffocating UN sanctions. The attitudes of the Iraqis toward the exiles were summed up by an Iraqi military officer thus (Quoted in Hashim, 2006)

> The Americans did not keep their word. ... They placed at the head of the country people who had been in exile and who had never shared our suffering. They gave them the right to pillage Iraqi wealth when, on their advice, they disbanded the army stopped paying our wages. It was a mistake. For every officer it has become a question of honor to resist the occupation. (p.119)

Furthermore, the exiles, and Ahmed Chalabi in particular, were typically viewed by the Iraqi people as lackeys of the Bush administration. The fact that the Department of Defense issued payments of $347,000 monthly to Chalabi's organization, the Iraq National Congress, only exacerbated the situation (Phillips, pp.2005, 210). As a consequence, the CPA that was created by the United States as a provisional government for Iraq was rejected by many Iraqis due to its close association with Iraqi exiles. In particular, the Iraqi people disapproved of the Pentagon's preferred Iraqi exile leader, Ahmed Chalabi, who in some opinion polls was even more despised than Saddam Hussein (Phillips, 2005, p.45, 164). The polls were vindicated in the Iraqi election of December 2005 when Chalabi received less than 1% of the vote and his party did not receive a single seat in the new Iraqi Parliament (www.washingtonpost.com/wp-dyn/content/article/2005/12/26/AR2005122600299.html).

Much has also been written about the plans of American neoconservatives in the Bush administration, including Dick Cheney, Donald Rumsfeld, and Paul Wolfowitz, to invade Iraq as part of a global military campaign to make the world safer by militarily deposing political regimes unfriendly with the United States and replacing them with democracies. Detailed discussions of the plans of the "Neocons" can be found in *Chain of Command* from Seymour Hersh (2004), Phillips (2005), Diamond (2005), Packer (2005), Clarke (2004), and Suskind (2004). Although the Bush administration essentially sold the war to the American public based on the threat of Saddam Hussein's Weapons of Mass Destruction, it is clear that the neoconservatives within the Bush administration had desired to depose Saddam Hussein militarily ever since the first Persian Gulf War of 1991, and that they viewed the 9/11 terrorist attacks as providing them with their opportunity. Furthermore, it is clear that the neoconservatives essentially believed that once Saddam Hussein was gone, the Iraqi people would quickly embrace democracy in Iraq. In the view of the neoconservatives, Iraq's situation was much like that of Nazi Germany and Imperial Japan at the end of World War II, and the United States only needed to militarily eliminate the authoritarian dictator for the people of the defeated country to quickly embrace American-style democracy (Packer, 2005, p.192).

If this was indeed the war motivation, then the Weapons of Mass Destruction pretense for the war was indeed disingenuous, a fact not lost on the Iraqi population. To make matters worse, there are numerous problems with the neoconservatives' supposition that Iraq in 2003 was analogous to Japan and Germany in 1945. Besides the obvious facts that Iraq is an economically lesser developed state with a Muslim culture and Japan and Germany in 1945 were not, there are numerous other factors that make Iraq in the present qualitatively different from the 1945 German and Japanese examples. Perhaps most important is the fact that the people of Japan and Germany after World War II were essentially faced with the choice of American-style democracy (with American protection) or probable domination by the not-so-benevolent Soviet Union under Joseph Stalin. Given such a choice (or threat), it is perhaps unsurprising that the Germans and Japanese embraced the American model rather than find themselves under the boot of Soviet communism. In 2005, however, there is no geopolitical rival to the United States akin to the Soviet Union that poses a similar threat to the people of Iraq. Instead, the competing paradigm most familiar to the Iraqi people is that of the Islamists. Given the apparently (to Iraqis) disingenuous character of the American invasion and the failure of the United States to forge Iraq into a safer, better place with greater opportunities, the competing paradigm of the Islamists appeals to many.

It is worth noting that the word "Islam" in the Muslim world is essentially analogous to "goodness incarnate," or all that is true, honest, and just, much as the words freedom, democracy, or even "Christianity," may be symbols of truth, honesty, goodness, and justice to those living in the West (Sayyid, 2003, p.48). That being the case, the supposition that a new Iraq should be based on "Islam" can be translated to many Iraqis as the supposition that a new Iraq should be forged based on all that is true, honest, and just. This, in the minds of many Iraqis, is an attractive contrast to the perceived disingenuous motives of the Americans.

Indiscriminate Killing and Harassment

Iraq abounds with stories of indiscriminate killing and harassment of Iraqi civilians by American troops, occurrences that can only provide fuel for the continued anti-American insurgency. American journalist George Packer (2005, p.220), for example, relates one story aired by CNN of a US Marine, who when confronted by a crowd of angry Iraqis, shouted at them, "We're here for your f*cking freedom! Now back up!" The obvious contradiction in the young Marine's statement is perhaps symbolic of the entire American effort in Iraq, where the US military has repeatedly violated the freedom of the Iraqi people while ostensibly bringing them freedom. Sometimes the American efforts have appeared as unnecessary harassment to the Iraqi people, while at other times they have merely appeared to be indiscriminate killing.

For example, as explained in the *Economist* (January 1, 2005)

> American marines and GIS frequently display contempt for Iraqis, civilian or official. Thus the 18-year-old Texan soldier in Mosul who, confronted by jeering school-children, shot canisters of buckshot at them from his grenade-launcher. 'It's not good, dude, it could be fatal, but you gotta do it,' he explained. Or the marines in Ramadi who, on a search for insurgents, kicked in the doors of houses at random, in order to scream, in English, at trembling middle-aged women within: 'Where's your black mask?' and 'Bitch, where's the guns?' (p.31)

Unfortunately, these are not isolated incidents, but part of a pattern of abuse that has worked to continually enrage the Iraqis and embolden the Islamists. For instance, an Iraqi urologist named Nimat Kamal complained to American journalist George Packer (2005, p.167) that soldiers searched him and his car outside his hospital every day even though the soldiers knew well who he was. In the words of Dr. Kamal, "They don't distinguish between a doctor and a terrorist." Dr. Kamal also complained that one of his relatives and his neighbor's twelve-year-old boy had been shot and killed when they inadvertently drove down a street that had been cordoned off by US soldiers (Packer, 2005, p.167).

As if to announce to the world that its methods in Iraq are indiscriminate, the US military placed signs on its vehicles in Iraq (in English and Arabic) warning Iraqi civilians not to come within fifty meters of the American vehicles or deadly force would be applied. For the 43% of Iraqis that are illiterate, it is doubtful that the signs were of much value. Furthermore, innocent Iraqis who happened to be in buildings from which insurgents fired on Americans were often indiscriminately killed when the American military leveled entire buildings to get the insurgents, taking no account of whether innocent persons might also be in the same buildings (*Economist*, April 10, 2004). As one Iraqi who lost his two-year-old granddaughter in September 2003 to bullets from US soldiers explained, "It is their routine. After the Americans are attacked, they shoot everywhere. This is inhuman—a stupid act by a country always talking about human rights" (Quoted in http://observer.guardian.co.uk/international/story/0,,1080989,00.html).

As the insurgency increased in intensity in 2003 and 2004, checkpoints became scenes of danger and tragedy as innocent Iraqis, sometimes families with children, were frequently slain by American gunfire when they failed to understand American signs, hand signals, and verbal warnings shouted in English. No one knows how many civilians died in such situations because the United States does not keep track of civilian deaths (Packer, 2005, p.236). George Packer (2005, p.158) relates another story of the fate of some Iraqi boys that ignored warning signs against swimming in the Tigris River. According to Packer, American troops scared some of the boys out of the water with warning shots, but a few swimmers who ignored the American warnings were then simply killed. In another story related by the *New York Times*, a 51-year-old man was kicked, beaten, and urinated on by American soldiers who arrested him (Packer, 2005, p.238). Another story was related to Western journalists by an Iraqi insurgent who stated that though there had been some American soldiers who had been friendly, "others treat us like dogs. I saw one put his boot on the head of an old man lying on the ground. Even Saddam would not have done such a thing" (Quoted in Hashim, 2006, p.20).

Reports also circulated Iraq of indiscriminate arrests of Iraqi citizens by American soldiers and the inability of the relatives of detainees to find out any information about them from the American authorities. American soldiers were even accused of confiscating the money, valuables, and luxury automobiles of Iraqi citizens accused of crimes. In the words of one man, Abdul-Zahra Abid, who spent eighteen months in Saddam's prisons, "They arrest people, they don't give information to families—like the Baath. The past and the present—there's no difference. There should be a difference" (Quoted in Packer, 2005, pp.203–204). In one particular incident in the Iraqi city of Baij in 2004, the Americans detained seventy men identified by an informant as "bad." As explained by the *Economist* (January 1, 2005)

In near-freezing conditions, they sat hooded and bound in their pyjamas. They shivered uncontrollably. One wetted himself in fear. Most had been detained at random; several had been held because they had a Kalashnikov rifle, which is legal. The evidence against one man was some anti-American literature, a meat cleaver and a whistle. American intelligence officers moved through the ranks of detainees, raising their hoods to take mug-shots: 'One, two, three, jihaaad!' (p.32)

One middle-tier American officer who witnessed the event commented on the mission to a correspondent from the *Economist* and stated the obvious that "When we do this, we lose" (Quoted in the *Economist*, January 1, 2005, p.32). The heavy-handed and seemingly indiscriminate American tactics connected the American occupiers to the Israelis in the occupied territories in the minds of some Iraqis. In the words of an Iraqi engineer named Mohamed Abbas, "Same soldiers, same Apaches, same way of apprehending people. Iraqis are becoming more aggressive, because they make the connection" (Quoted in Packer, 2005, p.167).

De-Baathification and the Dispossessed

The Iraqi insurgency also drew from Iraq's dispossessed. The Sunnis and Baathists who had occupied the preferred positions of power in Iraq for over four decades suddenly found themselves removed from power and diminished in importance. Former Baathists and members of the Iraqi military suddenly had little to lose, since they had been disenfranchised by the Americans, and had everything to gain by expelling those same American tormentors through insurgent attacks (Packer, 2005, p.308).

A further contributing factor to the Iraq insurgency was unemployment, estimated at 65% in 2003, much of it created by the twelve years of sanctions and by the war, and some of it created by the American de-Baathification policies under Paul Bremer (Phillips, 2005, p.155). Less than two weeks after taking over the responsibility for the American occupation from General Jay Garner, Bremer disbanded the Iraqi army and dissolved the Iraqi Ministry of Information, thus rendering approximately 400,000 people unemployed. Among these were at least 35,000 members of the bureaucracy, including thousands of school teachers who lost their jobs overnight. There was no consideration as to whether the dismissed party members were guilty of any crimes or not, creating a major sense of injustice among Iraqis in a culture that places a premium on justice. To make his decision even worse in the minds of Iraqis, Bremer left the people he rendered unemployed without pensions or salaries. With no jobs and no money, suddenly 400,000 militarily trained persons were wandering the streets of Iraq with a personal reason to despise the

United States. Many members of the military felt betrayed since they had offered only light resistance to the American invasion and many therefore expected to have a role in the new Iraq (Shadid, 2005, p.152 Packer, 2005, p.191 Phillips, 2005, pp.144–149). Worse still, it should be considered that the average Iraqi family includes six persons; hence, the firing of 400,000 people should have impacted approximately 2.4 million Iraqis, or 10% of the population (Phillips, 2005, p.142). It is difficult to conclude anything other than that the de-Baathification program was ill-conceived, overzealous, and contributed to the insurgency. In the words of Benjamin and Simon (2005)

> Through an overly ambitious de-Baathification program and the precipitous dissolution of the Iraqi army, America multiplied the number of those disgruntled by the fall of the regime, creating a large pool of tactical allies for the radicals. It seems that no one seriously contemplated the aftermath of the invasion going badly and the possibility of a real insurgency, or even the civil war that now appears to be looming, or how that would affect American standing in the Muslim world and, by extension, the effort to stem radicalization. (p.181)

Even in the more American-friendly northern city of Mosul, the dissolution of the Iraqi army led to an explosion of violence in the fall of 2003 (although it should perhaps be mentioned that Mosul also has approximately 1 million Sunni Arab residents, many of whom were former military personnel). Essentially, the people of Mosul felt betrayed by the Americans after they generally had not resisted the American invasion.

Perhaps the final proof that the de-Baathification program was wrongheaded is in the fact that approximately one year after Bremer's decision, the CPA began inviting former Baathists back to their jobs and attempting to reconstitute the Iraqi army in a desperate effort to get them to assist the American occupation army with providing domestic security (Phillips, 2005, p.153). In spite of the rehiring of the Baathists, as of May 2005, estimates of unemployment in Iraq ranged from an optimistic 25% to a pessimistic 50%. Regardless of which figure is closer to being correct, the overall economic situation by the end of 2005 appeared to have improved little since the end of the official war in May 2003. As a consequence, some insurgents against the American occupiers were engaging in attacks simply for a few hundred dollars in pay (*Economist*, May 7, 2005, p.21).

Ethnicity and Religious Cleavages

During the decades of authoritarian rule by Saddam Hussein, simmering hostilities between Iraq's religious and ethnic groups were kept somewhat in check through the heavy hand of Saddam's brutal re-gime, although the Sunni dominance was never viewed as legitimate by the majority in the Kurdish North or the Shiite South. The Ameri-can invasion removed the illegitimate Sunni dominance, but also re-moved the primary force that was keeping ethnic hostilities in check and therefore enhanced the possibility that ethnic and religious ani-mosity would boil over into full blown civil war (Phillips, 2005, p.5). The possibility of ethnic conflict and perhaps even dissolution of the country was recognized by numerous Western scholars, American policymakers, and experts on Iraq. In fact, the possibility of ethnic civil war and the dissolution of the country was part of the reason that Vice President Dick Cheney, one of the most ardent supporters of the 2003 invasion, argued against invading Iraq and ousting Saddam at the end of the first Gulf War in 1991 (Phillips,2005, p.23).

The crux of the ethnicity problem is that many Iraqis lack a well-developed sense of national identity, seeing themselves first as Kurds, Sunnis, or Shiites, rather than Iraqis. Arab Sunnis, only approxi-mately 20% of the population, have dominated Iraq politically since World War I and prefer not to be subordinate to the other groups after being accustomed to a preferred political position. The American in-vasion removing their preferred position has thus created a serious identity crisis for them (Hashim, 2006, p.67). In the words of one former member of Iraqi Intelligence, "We had dreams. Now we are the losers. We lost our positions, our status, the security of our fami-lies, stability. Curse the Americans, Curse them" (Quoted in *Washing-ton Post*, January 13, 2004, p.1). The man then expressed his disdain for the Shiites and what he viewed as an inevitable imposition of Shi-ite theocracy on the Sunni population. In his words, "These people with turbans are going to run the country. What do they know?" (Quoted in *Washington Post*, January 13, 2004, p.1). Another Iraqi man expressed his sentiments toward Shiite dominance of Iraq when he exclaimed to Western journalist Nir Rosen that "I will kill myself if they (Shiites) rule. ... They hate us and we hate them" (Quoted in Hashim, 2006, p.71). Similarly, Shaikh Abdallah Dakhil al-Farraj al-Jibouri, a leader of one of the largest Sunni tribes, stated of the Shiites that, "They cannot rule Iraq properly. The Shiites are backwards. They are barbarian savages, they do not know true religion, theirs is twisted, it is not the true religion of Mohammed" (Quoted in *New York Times*, August 10, 2003). Finally, as Iraq erupted into violent bombings at mosques in 2003, one Sunni worshiper at a bombed out Baghdad mosque immediately blamed the Shiites for the bombing, stating that "It was the Shiites who did this. The Shiites are worse than the Jews" (Quoted in *Los Angeles Times*, December 10, 2003, p.1).

Thus, the Sunni insurgency can be viewed partially as religious animosity against the Shiites, partially as an attempt to retain their identity, partially as an attempt to expel the American invaders, and partially as an effort to prevent the emergence of Shiite rule. The United States has only exacerbated the problem of Sunni antagonism against Shiites by raiding the homes of Sunnis with Shiite militias and manning the new Iraqi National Guard and Security police primarily with Shiites (*New York Times*, May 8, 2005). The situation was made even worse when the Shiite policemen sometimes turned out to be little more than ill-disciplined "death squads" on a rampage against Sunnis (Hashim, 2006, p.380). The Sunni town of Haditha, for instance, was not known for insurgent activity until the new Iraqi government sent Shiite security police to patrol the town. Afterwards, Haditha became a hotbed of Sunni insurgency aimed at the Shiite policemen (www.guardian.co.uk/Iraq/Story/02,2763,155369,00.html).

American attitudes have further enraged the Sunnis by essentially favoring the Shiites and Kurds (who have been less resistant to the US occupation) over the Sunnis. Even Adnan al-Janabi, the Minister of State in the Iraqi interim government of Iyad Allawi, argued that the Americans "made every single mistake they could have thought of to alienate the Sunnis. The US is behaving as if every Sunni is a terrorist" (www.guardian.co.uk/Iraq/story/0,2763,1398636,00.html).

Kurds, on the other hand, generally welcomed the American invasion so as to liberate them from the rule of Saddam Hussein, but view the United States as treacherous for treating the Arabs the same as the Kurds, who had been on the American side from the beginning. Due to their collaboration with the United States., the Kurds are clearly favored by them, and therefore are hated by the Sunnis for their "collaboration." The Sunni-Kurdish antagonism is not new, however. The Kurds suffered persecution at the hands of the Sunnis under the Baathist regimes and have no desire to return to Arab subjugation after twelve years of American-protected autonomy after the Persian Gulf War. For example, at the close of the Iran-Iraq war in 1988, Saddam launched a campaign against the Kurds that included the use of chemical weapons and led to the deaths of over 180,000 Kurds (Phillips, 2005, p.23). With such a history, the Kurds should perhaps be expected to reject any proposal that would again lead to Sunni Arab domination of the Kurdish population. In fact, in December 2003, the leader of one Kurdish Party, Massoud Barzani, published an article in a Kurdish newspaper where he proclaimed that "Kurds will not accept less than their existing situation" (which includes almost complete Kurdish autonomy) and warned that the "imposition of an unacceptable formula' could lead the Kurds to "resort to other choices," an obvious threat of Kurdish revolt (Quoted in Diamond, 2005, p.162).

Kurds are also Sunni Muslims, however, and are therefore just as likely to consider the Shiites to be barbarian apostates and backstabbers as are the Arab Sunnis (Hashim, 2006, pp.72–73). For example, a senior Kurdish official in Barzani's Kurdistan Democratic Party (KDP), one of the two largest Kurdish Parties, said of the Shiite prime minister, Ibrahim al-Jaafari, "Jaafari is like the Baath, he will seek to use his position to construct an Islamic state. He wants all of Iraq to be an Islamic state, with a modern face. That is why we do not like him" (Quoted in Hashim, 2006, p.362).

Shiites, who compose 60% of the population, have incentive to embrace democracy based on popular vote since it would give them what they view as rightful control over Iraq after decades of Baathist subjugation of the majority. It is questionable, however, whether any form of Shiite democracy will much resemble Western democracy, due to the general Shiite belief that the Government must be subordinate to the ulama in one form or another. There are also simmering hostilities between Shiites and Sunnis stemming from the decades of Sunni oppression of Shiites under Saddam Hussein. When provided the opportunity after the first Persian Gulf War in 1991, Shiites not only rebelled against Saddam Hussein, but executed local Baathist leaders in southern Iraq, including a provincial governor, a chief of police, and a local head of the Baath Party. When Saddam retaliated, his reprisal was merciless, and some estimate that 200,000 Shiites were killed (Phillips, 2005, p.24). The ill feelings and distrust among Shiites for Sunnis has lingered. For example, after the bombing of a Shiite mosque in Baghdad, a Shiite cleric immediately blamed Sunnis and encouraged a civil war against them. In the words of the cleric (Quoted in *Philadelphia Inquirer*, December 12, 2004, p.1)

> The suicide bomber wore the devil's beard, and he wore clothes from the people of hell...Those who want you to have a peace agreement with these criminals, they are telling you that they are carrying explosive materials and they want to kill you; and you think you should have a peace agreement with them.

When smaller minorities of Turkomen, Iranians, and Armenians are thrown into the mix, the potential for ethnic or religious conflict, if not all-out civil war, is great. The exact or even approximate population of the Turkomen in Iraq is unknown, and the 1997 census showed that there were only 600,000, but other sources suggest that there may be as many as 3 million (12% of Iraq's population). The Tukomen and the Kurds, who occupy some of the same territories in Northern Iraq, are historic enemies due to a history of Turkish oppression of Kurds in Turkey. One Kurdish leader, for example, informed American officials a month before the American invasion that "if we have to choose between Turkish domination and what we have now, then we'd rather live with Saddam" (Quoted in Phillips, 2005, p.115). The Turkomen also proved that they too would not be a quiet minority, when a few days after the fall of Saddam Hussein, they killed the Kurdish mayor of a Turkomen town after he had raised a Kurdish flag outside his office (Hashim, 2006, p.371). The Turkomen also served notice that they will not be quietly ignored when they protested against the Iraqi Interim Constitution through a hunger strike (Phillips, 2005, p.190).

The potential for ethnic conflict in Iraq is exacerbated by the oil factor, since most of Iraq's oil is in the Shiite South and Kurdish North, rather than the Sunni Triangle. Lacking oil on their own land, one can expect Sunnis to demand an equitable distribution of revenues from the oil in the north and south, while Kurds and Shiites perhaps should be expected to prefer that each group keep the oil underneath their own feet and thus leave their former Sunni oppressors without (Diamond, 2005, p.168).

Finally, it should be noted that the three areas of Iraq that are generally thought of as Kurdish, Sunni, and Shiite, are far from completely segregated along those ethnic and religious divisions. For instance, Mosul, in Northern Iraq, has a population that includes over a million Arabs, many of whom were former Baathists. Similarly, the city in Iraq with the largest Kurdish population is actually Baghdad, with over 1 million Kurdish residents. In the Shiite South, there are over a million Sunnis in the "Shiite" city of Basra. Finally, the most radical element of the Shiite community at present, the militant followers of Muqtada al Sadr, reside in Baghdad. Given this degree of integration, Iraq would not be so easily segmented into three separate countries based on religion and ethnicity, though it is also questionable whether all can live peacefully under one roof without massive amounts of central government coercion such as that applied by the Baathists under Saddam Hussein (Hashim, 2006, pp.225, 227).

Kirkuk

Kirkuk is a multiethnic town near the Southern border of Kurdistan endowed with oil fields outside the city that may comprise almost 10% of Iraq's total reserves. The Kirkuk oil fields have been tremendously productive in the past and produced an estimated 10 million barrels in 1998 during the time of strict sanctions on Iraq (Phillips, 2005, p.166). According to the 1957 census, Kirkuk was 40% Turkoman and 35% Kurdish, with Arabs making up less than one fourth of its population. During the 1980s, however, Saddam Hussein attempted to wrestle control of the city for Sunni Arabs by offering Arab families a free house and 10,000 dinars if they would move to Kirkuk. Simultaneously, Saddam forbade Kurds from building or purchasing houses in Kirkuk, and any family that could not prove residence from the 1957 census was subject to expulsion. After 1980, only the Arab language was taught in the schools of the predominantly Kurdish town. Eventually, 120,000 Kurds and other non-Arab ethnics were forcibly removed from Kirkuk while over 53,000 Arabs moved into the city during Saddam's reign (Packer, 2005, pp.341–356). The predictable result is that Kurds are now returning to Kirkuk to claim their property, sometimes chasing out Arab occupants. Iraqi courts are backlogged with property cases, and a year after the fall of Saddam Hussein, the United States had not yet begun to provide solutions due to the failure of the US Department of Defense to implement a property claims and compensation system (Phillips, 2005, p.167).

Kurds remain despised by many Arabs (including Shiite radical Muqtada al-Sadr), as Western collaborators and apostates, and have been forced to flee many Arab cities for Kirkuk, where a shortage of housing has subsequently developed. Failing to take the high road after their experience as a persecuted minority under the Baathist regime, Kurdish authorities in Kirkuk demanded the expulsion of all Arabs from Kirkuk, even those born in the city, so as to make room for the Kurdish refugees. Perhaps not surprisingly, Kirkuk has suffered a rise in insurgent attacks and suicide bombings and a campaign of assassination of the city's Kurdish leaders (Packer, 2005, pp.341–356).

Saddam Hussein's Planned Insurgency

Intelligence information gathered by the CIA and the UN both before and after the American invasion of Iraq suggests that at least a segment of the Iraqi insurgency against the American occupation was planned by the Baath Party under Saddam Hussein. According to Salah al-Mukhtar, a senior Baathist official in exile in Yemen (Quoted in Hashim, 2006)

> At the beginning in the year 2002, the Baath party has completed the training of about 6 million Iraqi citizens to fight urban warfare by the so-called Al Quds Army. President Saddam Hussein has managed all preparation, including storing about 50 million of guns, big, medium and small sizes with their necessary ammunition to fight against the occupation for ten years. ... In light of what I have said, you can reach the conclusion that the resistance was prepared mainly by the political leadership of Iraq. (p.134)

Evidently, each Iraqi village, town, and city became its own independent citadel of small arms with large caches of assault rifles, machine guns, mortars, and rocket-propelled grenades that were kept under guard by the Baathists (Gordon and Trainor, 2006, p.62). In the words of one retired Iraqi general who predicted the insurgency prior to the American invasion, "the considerable difference in power between Iraqi forces and the US-led alliance would naturally result in Iraqi forces resorting to guerilla warfare" (Quoted in Hashim, 2006, p.1).

It appears from interviews with captured Iraqi leaders, however, that the purpose of the small weapons stockpiles was primarily to arm Saddam's Fedayeen militia units for the purpose of putting down local insurrections. Evidently, Saddam feared indigenous uprisings against his regime more than he did foreign invasions (Gordon and Trainor, 2006, p.62). Consequently, with such large volumes of small weapons stockpiled throughout the country, the American army faced unexpected guerrilla tactics at the outset of the 2003 invasion as paramilitary forces led by Saddam's son Qusay launched hit-and-run attacks and booby traps with "Improvised Explosive Devices" (IEDs). The guerrilla tactics prompted Lieutenant General William Wallace to state that "The enemy we're fighting is a bit different from the one we war-gamed against" (Quoted in Packer, 2005, p.298). Wallace's statement is consistent with the report of the Iraq Survey Group in late 2004 that concluded that although Saddam Hussein possessed no weapons of mass destruction, he essentially planned a defense of his regime based on his beliefs (thus far proving to be correct) that Iraq was susceptible to sectarian violence and the Iraqi people would not tolerate an American occupation. Pursuant to those ends, Saddam and his commanders studied Vietnamese manuals on guerrilla tactics and had Iraqi intelligence train guerrillas in camps outside Baghdad. Months before the United States invaded, Iraqi commanders then removed all of the weapons from the training bases and hid them in farms and houses in multiple locations to be used in the planned insurgency (Packer, 2005, p.299).

Neither Saddam Hussein nor his sons, however, would be the charismatic leaders of the Iraqi insurgency, perhaps at least in part due to their own incompetence. One Iraqi officer, Colonel Raaed Faik, for instance, complained that the orders of Qusay (who commanded the Republican Guard) were the orders "of an imbecile. ... Qusay was like a teenager playing a video war game" (Quoted in *Los Angeles Times*, August 11, 2003, p.1). Another Iraqi officer, General Ahmed Rahal, complained that Saddam's regime did not adequately prepare for guerilla war in that they did not mine Iraq's roads and bridges (Hashim, 2006, p.12). Perhaps not surprisingly then, Saddam's sons were quickly killed by the US military and Saddam himself was captured, with the result that the insurgency quickly became a fragmented network with no clear central command, although the American media increasingly gave the impression in the early days of the insurgency that "elements loyal to Saddam" were in command.

Journalists on the scene, however, painted a picture of disorganiza-
tion and chaos among insurgents in the early days of the American occupation. In the words of David Zucchino, an imbedded journalist for
the *Los Angeles Times,*

> The Iraqis seem to have no training, no discipline, no coordinated tactics. It
> was all point and shoot. A few soldiers would pop up and fire, then stand
> out in the open ground to gauge the effects of their shots. The big coax
> rounds from the tanks and the Bradleys sent chunks of their bodies splat-
> tering into the roadside .... Soldiers and civilian gunmen were arriving now
> in every available mode of transportation—hatchbacks, orange-and-white
> taxis, police cars, ambulances, pickups, big Chevys, motorcycles with side-
> cars. Major Nusio, the battalion executive officer, opened fire on a huge
> garbage truck with a soldier at the wheel. He was thinking to himself as the
> soldier keeled over and the truck crash-landed: 'A garbage truck? These
> people are so stupid—stupid but determined (Quoted in Zucchino, 2004,
> p.14).

Since the capture of Saddam, the Jordanian Islamist Abu Musab al-
Zarqawi, who had ties to al-Qaeda, but not Saddam, has often been
portrayed in the American media as the central insurgent commander, although he was an al-Qaeda-affiliated Islamist, and not a
Baathist, and it therefore seemed unlikely that he commanded the
same group that was loyal to Saddam. At any rate, the capture of Saddam Hussein and the rest of the famous American "deck of cards" had
no recognizable impact on the insurgency. Instead, the insurgency increased as the outstanding faces in the deck of cards decreased, suggesting that other elements were at play besides Baathist regime
loyalists (Packer, 2005, p.302).

A major reason that the capture of Saddam and other leading
Baathists had little impact (as did the later elections and formation of
a new Iraqi government) is that the insurgency was not solely
Baathist, but lacked a unifying ideology and was composed of multiple
groups with multiple goals; the only unifying factor perhaps being the
desire to expel the Americans (Hashim, 2006, p.13). The insurgents
would draw fighters both from the Sunni and Shiite segments of the
Iraqi population, both secular and religious, and from foreign fighters
of jihad (Packer, 2005, pp.302–303). Colonel David Teeples (Quoted
in *Los Angeles Times*, February 9, 2004, p.1) explained the relations
between the foreign jihadists and Saddam's regime thus

> The jihad people who came in had their own agenda. They were not con-
> nected to former regime loyalists, but to Islamic extremists. But as this
> thing evolved, it became obvious that the best network for anyone coming
> from outside to fight would be to contact former regime loyalists. Those
> were the people who knew who to call, where to find safe houses, where to
> get their hands on money, weapons, transportation. They had intelligence
> on where the coalition troops were moving convoys, where the troops were
> stationed, where mortars could be set up.

Thus, the insurgency has become one where Islamists are often working in concert with Baathist supporters of the former regime. In many cases, however, the insurgents are neither Baathists nor foreigners. In the American siege of Fallujah in November 2004, for instance, the Americans took 2000 prisoners in the predominantly Shiite, and therefore not traditionally Baathist town. Only thirty of the insurgents turned out to be foreigners, thus suggesting that the primary thrust of the insurgency is from Iraqi nationals rather than foreigners (*Economist*, January 1, 2005, p.31). Similarly, of 5500 suspected insurgents held in prison by coalition forces in September 2004, only 130 to 140 were foreigners (*Economist*, September 25, 2004, p.58). Instead of fighting just elements loyal to Saddam or just foreign jihadists, the American invasion had the impact of bringing together Baathists loyal to Saddam with dispossessed Shiites and foreign jihadists united with the singular goal of ousting the Americans. In the words of Abdullah Fahad, the former mayor of the Iraqi town of Baij (Quoted in the *Economist*, January 1, 2005)

> There are terrorists here, not from Syria, not from Mosul, but from Baij. Some are Baathists and some are Islamists and before they hated each other but now they work together and they tell people that if they don't work with them they will kill them. (p.32)

Whether Shiite, Baathist, or foreign jihadist, however, the insurgents well understood that the battle was not about body counts, but was for the hearts and minds of the Iraqi people and that the failure of the Americans to provide security would work to the advantage of the insurgents. For an insurgency on the scale of the one in Iraq to work, it requires a significant amount of support from the civilian noncombatant segment of the population in the form of safe houses, misinformation to the occupying power, and sometimes merely looking the other way (Hashim, 2006, p.xxiii). By 2005, it appears that the insurgents had plenty of all types of popular support in the Sunni Triangle. Although polls vary, it is estimated that up to 85% of respondents in the Sunni Triangle in 2004 and 2005 may have supported the insurgent attacks on the United States (Hashim, 2006, p.131).

The failure of the Americans to prepare in advance for a widespread security meltdown was a major reason not only for the fact that they lost the battle for the hearts and minds, but also a major reason that a successful insurgency was possible because it gave the insurgents a receptive population to work within (Packer 2005, pp.306–307). In fact, by the end of 2004, there were signs that the Americans had given up the battle for hearts and minds. In the words of American General George W. Casey, the commander of the coalition forces in Iraq (Quoted in the *Economist*, January 1, 2005), "Our broad intent is to keep pressure on the insurgents as we head into elections. This is not about winning hearts and minds; we're not going to do that here in Iraq. It's about giving the Iraqis the opportunity to govern themselves." Unfortunately, it appears that the United States cannot govern Iraq sufficiently until the Iraqis can govern themselves without the support of the hearts and minds of the Iraqis.

American Backlash and Escalation

After the fall of Saddam Hussein, the US Army's First Infantry Division began using a schoolhouse in Fallujah, a city of approximately 300,000 in the Anbar province of the Sunni Triangle, as military barracks. Local residents took to the streets in protest and a confrontation with US troops ensued in a situation similar to the Boston Massacre. US troops fired into the crowd and seventeen Iraqis were killed, thus sparking guerrilla resistance against the Americans in Fallujah (Phillips, 2005, p.195). On March 31, 2004, violence again escalated when four American civilian contractors were killed and their bodies mutilated and burned as Fallujah residents retaliated for the earlier violence. President Bush quickly ordered retaliation, reportedly stating, "I want heads to roll" (Quoted in Packer, 2005, p.323). The US Marines were instructed to surround Fallujah, retake it, and hunt down the killers of the civilian contractors. Critics would suggest that the American action in Fallujah was an over-reaction to four American deaths, but the images of the mutilated and burning American bodies had an extraordinary impact on the American public. Arab satellite TV reported hundreds of civilian deaths in and around Fallujah, inflaming opinion against the United States all over Iraq and the entire Middle East region. The fighting created an alliance of Sunni and Shiite insurgents against the Americans for the first time, as Shiite mosques organized blood drives and aid convoys for their besieged Sunni compatriots. In two weeks of April 2004, forty-eight Americans were killed, suggesting a major escalation of combat. The United States then withdrew from the bloody assault that had made front-page news in the United States (during an election year) and left Fallujah to the insurgents until a new division of marines would take the city in November that year after President Bush had won reelection (Packer, 2005, p.324). When the United States did move back into Fallujah on November 8, 2004, 2085 insurgents were killed and 1600 were taken prisoners. Again, when it is considered that the average Iraqi family is approximately six people, one can assume that over 20,000 Iraqis became sworn enemies of the United States as a result of the Fallujah offensive alone (Phillips, 2005, p.216). To make matters worse, after the American forces withdrew from Fallujah and returned to the safety of the Green Zone, insurgents essentially moved back in and took control of the town. Since the violent battle in November 2004, insurgents have blown up a Fallujah police station twice and kidnapped and executed a contractor involved in the building project (Hashim, 2006, p.335).

Abu Ghraib

At a Press Conference in the Rose Garden in May 2004, President George Bush boasted that one of the major achievements of the United States in Iraq was that "there are no longer torture chambers or rape rooms" (*The Economist*, May 8, 2004, p.34). A week later, a scandal erupted involving American abuse of Iraqi prisoners at Saddam Hussein's Abu Ghraib prison. Iraqi prisoners had been sodomized with broomsticks, one had been beaten to death, and photos were circulated throughout the media of naked Iraqi prisoners in humiliating and compromising positions. One photo showed an American soldier with a smirk on her face and a dog leash around the neck of an Iraqi man. Another showed a hooded Iraqi man wearing something resembling a blanket standing on a box with electrical wires attached to his testicles. Regardless of American explanations and contentions by the Bush administration that the abuses were isolated incidents, the revelation destroyed American credibility in the minds of most Iraqis, and memos on torture and the Geneva Conventions written by the President's Counsel (later Attorney General) Alberto Gonzalez, that essentially condoned torture, only added fuel to the fire. No high-ranking American official was held accountable for the abuse and only low-level enlisted personnel faced charges stemming from the scandal. For the Iraqis, the implications of the scandal were clear enough; there was little difference between the Americans and Saddam Hussein (Packer, 2005, pp.325–326). A cartoon in *al-Hayat*, a leading Arab newspaper, depicted the prison at Abu Ghraib with a sign that read, "Under New Management," sentiments that angered the Bush administration, but were shared by most of the Muslim world (Phillips, 2005, p.204).

For Muslims, Abu Ghraib symbolized the hypocrisy of American policies, since the United States was supposedly occupying Iraq in order to bring freedom to the Iraqi people, but had shoved aside the Geneva Conventions that had governed the treatment of prisoners of war for decades and evidently condoned maltreatment of Muslim prisoners. Radical Islamists in Iraq and throughout the Muslim world quickly utilized Abu Ghraib as a rallying cry and recruiting tool for jihad. For example, one radical Imam in Paris, Farid Benyettou, was arrested in Paris on charges of recruiting young boys for terrorism (some as young as thirteen) and sending them to Iraq. Benyettou's lawyer described his client's approach to recruitment thusly (Quoted in the *Los Angeles Times*, April 2, 2005)

> He would talk to his disciples about Abu Ghraib, the abuse of Muslims and say, 'What are you going to do about it?' He was like a...guru who claimed to know the sacred texts ... and he convinced them that the texts said it was their duty to go to Iraq to fight for the cause.

Three of Benyettou's recruits were known to have died in Iraq, and another, a thirteen-year-old boy named Salah, was working with jihadists in Syria preparing fighters for the conflict in Iraq (*Los Angeles Times*, April 2, 2005).

Islamist Religious Motivations

Abu Ghraib aside, the American invasion of Iraq in 2003 clearly provided a major boost to the rise of Islamism in Iraq (especially in predominantly Shiite areas) due to the fact that the downfall of Saddam Hussein endowed the Iraqi people with a new freedom to express their religion openly (*New York Times*, April 23, 2003, p.A13). As one former Iraqi officer explained (Quoted in Hashim, 2006, p.119), "In 1990, many soldiers returned to religion. But we were forced to pray in secret. And we could not grow a beard. If we attended the mosques too regularly, we were thrown into prison." With Saddam out of the way, suddenly the radical Islamists were free to practice their religion and politics openly in Iraq.

The American invasion did more for Islamism than just allow the Iraqi people to practice their religion freely, however. Instead, it provided Islamists with a new infidel enemy in their midst to rally the people against with the teachings of Islam serving as a basis for the opposition. The illegitimacy of American rule in the eyes of the Islamists is predicated on the fact that the Americans are not Muslims, but are instead "infidels." That being the case, American rule cannot be viewed as legitimate by Islamists, since their interpretation of the Koran is that only Islam can confer legitimacy in government and the government imposed by the Americans resembles a Western model most certainly does not gain its legitimacy from Islam (Lewis, 1988, p.103). As explained by one radical Islamic cleric (Quoted in www.salon.com/news/feature/2004/12/16/iraqi_insurgents/print.html)

> We fight the Americans because they are nonbelievers and they are coming to fight Islam, calling us terrorists. ... We fight for our land, against those who are fighting Islam, for our country and for our women. Our goal is to fight whoever fights us and not just the Americans. And we want this country to be ruled by the Tawhid and Sunna. If that doesn't happen, that means all of us will die because we fight until the last breath.

This type of Islamist thinking that has become so prevalent in the insurgency was evidently unanticipated by American war planners. As previously discussed, prior to the Persian Gulf War and the twelve years of economic sanctions that followed, Iraq was widely considered to be among the most secularized countries in the Middle East. For instance, Saddam Hussein's Deputy Prime Minister, Tariq Aziz, was one of the Arab world's best-known Christians and Saddam Hussein allowed the broadcast of Christian Easter services on State television (*Economist*, August 7, 2004). As a consequence, American officials did not expect a religious insurgency in Iraq after the American invasion, evidently believing their own propaganda that the Americans would be greeted as liberators with sweets and flowers. American war planners were aware that Islamists, such as Jordanian terrorist Abu Musab al-Zarqawi, were in the country ready to fight Americans, and they knew of al-Zarqawi's importance at the time in the Islamic world, but a top Pentagon intelligence official admitted to Daniel Benjamin and Steven Simon that

> no one believed that the radicals would get much of a foothold in Iraq, which was considered to be too secularized, a 'country of accountants' as some said before the war. In terms of predicting a jihadist insurgency, we flat out missed that. We thought it would be a Baathist/Sunni (nationalist) insurgency that would be easily contained (Quoted in Benjamin and Simon, 2005, p.34).

Such a statement merely reveals the ignorance of the American war planners concerning the importance of Islam in Iraq. Some of the simplest survey techniques in Iraq prior to the invasion could have revealed a very different picture. For instance, an August 2003 poll of the Iraqi people commissioned by the United States revealed that 87% wanted religious groups to share power in government, and 33% in Basra and Baghdad, 43% in Fallujah, and 92% in Shiite Najaf favored an "Islamic State" (Diamond, 2005, p.48). With this kind of information, the war planners should have known that religious resistance to Western-style democracy, not to mention religions resistance to the invasion and occupation, was to be expected.

It is possible, however, that the Bush administration is guilty of more than mere ignorance. Benjamin and Simon (2005, pp.178–180) for instance, go even further to suggest that the Bush administration officials knew that the radical Islamists Abu Musab al-Zarqawi and the group Ansar al-Islam (supporters of Islam) were in the country, but preferred to leave them there so as to use them as proof that there was a connection between Iraq and al-Qaeda (in spite of the fact that the area of the country where Ansar al-Islam was operating was in the Kurdish no-fly zone and had not been controlled by Saddam Hussein since the Persian Gulf War). There is some evidence that Saddam

Hussein actually aided Ansar al-Islam against his other Kurdish enemies, thus validating Bush's claim that there was a Saddam Hus-
sein/al-Qaeda connection, although it was aimed at the Kurds rather
than the Americans (Phillips, 2005, p.28).

The CIA investigated the Saddam/al-Zarqawi connection, however,
and concluded that there was little evidence of a relationship between
the two men, that there was no collaborative relationship between
Saddam Hussein and al-Qaeda, and there was no evidence indicating
that Iraq cooperated with al-Qaeda in developing or carrying out attacks against the United States. Furthermore, the CIA concluded that
Saddam Hussein was unlikely to supply weapons of mass destruction
to terrorists; first of all, because it has become obvious that he did not
have them, but second, because it is clear that the Islamic terrorists
might have used them on Saddam himself since the religious zealots
of al-Qaeda viewed him as an apostate (*New York Times*, October 10,
2004). Instead, CIA analysts expressed concerns prior to the American invasion of Iraq that an American invasion would turn Iraq into a
"laboratory for terrorists," which is essentially what has happened
(*Washington Post*, September 9, 2003).

Islamists and Al-Qaeda Related Groups

Ansar al-Islam is a group in Iraq with al-Qaeda connections as the
Bush administration alleged; however, it is also a somewhat separate
movement from the main Sunni insurgency in Iraq. Ansar al-Islam is
also a relatively new player in Iraq and was formed in 2001 (two years
before the American invasion) in a merger between the Islamic
Movement of Kurdistan and another al-Qaeda-affiliated Kurdish
group known as Jund al-Islam. The group's goals were to create an
autonomous Kurdish Islamic State in northern Iraq, and they were
thus opposed to Saddam Hussein, who opposed an independent or
autonomous Kurdish region and also opposed the major Kurdish Parties due to their secularism (Clarke et al., 2004, p.39).

Ansar al-Islam has exhibited tremendous potential for danger,
however, in that the group worked with al-Zarqawi and al-Qaeda in
Iraq in a failed attempt to produce chemical weapons prior to the US
invasion. The group has also carried out attacks on the United States
and the new Iraqi government established by the Americans after the
capture of Saddam Hussein. Its most successful attack, however, was
not directed at the Americans, but at the major secular Kurdish political parties during a meeting involving those parties (none of which
were radical Islamist) in February 2004, where 109 people were killed
and 235 were wounded (Clarke et al., 2004, p.39). In spite of their
connections to al-Qaeda, Ansar al-Islam does not appear to be the

most important group behind the Iraqi insurgency at present since the insurgency appears to be primarily Sunni driven and Ansar al-Islam is driven primarily by Kurdish nationalism in addition to its Islamism.

The most important segment of the insurgency in Iraq, however, is clearly both Islamist and nationalist in character, and al-Qaeda is involved, but Saddam Hussein, on trial at the time of this writing for his crimes against humanity, is not part of the religious insurgency (although his former Baathist Party is involved). In fact, Saddam evidently warned the Baath Party against close links with foreign religious extremists (Hashim, 2006, p.142). Nevertheless, Iraq is now the central front in the jihad for the Islamists of al-Qaeda and other similar international Islamist groups.

Two indicators within Iraq of the Islamist nature of the Iraqi insurgency are the presence of foreign fighters (who, if not religious, are clearly not fighting for Iraqi nationalist reasons) and the number of suicide attacks, which have been more widespread in Iraq than in any war since the Japanese Kamikaze attacks of World War II. In comparison, for example, Israeli officials documented approximately ninety suicide bombings between 1993 and 2005. Meanwhile, there were an estimated ninety suicide bombings in Iraq in the month of May 2005 alone (*Washington Post*, July 17, 2005). Given that suicide in Islam is forbidden, but "martyrdom" in jihad is not, the suicide bombings can only be explained as martyrdom in Islamic jihad. Although all parties agree that most insurgents are Iraqis, in September 2004, Iraqi Prime Minister Iyad Allawi estimated that 30% of insurgents were foreign fighters (*Los Angeles Times*, September 28, 2004). While this may be an overestimate, the presence of so many foreign fighters indicates that a large segment of the insurgency is religious since there is simply no other force (certainly not Iraqi nationalism) that would compel so many non-Iraqi individuals to join the fight.

Instead, many Iraqi insurgents state the same goals as Osama bin Laden and al-Qaeda. For example, Sheikh Abd-al-Salam Bin-Osman al-Khattabi, the head of the Ahl al-Sunnah-wa-al-Jama'ah Association, a Sunni Salfist group, called for the establishment of an Islamic government in Iraq as a prelude to the liberation of other Muslim lands from infidels and apostates and the eventual reestablishment of the caliphate (Hashim, 2006, p.123). Similarly, a group known as Jaish Ansar al-Sunnah has issued statements declaring that jihad in Iraq is the individual duty of every Muslim and the jihad cannot end until sharia has been applied in Iraq (Hashim, 2006, p.123). Other Islamist insurgent groups include Munazzamat al-Rayat al-Aswad (Black Banner Organization), which has called for sabotage of the Iraqi oil industry, Mujahideen al-ta'ifa al-Mansoura (Mujahideen of the Victorious Sect) Kata'ib al Mujahideen fi al-Jama'ah al-Salafiyah fi al-'Arak (Mujahideen Battalions of the Salafi Group of Iraq) who consider themselves to be followers of Osama bin Laden's mentor, Abdullah Azzam, the Armed Islamic Movement of al-Qaeda Organization, Fallujah Branch, Jaish Muhammad (Army of Muhammad), which threatens to blow up embassies of countries that interfere in Iraq, and the Islamic Army of Iraq, which is a Salafist organization with ties to al-Qaeda (Hashim, 2006, pp.170–175). With this much activity and so many groups emerging in such a brief time frame, it suggests that new jihadist groups can be expected to continue to form and reform in Iraq until the Americans withdraw.

Abu Musab al-Zarqawi and Strategy

Perhaps the most important jihadist group in Iraq from the US invasion through the spring of 2006 was that of Abu Musab al-Zarqawi, the Jordanian leader of al-Qaeda in Iraq, who was killed in a U.S. bombing attack in June 2006. Al-Zarqawi was a Jordanian militant drawn to the jihad in Iraq who at first evidently attached himself to Ansar al-Islam before forming his own group which eventually became known as al-Qaeda in the Land of Two Rivers (Iraq) (*New York Times*, July 13, 2004, A8). Al-Zarqawi was a Palestinian refugee who grew up in Jordan, but departed to join the jihad in Afghanistan in the 1980s where he developed ties with al-Qaeda. The ties became even more clear in December 2004 when Osama bin Laden praised al-Zarqawi and recognized him as the leader of al-Qaeda in Iraq (Hashim, 2006, 143). Like other Islamists, al-Zarqawi's goal was to overthrow current "apostate" Muslim regimes and reestablish the Islamic caliphate. Al-Zarqawi was a follower of Takfiri ideology, under which all non-Muslims, as well as Shiites, are considered apostates who should be killed if they do not convert. Al-Zarqawi viewed God as sovereign and therefore viewed Western democracy as an evil form of polytheism where rule by God through sharia is supplanted by rule through the people (Clarke et al., 2004, pp.34-35).

Al-Zarqawi created his terror group in 2003 with the primary goal of causing the failure of the American project to bring democracy to Iraq. In doing so, al-Zarqawi hopes to create the conditions for the establishment of an Islamic government in Iraq based on the sharia. Consequently, al-Zarqawi denounced the American plans to install democracy as a "conspiracy of crusader harlots" and threatened to behead the children of those who dared to vote. During American-sponsored Iraqi elections, anonymous fliers were distributed by al-Zarqawi's group throughout Baghdad threatening the lives of those who voted. Al-Zarqawi declared war on what he termed "this evil principle of democracy and those who follow this wrong ideology" and threatened to "wash the streets of Baghdad in the blood of voters" (*New York Times*, January 24, 2005, pp.A10). Although al-Zarqawi and his successors thus far have been unsuccessful in bringing elections to a halt, such intimidation by religious zealots has made voting extremely risky for many people in the Sunni Triangle. In fact, the intimidation was so intense that a team of international election observers monitored the first round of Iraqi elections from Jordan, rather than from Iraq itself (Packer, 2005, pp.414–415).

Al-Zarqawi, like many other Islamist insurgents, was not squeamish about the killing of innocent bystanders while waging his jihad against the Western infidels. In the words of another Iraqi insurgent leader, "al-Zarqawi does not give a damn about Iraq; he is prepared to kill 10 Iraqis if in doing so he can kill one American" (Quoted in Hashim, 2006, p.209).

Another strategy (largely successful) of the religious insurgents has been to isolate the American occupiers in Iraq by driving other foreigners, whether foreign armies or civilian contractors, out of the country through the means of terrorism, murder, mayhem, and atrocity. The strategy has thus far proven to be somewhat successful as civilian contractors, foreign armies (such as Spain's), and international organizations (such as the UN and the Red Cross) were forced to pull out of Iraq in 2003 due to the danger posed to their people (Diamond, 2005, p.13 Phillips, 2005, p.9). For example, in April 2004 after hostage-taking escalated and Islamist Web sites displayed the gruesome beheadings of hostages from Bulgaria, Italy, and South Korea as well as the United States, France and Germany warned their citizens to leave Iraq, Russia withdrew 600 workers, and Brown and Root, a division of Halliburton, suspended all convoys into Iraq (Phillips, 2005, p.202).

In the case of the Spanish army, an Islamist message board associated with al-Qaeda known as "the Information Institution in Support of the Iraqi People" contended that Iraq was the key battleground in the global jihad and the best way to damage the United States was by inflicting enormous economic costs in Iraq. Spain, it was argued, was America's weakest partner in the struggle due to the war's unpopularity in Spain; consequently, the author urged that jihadists should strike several major blows against the Spanish forces, after which it would be forced to withdraw (Lia and Hegghammer, 2004, p.355). The strategy, of course, proved successful due to the efforts of Islamists in Spain (rather than those in Iraq), whose 2004 bombings of the Spanish rail system led to the collapse of the government and the Spanish pullout of Iraq.

After the American transfer of political power to the new Iraqi government in June 2004, al-Zarqawi and his group began attacking "collaborators" with the infidels through attacks on the new Iraqi interim government in the forms of assassinations and attacks on government infrastructure. Al-Zarqawi also indicated in a letter to al-Qaeda facilitator Hasan Ghul that he would attempt to instigate a civil war in Iraq by attacking Shiite targets to such a degree that they would begin attacking Sunnis in retaliation. The escalation of violence that would result from such tactics is purposed to render Iraq ungovernable and thus prevent the United States from realizing their goals of Western democracy and profitable oil flows from Iraq (Clarke et al., 2004, pp.35–38). Pursuant to these goals, al-Zarqawi's group has essentially waged a war with the Badr Corps, the Militia of the Supreme Council for Islamic Revolution in Iraq (SCIRI), a Shiite Party connected to Iran. In retaliation, SCIRI has essentially launched a war of assassination against prominent Sunnis, thus escalating sectarian violence (Hashim, 2006, pp.247–249).

Al-Zarqawi's group has been successful in producing major mayhem, most notably when they attacked Shiite pilgrims and worshippers in Baghdad and Karbala during the festival of Ashura in March 2004, killing 143 and wounding 400 (Clarke et al., 2004, pp.35–38). Similarly, in January 2005 Sunni extremists launched suicide-bombing attacks against a Shiite mosque and a wedding party in Baghdad, killing 22 people (*Economist*, January 29, 2005, p.7).

Al-Qaeda in Iraq's attacks on Shiites are also motivated by religious differences since Zarqawi and his radical Sunni successors view them as polytheists who worship idols and deviant apostates who have strayed from true Islam (Hashim, 2006, p.47). Al-Zarqawi credited Shiites with a long history of treachery, most significantly as traitors to Islam who allowed the Mongol leader Hulagu to destroy the caliphate in Baghdad in 1258. In the words of al-Zarqawi himself concerning the Shiites, "By god, nobody is as cowardly as those people. Their early forefathers were labeled as cowardly and treacherous" (Quoted in Hashim, 2006, p.182).

The efforts of al-Zarqawi and al-Qaeda in Iraq at engendering sectarian strife have been somewhat successful in that they have engendered resentment from many Iraqis against al-Qaeda and foreign fighters in general due to their indiscriminate killing, since it appears that most Iraqis oppose the indiscriminate slaughter of innocent civilians. For instance, the commander of the insurgent group, the First Army of Muhammad prophetically stated that al-Zarqawi is "mentally deranged, he has distorted the image of the resistance and defamed it. I believe his end is near" (*Washington Post*, October 13, 2004, p.1). That this commander was correct in his assertion that al-Zarqawi would not last long is most likely irrelevant, however, since the pattern appears to be that as soon as one face in the "deck of cards" is eradicated, another face emerges to take its place. Such is the nature of a war of ideologies.

Islamists and Mass Media Propaganda and Recruiting

Islamists proudly display evidence of their attacks on Americans on the Internet so as to demonstrate their resolve and virtue, as well as to provide evidence that they are winning. They also post pictures of Iraqis killed at the hands of Americans so as to play on people's emotions and thus boost their recruiting. That the American invasion of Iraq has provided a boon to Islamist recruiters should be obvious to all. For specific evidence, Israeli scholar Reuven Paz analyzed the biographies of 154 foreigners who died in Iraq. Paz concluded that the fallen insurgents were not seasoned veterans from the jihad of Afghanistan or elsewhere, but new, young, recruits who had never taken part in any terrorist activity before the American invasion of Iraq. In other words, the American invasion is spawning Islamic terrorists and the terrorists in Iraq have emerged in response to recent political developments, rather than as a response to a life-long commitment to jihad (*Boston Globe*, July 17, 2005). In a similar study of some three hundred Saudis captured in Iraq, Saudi scholar Nawaf Obaid concluded that

> the largest group is young kids who saw the images on TV and are reading the stuff on the internet. Or they see the name of a cousin on the list or a guy who belongs to their tribe and they feel a responsibility to go. (*Boston Globe*, July 17, 2005)

An Imam from a British Mosque in Beeston, United Kingdom, from where one of London's transportation bombers, Mohammad Sidique Khan, resided, concurred that the American invasion of Iraq created jihadist sentiments among his congregation. In the words of the Imam, "A big thing is Iraq and Afghanistan. Lots of youngsters, whether they have Islamic knowledge or not get automatically affected. It triggers something" (Burke, 2004, p.135).

Captured jihadists themselves have confirmed the observations of Obaid and Khan. One insurgent captured in Iraq, Walid Muhammad Hadi al-Masmudi, cited television as the primary influence on his decision to leave his native Tunisia and go to Iraq. In the words of al-Masmudi (Quoted in Hashim, 2006)

> We also watched clerics on television and on Al-Jazirah declaring jihad I Iraq ... there was a statement, fatwa, by a list of 40 scholars from the Arab and Islamic world on Al-Jazirah. ... They used to show events in Abu Ghraib, the oppression, abuse of women, and fornication, so I acted in the heat of the moment and decided ... to seek martyrdom in Iraq. (p.144)

Another Tunisian jihadist captured in Iraq, Muhammad bin Hassan Rabih, also cited the images on Al-Jazirah and the abuses at Abu Ghraib in particular as the reasons he left his homeland to go to Iraq to wage jihad (Hashim, 2006, pp.144–145).

Turn to Religion in a Time of Chaos

It is not surprising that the Iraqi people would turn to religion in a time of uncertainty, calamity, and chaos. After all, a similar phenomenon has been observed throughout history in Western societies. For example, American religiosity was at its highest recorded peak in the 1950s after the twin calamities of the Great Depression and World War II (Johnstone, 1992, p.240). That Iraqis would turn to religion after more than twenty years of calamity caused by the war with Iran, the Persian Gulf War, and twelve years of strangling economic sanctions, merely fits a predictable historical and sociological pattern. The return to religion in Iraq also received a major boost from Saddam Hussein himself in 1993 when Saddam instituted a government-led "Faith Campaign," the purpose of which was to foster support for his regime through religion. According to Amatzia Baram at the United States Institute of Peace, Saddam knew that large segments of the Iraqi public were turning to religion during the difficult years of sanctions after the Persian Gulf War, so he "decided to jump on the bandwagon" (www.usip.org/pubs/specialreports/sr134.pdf.). Given that the religion of Iraq is Islam, which contains the calls for jihad against infidel invaders, an insurgency should have been expected, and it should have been expected that the insurgency would be driven by Islam. According to George Packer (2005, p.309) that is indeed exactly what happened. In the words of Packer

> the most potent ideological force behind the insurgency was Islam and its hostility to non-Islamic intruders. Some former Baathist officials even stopped drinking and took to prayer. The insurgency was called mukawama, or resistance, with overtones of religious legitimacy; its fighters became mujahideen, holy warriors; they proclaimed their mission to be Jihad.

Ahmed Hashim (2006, p.99) essentially concurs with Packer, arguing that many former Baathists blended nationalism and Islamism in forging their resistance against the United States. Hashim quotes a Fallujah resident and former army officer, Sheikh Abu Bashir, who argues that the biggest mistake made by the United States was the dissolution of the army, but also added that God had ordered him to resist the American invasion forces (Hashim, 2006, p.99).

As American planners should have expected, religion, one of the most important societal social structures in Iraq, along with family and tribal affiliations, was one of the few societal structures that remained intact after the fall of Saddam, and provided continuity, direction, and meaning in a time of uncertainty (Shadid, 2005, p.232). It appears that the fall of Saddam Hussein created somewhat of a power vacuum in Iraq that the US was unable to quickly fill with a legitimate new Iraqi government. Into this vacuum, it is unsurprising that religion would surge forward to fill the void. Ahmed Hashim (2006, p.112), argues that a major surge in the influence and power of Sunni clerics in Iraq occurred due to the absence of any Sunni political entities that could truly represent the Sunni community. In the words of radical Sunni cleric Sheikh Nadhim Khalil, "Only mosques represent the Sunnis" (Quoted in Hashim, 2006, p.113). In the absence of any other legitimate political authorities in the eyes of Iraq's Sunnis, the mosques, which have traditionally served as a means of disseminating political information in Muslim societies, quickly became centers for the spread of radicalism and recruitment. Many Imams mirror the words of Sheikh Nadhim Khalil, who stated that "The occupation is like a cancer, and it has to be removed" (Quoted in Hashim, 2006, p.113).

Hashim also argues that the rise of the importance of religion in Iraq is due to the spiritual needs of the Iraqi Sunnis who had lost their identity and status. Sunnis tended to perceive that the Americans were specifically targeting the Sunni community, a perception that was only made worse when the United States began arresting anti-American Sunni clerics, such as Sheikh Mahdi Ahmed al-Sumaidi, who was detained after a weapons cache was discovered in his mosque (Hashim, 2006, pp.113–114).

Additionally, part of the rise of Islam in Iraq can be attributed to a widespread perception among the Iraqi people that there is a high degree of integrity among the clerics, who refused to legitimate or cooperate with the occupation (Hashim, 2006, p.112). In the words of one Baghdad man (Quoted in *Seattle Post-Intelligencer*, May 11, 1999, p.1), "I have more confidence in the religious leaders now. We are Muslims, and I believe religion is the truth. During this crisis, it was the religious leaders who tried to solve things." Thus, when clerics, such as those at the Khaleed ibn Walid mosque in Fallujah, praise the killing of American soldiers and denounce them as "occupiers," it has a great impact upon the people in general. In the Fallujah case, the Americans then exacerbated the situation by arresting clerics that denounced the American occupation and thus further fanning the flames of revolt (Hashim, 2006, pp.28–29).

Islam, like most other religions, is greatly open to interpretation and therefore can be easily tailored to fit specific situations in specific places at specific times. Consequently, Islam has been used to galvanize the poor in Palestine and Southern Lebanon against what they view as Jewish oppression. In Egypt, the Muslim Brotherhood uses Islam to rally the people against Western decadence and governmental corruption and apostasy. In Iraq, Islam has become a means to rally the people against the American occupation. Similar to the situation in Palestine, Islam has provided a rallying cry for the disenfranchised drawn to the simplicity of a struggle against the infidels and enemies of God (Shadid, 2005, p.288). In the words of Benjamin and Simon (2005)

> By invading Iraq, the United States provided the jihadists with the ideal opportunity to fulfill their obligations and drive an occupying army out of the lands of Islam. There would be roughly 150,000 Americans spread thinly over a wide-open country. This was an entirely different picture from the U.S. deployment in Saudi Arabia, where just 5,000 troops were stationed, most of them in remote desert camps where ordinary Saudis would never see them. From the perspective of the jihadists, the targets were being delivered for the killing. The American occupation of Iraq gave the radicals an unprecedented chance, in bin Laden's words, to help 'establish the rule of God on earth.' (p.34)

To make matters worse, the chaos created by the war provided a major recruiting tool for those who favored jihad. Daniel Benjamin and Steven Simon (2005, pp.95–96), for example, explain the impact of war in Iraq for the recruiters of jihad thus

> Islamist radicalism thrives on war. Atrocities help to create and attract new militants, and the experience of the fight expands their capabilities, giving them skills and inspiration for the next battle. This has been the case in Afghanistan, Bosnia, Kosovo, Kashmir, and Chechnya. All of these conflicts, to some degree or another, started out with religion playing a relatively small role, but eventually the question of religious identity moved to the center, driving the parties to greater violence. In the Balkans, hundreds of thousands died; in Afghanistan, the tally has run into the millions. The jihad lives off these conflicts—they are, in a way, the undersea plumes that nourish monsters. They also tend to expand, overflowing their boundaries, spreading destruction.

Iraq thus far appears to be conforming to the pattern described by Benjamin and Simon as violence appears to breed more violence, more calls for jihad, and more jihadists heed the calls to join the Holy War.

Internationally, radical clerics and jihadists have issued numerous calls for Holy War against America in Iraq. Most notably, in February 2003 (the month before the American invasion of Iraq), Osama bin Laden, still perhaps the most important jihadist in the world, at least in a symbolic sense, laid the groundwork for an al-Qaeda-led insurgency when he called for guerrilla-war strategy in Iraq after the pending American invasion as opposed to a strategy of conventional fighting. In the words of al-Qaeda leader Osama bin Laden, (http://news.bbc.co.uk/2/hi/middle_east/2751019.stm)

> We also recommend luring the enemy forces into a protracted, close, and exhausting fight, using the camouflaged defensive positions in plains, farms, mountains, and cities. The enemy fears city and street wars most, a war in which the enemy expects grave human losses.

Osama, however, was not alone in his call for jihad in Iraq. Radical Islamist Internet message boards have been lighting up with similar calls for believers to join the jihad in Iraq even since the US invasion. As one Islamist wrote on a radical web site in the fall of 2004 (www.ansarnet.ws/vb/showthread.php?t=14236)

> al-Qaeda has gained a new land: The Country of Two Rivers. The distances separating the black banners (of al-Qaeda in Iraq) and Jerusalem became shorter. ... The Jihad in the world has united under the banner of al-Qaeda: Although the names have not been unified, the thoughts have come close enough to the degree of unification. This was noticed in Chechnya, Algeria, Kashmir, Iraq, and Allah willing, in Palestine.

Inside Iraq, the impulse to jihad has been similar as radical Imams began calling for jihad against the United States as soon as the Americans arrived. For example, Baghdad Salafi cleric, Sheikh Fakrhri al-Qaisi, argued that Iraqi Muslims had no choice under Islam but to engage in jihad. In the words of al-Qaisi, "Infidels are occupying a Muslim country, the jihad is therefore automatic as a right of legitimate defense. We have no need to launch a general appeal for a holy war" (Quoted in Hashim, 2006, p.114). Similarly, Sheikh Ibrahim al-Nama'a of Mosul preached the following to his followers (Quoted in Hashim, 2006, p.116)

> In invading a Muslim territory, the objective of the infidels has always been to destroy the cultural values of Islam. With them they bring nationalism, democracy, liberalism, communism, Christianity. ... Today the Iraqis suffer. Now Iraq is occupied precisely because it has forgotten the divine teachings and has not followed the principles of Islam. We have been delivered of the injustices of one man (Saddam), but this does not mean we must accept the American-British domination.

Al-Nama'a clearly teaches that the American invasion was not a liberation of the Iraqi people (although he acknowledges the end of the tyranny of Saddam), but a war against Islam and an attempt by the Americans and British to pollute or destroy Iraqi culture. In such a perception, jihad becomes the only option for the devout Muslim. If al-Nama'a were alone in his thinking, then perhaps there would be little danger; however, Al-Nama'a's sentiments are frequently echoed by the insurgents themselves. One Islamist insurgent (known only as Ahmed) described his motives for jihad in Iraq thusly (Quoted in www.smh.com.au/articles/2003/08/15/1060936052309.html)

Our fighters are protecting our religion. We cannot allow foreigners to occupy our country. The Americans do not respect us, so we cannot respect
them. They are a cancer of bad things: prostitution, gambling and drugs.
This struggle is not about Saddam. It's about our country and our God. Our
aim is not to have power or to rule the country. We just want the U.S. out
and for the word of Allah to be the power in Iraq.

Another Iraqi insurgent, Abu Abdul Rahman explained the jihad using extremely similar terms. In the words of Rahman (Quoted in
www.guardian.co.uk/international/story/0,3604,1374581,00.html)

Thanks to the Americans for getting rid of Saddam, but no thanks for stay-
ing in Iraq. The idea of jihad came step by step as I watched what the
Americans were doing to our country. ... Our goal is to get the invaders out
of our country, and from all the Arab countries, and I hope that after we get
them out we will have a couple of moments of peace in our lives.

The call for jihad, unfortunately, has proven to be much more than
just words in mosques and on Internet message boards and the conflict over time appears to have become more and more religious in
character. Furthermore, as foreign jihadists stream into Iraq and
funds from international Islamic radical groups pour into Iraq, the
conflict clearly has spread beyond its borders and had global impact,
with Iraqi Islamists uniting with foreign fighters to resist the United
States under the cloak of Islam. In the words of one former Iraqi military officer now turned jihadist against the United States (Quoted in
Hashim, 2006, p.119)

We are fighting under the flag of Islam. ... Muslims in several Arab countries have called for a jihad. We can therefore count on internal and external support. Sheik Osama bin Laden has launched an appeal to liberate
Iraq. He is a man of principle. If he wants to help us fight our enemy, we
will be pleased to accept.

Conspiracy Theory and Anti-Semitism

Iraq has an unfortunate recent history of strong anti-Semitism that
has contributed to the Iraqi insurgency as Iraqis combine their anti-
Semitic beliefs with traditional conservative conspiracy theories and
connect the American invasion with some sort of Jewish plot. The
anti-Semitism in Iraq is so strong that upon the establishment of the
State of Israel in 1948, approximately 100,000 Jews were expelled
from Iraq. Saddam Hussein himself raided a Jewish shrine in Baghdad in 1979 and disposed of ancient Torahs that were thousands of
years old, one said to have been written by Ezekiel himself (Diamond,
2005, pp.3–4). In such an environment, young Iraqis who had been
raised in Saddam Hussein's anti-Semitic propaganda state tend to
view the Jews as evil incarnate, and therefore often connect anything
and everything they oppose with some sort of Jewish plot. The goals

of the religious insurgents from the beginning were clearly linked to the Islamist worldview of "plot mentality," anti-"infidel" Islamic jihad, and anti-Semitism. This mentality can be seen in the radical Islamists' call to kill all Americans and any foreigners supporting them. The ultimate goal of the jihadists is the expulsion of the infidels from Iraq. As a consequence, the religious insurgents referred to American soldiers and contractors, as well as Iraqis working with the occupation forces, as "Jews" (Packer, 2005, p.288). For example, American Captain Gerd Schroeder, commander of Bravo company, reported that when he sent interpreters into the Baghdad mosques to see what was being preached, the message of the day was, "If you're not killing the Americans and the Jew pigs, you're not a true Muslim" (Quoted in Shadid, 2005, p.201). Not uncoincidentally, many insurgents view the American invasion as part of an American plot to prop up Israel, destroy Islam, take over Muslim lands, and steal Muslim oil. One Egyptian jihadist, for instance, argued that (Quoted in Hashim, 2006, p.13), "if Arabs did not fight the United States in Iraq, other Arab countries would be next on the list ... if they take Tikrit, then is Cairo next?" There is obviously tremendous irony in this statement in that it resembles the arguments offered by the Bush administration in justification of the American invasion of Iraq; specifically, the contention that the United States is fighting the Islamists in Iraq so that they would not have to fight them at home.

Rise of the Shiite Ulama

The Shiite ulama, already a legitimate source of government authority in Shiite Theology, but suppressed under Saddah Hussein, found that the greatest impediment to their power had been removed with the fall of the regime of Saddam Hussein and quickly moved to fill the power vacuum. The removal of Saddam's oppression was not the only benefit; however, the Shiite ulama gained further credibility in the eyes of the Shiite people when they organized the establishment of one hundred roadblocks in the impoverished Shiite neighborhoods of Baghdad to deter looters during the chaos that accompanied the American invasion. In other words, the Shiite religious leaders were at least partially and visibly able to do what the American superpower could not, and thus gain the support of people that might not have otherwise turned to religion (Shadid, 2005, p.157).

Unfortunately for the Americans, those same Shiite religious leaders have not overwhelmingly embraced peace or the American occupation. Instead, the Shiite Supreme Council for Islamic Revolution in Iraq (SCIRI), a group that Sunnis view as a front for Iran, issued the statement, "We refuse to put ourselves under the thumb of the Americans (Quoted in Phillips, 2005, p.137). Instead, SCIRI, which has directly received support and arms from Iran, advocates Theocratic rule for Iraq (Hashim, 2006, pp.247–248). Similarly, Ayatollah al-Haeri, the spiritual mentor of the radical Shiite cleric Muqtada al Sadr, issued a fatwa on April 8, 2003 instructing Iraq's Shiite clerics to "raise people's awareness of the Great Satan's plans and of the means to abort them" and to "seize as many positions as possible to impose a fait accompli for any coming government" (*New York Times*, April 26, 2003, A1). These positions were obviously a far cry from the "sweets and flowers" with which Ahmed Chalabi promised the Shiites would greet the American troops.

The Shiites have not limited their violence exclusively to the American occupiers, however. SCIRI is essentially a Shiite umbrella group founded in Iran in 1982 that advocates Shiite religious control of Iraqi politics. SCIRI includes not only Shiite clerics and fielding Party candidates in elections for Iraq's elected assembly, but also a 10,000-man militia known as the Badr brigade that has been known to exact vengeance on Sunnis and credited with sectarian violence. For instance, after the death of Shiite cleric Ayatollah Muhammad Baqer al-Hakim along with hundred others in a car bombing in Najaf in August 2003, SCIRI Badr militiamen loyal to al-Hakim killed Baathists in the streets of Najaf in retaliation and declared that the death of their leader would be avenged in blood (*Economist*, September 6, 2003, p.39).

Muqtada al Sadr

Among the important Shiite clerics who quickly became linked to the insurgency is Muqtada al-Sadr, a fiery young (early thirties) Iranian-backed Shiite cleric and sayyid (descendant of the Prophet), who opposed the American occupation of Iraq, and quickly arose as one of the most important Shiite components of the Iraqi resistance to the US occupation.

Al-Sadr is an important cleric in Shiite theology due to his lineage that he traces to the sixth Shiite imam, Jaafar al Sadiq, a famous Shiite leader in the eighth century. Additionally, Muqtada al-Sadr's great uncle, Ayatollah Mohamed Baqr al-Sadr, had been considered the greatest Shiite scholar of the previous generation until enduring torture and assassination at the order of Saddam Hussein in 1980. (Packer, 2005, p.264).

Mohamed Baqr al-Sadr's nephew and Muqtada al Sadr's father, Mohammed Mohammed Sadiq al-Sadr was also a Grand Ayatollah, the highest Shiite clerical rank, who had spent time in Saddam Hussein's prison before Saddam released thousands of political prisoners in 1992; consequently, not only was Muqtada's father a sayyid and a Grand Ayatollah, the elder al-Sadr had also suffered at the hands of Saddam for his faith and was greatly revered. In the views of Baghdad's Shiites, Sadiq al-Sadr, was blessed by God and his word was therefore unquestioned by Shiites in Sadr City, an impoverished predominantly Shiite area of Baghdad (Packer, 2005, p.264).

Mohammed Sadiq al-Sadr then built up a significant following among the dispossessed Shiites in the South. Sadr's followers even attributed superhuman powers to him. Some Shiites believe that on Judgment Day at the end of the world, God will see everyone as he truly is. To God on that day, a liar will appear to God as a dog, an arrogant man as an insect, and a drinker as a pig. Some Shiites believed, however, that Ayatollah Mohammed Sadiq al-Sadr was able to see humans as God would see them on Judgment Day while he was still alive (Packer, 2005, p.264).

In spite of his earlier prison experience at the hand of Saddam Hussein, in the late 1990s, Sadiq al-Sadr began preaching against the regime of Saddam Hussein, a clear path toward martyrdom. In doing so, Sadr broke with Ayatollah Sistani's policy of being politically silent, and proclaimed the Khomeini view of the clergy's central role in politics. When Sadiq al-Sadr and two of his sons were predictably ambushed and killed by Saddam's men on the road between Najaf and Karbala, his youngest son, Muqtada, became heir to his following. Young Muqtada therefore benefited from the holiness of his father, and the adoration of the Shiites for his father was transferred to him after his father's death (Shadid, 2005, pp.171–173).

When news of the elder Sadr's death reached the streets of Baghdad, Shiites filled the streets of Baghdad in both grief and demonstrations in defiance of a curfew issued by the Baathists. The Republican guard quickly moved in and put down the unrest, killing and arresting protestors. Muqtada al-Sadr quickly assumed a leadership position in his father's movement, but the movement essentially moved underground so as to prevent further government oppression (Shadid, 2005, pp.171–173).

After the fall of Saddam, Muqtada al-Sadr's movement made the move from underground to the streets and provided food and other essential services to impoverished Iraqis. Sadr's militias protected mosques, acted as traffic police, and collected garbage in Baghdad, thus winning support of Baghdad's dispossessed Shiite population (Phillips, 2005, p.198). In Sadr City, an impoverished part of Baghdad where Sadr's mosque is located, it is estimated that unemployment hovers at approximately 70%; consequently, Sadr's is a hero to Iraq's most downtrodden population (Hashim, 2006, p.252).

Sadr quickly denounced the American invasion as an "occupation" rather than "liberation," condemned American mismanagement for allowing looting, and denounced the failure of the Americans to support the Shiite uprising in 1991. Sadr called for a restoration of religion's primacy in life, and denounced Western consumerism and globalism; consequently, nationalism and the notion that Shiite Islam should defend Iraq against foreign invasions. Additionally, Sadr advocates the establishment in Iraq of an Iranian-style Islamist Theocracy (Diamond, 2005, p.214). In the words of Sadr, "We want to establish an Islamic state because this is our first objective" (Quoted in Hashim, 2006, p.251). Even Sadr, however, has displayed some pragmatism, also stating that the establishment of a Shiite Islamic state would be very difficult in Iraq (due to religious diversity); consequently, Sadr has clarified his position, arguing that "We are not calling for establishing an Islamic state but we want the Islamic religion to be the source of legislation" (Quoted in Hashim, 2006, p.251).

Sadr effectively uses Shiite religious symbolism to rally the masses. Sadr's men prominently display the Iraqi flag with the slogan "God is the greatest," symbolizing the blending of religion and State (Shadid, 2005, pp.174, 178–179). Furthermore, Sadr's militia, the Mahdi Army, is also symbolic since the "Mahdi" in Shiism is the hidden Twelfth Imam, the messianic figure who is expected to return to save the world. Sadr used the symbolism even further to argue that the Americans knew of the impending appearance of the Mahdi and had invaded Iraq in an effort to seize and kill him. Sadr further argued that he could not disband his militia as the Americans demanded because the militia was not his alone, but belonged to the Mahdi, who commanded it (Diamond, 2005, p.214).

Sadr also connects the American occupation to Zionism and Israel, undoubtedly because many Iraqis believe the American invasion was launched for Israel's benefit. In the words of Sadr (Quoted in Hashim, 2006)

> See how Israel is sucking up the wrath of noble resistance fighters and converting it into infighting between sons of the same people. It does so by planting traitors and spreading love of power in order to consolidate its imperialistic planning and spread beyond Palestine by any means. ... All of this is increasing the tension in the Middle East. If America claims that it wants to spread peace in the Middle East, why doesn't it threaten Israel with occupation and war? Or is it only equal to dealing with the Arabs and Muslims and fears and even stands in awe of Israel? America supports Israel in all its decisions and its attacks against our oppressed people, the people of oppressed Palestine. America is for violations against the Arab and Islamic countries, such as Lebanon and Palestine. (p.259)

Sadr's movement was essentially a street movement rather than an intellectual one, however, and it was largely composed of young, unemployed, and uneducated men. Sadr's Mahdi Army is essentially the result of the generation of oppression under Saddam that created a segment of young, poor, and dispossessed Shiite men (Packer, 2005, p.313).

Like other Islamists, Sadr has called for Islamic purification and organized street gangs to enforce sharia in Sadr City. As a result, liquor stores, Western music stores, and Western clothing stores in Sadr City were attacked and closed. Predictably, women, as instructed by Sadr, immediately returned to wearing veils, and those who did not found themselves attacked by Sadr's followers (Shadid, 2005, p.179). Sadr's version of sharia, however, turned out to be more strict than simply the veil. Much as women experienced in Afghanistan under the Taliban, Iraqi women in Sadr City suddenly found themselves threatened by Sadr's militiamen just for being out of the house without male chaperones (Packer, 2005, p.409). Sadr's men took over schools and hospitals and intimidated the hospital staff members and school teachers and administrators into enforcing his version of sharia. Sadr also set up extralegal courts that imposed punishments for sharia violations, including death sentences. On July 20, 2003, 10,000 of Sadr's followers protested harassment by American troops on the streets of Najaf, a city that is home to two of Shiite Islam's holiest shrines. Seizing the moment, several days later Sadr pledged in front of an even larger crowd to form a religious army to drive the US troops from Najaf (Diamond, 2005, p.44). In October 2003, Sadr even declared himself to be the legitimate government of Iraq. In March 2004, Sadr's militiamen attacked and destroyed a village of gypsies in Southern Iraq when they refused to turn over a woman accused of violating sharia by Sadr's morality police. Sadr's militiamen attacked the town with mortars and rocket-propelled grenades, destroying 150 homes and leaving 1000 people homeless and without possessions (Diamond, 2005, p.212).

In the fall of 2004, the American authorities decided to put an end to the Sadr nuisance and decided to arrest him for the murder of a rival cleric, Abdel-Majid Khoie, on April 10, 2003, the day that Baghdad fell to the US armed forces. US officials also suspect that al-Sadr may have been involved in an attack that wounded Ayatollah Mohammed Saeed al-Hakim, and a car in bombing in Najaf in August 2003 that killed Ayatollah Mohammed Bakr al-Hakim, the head of SCIRI (Phillips, 2005, p.199). Mohammed Bakr al-Hakim had been a moderate cleric who favored working with the CPA and was, therefore, clearly killed for being a "collaborator" (Diamond, 2005, p.46). In the case of Khoie, he was beaten and stabbed at the Shrine of Ali by Sadr's men and a subsequent order to kill Khoie evidently came from Sadr himself (Shadid, 2005, p.192). Witnesses reported that they heard Sadr give an order in reference to Khoei to "Take this person away from here and kill him" (Packer, 2005, p.313).

In July 2004, after the signing of the interim law by the new Iraqi Governing Council in March of that year, Sadr called for the expulsion of Americans from Najaf and the dissolution of the Governing Council, an advisory panel of twenty-five Iraqis appointed by American Paul Bremer. Sadr's goal included not only expelling the Americans, but Sadr again also insisted that he and his followers were the rightful rulers of Iraq (Shadid, 2005, p.258). Sadr also began using the rhetoric of Hezbollah, the Iranian Shiite terrorist group that gained respect throughout the Islamic world for their success in forcing Israel to withdraw from Southern Lebanon in 2000, in a further attempt to enhance his own sense of legitimacy. Sadr used the Hezbollah slogan, "Crush them under your feet" on his posters and thus drew parallels between his own movement and the greater struggle against Israel (Shadid, 2005, p.365). Sadr also called for martyrdom and announced himself ready to sacrifice his own life for the expulsion of the invaders (Shadid, 2005, p.375).

Sadr's call to expel the Americans is especially important since to observant Shiites, the pronouncements of a cleric such as Sadr carry the force of law. As a consequence, American attempts to silence Sadr, such as the arrest of his top lieutenant, Mustafa Yaquoubi, and the closing of his newspaper, *Al-Hawza*, by the CPA on March 28, 2004, were generally viewed by Shiite Muslims as an American attack on Islam. *Al-Hawza* had inflamed American wrath by printing the names of "collaborators" with the Americans, accusing the Americans of deliberately hitting mosques with rockets, and accusing American consulate Paul Bremer of deliberately starving the Iraqi people (Packer, 2005, p.322). A week before the closing of the newspaper, Sadr had inflamed American wrath with a sermon where he praised the 9/11 attacks as a "gift from God" (Quoted in Diamond, 2005, p.231). Bremer had decided to arrest Sadr in October 2003, but Ayatollah Sistani sent Bremer a message warning that any such arrest would only enhance Sadr's stature and further inflame Shiites (Phillips, 2005, p.199). Nevertheless, Iraq's new interior minister issued an arrest warrant for Sadr in November 2003, and Sadr responded by ordering his Mahdi Army to resist the United States (Phillips, 2005, pp.199–200).

Instead of silencing Sadr, the American actions had the impact of uniting both Shiite and Sunni Muslims against the American infidel invaders and the closing of *Al-Hawza* also appears to have been a major precipitant to Sadr's Shiite insurgency against the American occupation (Shadid, 2005, p.375 Packer, 2005, p.297). After the closing of the paper and the arrest of Yaqoubi, Sadr's Mahdi Army launched major attacks on CPA offices in Kut, Nasiriya, Najaf, and Karbala, where Ukrainians, Italians, and the Spanish forces were unable to hold their ground (Packer, 2005, p.323). Jack Straw, Britain's foreign minister, reacted by stating that

> It is plainly the fact today that there are large numbers of people, and they are people on the ground, Iraqis and not foreign fighters, who are engaged in this insurgency. ... The lid of the pressure cooker has come off. (Quoted in the *New York Times*, April 10, 2004, p.A7)

On April 4, 2004, Sadr called on his militia to "Terrorize your enemy. God will reward you well for what pleases him" (Quoted in *Washington Post*, April 11, 2004). Shortly thereafter, Sadr's militia ambushed an American military patrol in Sadr City, killing eight. Consequently, Bremer declared Sadr an outlaw and announced a warrant for his arrest (Diamond, 2005, p.232). Further violence was temporarily abated when the United States agreed to withdraw from Najaf and suspend the warrant for Sadr's arrest if Sadr would dissolve his Mahdi Army. The United States fulfilled its part of the bargain, but Sadr renewed his insurrection three months later anyway, so in the end, the US efforts had perhaps done little other than fan the flames of Shiite rebellion (Phillips, 2005, p.201).

Ayatollah Ali Sistani

Muqtada al-Sadr's main competitor for Shiite power in the Iraqi South is the Grand Ayatollah Ali Sistani, whose influence among Shiites in Iraq perhaps cannot be understated. Unlike the Sadr klan, Sistani did not challenge Saddam's regime and instead practiced a Shiite theological concept known as taqiyya, or the principle of hiding one's beliefs to avoid persecution or harm. Sistani is also considered to be a "quietist," a Shiite tradition that discourages political activism among senior clerics. Instead, Sistani's goals are to ensure that the principles of Shiite Islam are respected in Iraqi public life (Hashim, 2006, p.241). Sistani's followers did form a militia, but its purpose was not to resist the Americans, but to protect Sistani from assassination by the unpredictable Muqtada al-Sadr (Diamond, 2005, p.215).

Like Sadr, however, Sistani is an Islamic conservative who forbids the playing of chess and backgammon, argues that men and women should not mix socially, insists that women wear head scarves, and rejects the idea of music for "entertainment." Sistani also opposes the import of Western consumerism, which he views as decadent. Finally, Sistani argues that secularism is the greatest threat to Iraq and to Iraqi culture (www.Sistani.org).

Sistani has far greater clout than Sadr among most Shiites in Iraq due to his status as the highest-ranking Ayatollah in Iraq. Sistani's position as Grand Ayatollah also means that he is vested with the power to interpret the Koran for all Shiites. Due to the Shiite stress on unity and the hierarchical nature of Shiism, Sistani's stance toward the Americans has great influence on the position of Shiites in general toward the American occupiers. In the words of Larry Diamond (2005, p.127), among many Shiites in Southern Iraq, there is a determination

> even among highly educated people to do, unthinkingly, whatever Ayatollah Sistani instructed—particularly if his message came in the form of a fatwa. One Iraqi told his focus group leader that even questioning a ruling from Sistani would be a sin. … In one focus group, a Shiite religious cleric had questioned Sistani's stance and his supreme power; he was driven out of the group and was afraid to return. The group leader later asked another Shiite participant, 'Why does everyone feel that they need to follow Sistani? Why not make up your own minds?' he replied, 'We are afraid, if we disagree, of what might happen to our families.

With this type of sway over the Iraqi Shiites, if Sistani had demanded open revolt, the American occupation may have gone even worse than it has. Fortunately for the Americans, Sistani has not advocated open revolt. He did, however, refuse to receive CPA officials, whom he viewed as illegitimate because they were unelected. Sistani appears to be well aware that true democracy in a country that is 60% Shiite could only work to enhance Shiite power. Sistani also issued a fatwa insisting that the new Iraqi constitution must be written by an elected, rather than appointed body such as the American-created Iraqi Governing Council (Phillips, 2005, pp.173, 178). In the words of Sistani (Quoted in Phillips, 2005)

> There is no guarantee that the council would create a constitution conforming to the greater interests of the Iraqi people and expressing the national identity, whose basis is Islam, and its noble social values. (p.178)

Given Sistani's clout as a Grand Ayatollah, his fatwa had immediate impact. Banners inscribed with the words of Sistani's fatwa on the constitution could be seen hanging from walls throughout Shiite sections of Baghdad in 2003 (Packer, 2005, p.213). With Sistani publicly in opposition to the Governing Council, it was not surprising when on December 1, 2003, the Oxford Research group released a nationwide survey that found that approximately three fourths of Iraqis rejected the legitimacy of the Governing Council (*USA Today*, December 4, 2003).

While Sistani's call for a constitution written by an elected body appears to be consistent with American democratic principles, in this case in the long run it is not, since the true democratic elections advocated by Sistani could only lead to a constitution written by Shiite clerics and based on sharia. When American administrator Paul Bremer belatedly attempted to meet with Sistani concerning the matter, Sistani conveyed that his position was nonnegotiable by refusing to meet with Bremer. Sistani then issued statements dismissing American plans as "fundamentally unacceptable" and proclaimed "We see no alternative but to go back to the people for choosing their representatives" (Phillips, 2005, pp.178–179).

Sistani caused further trouble for the Americans in March 2004 when he opposed the interim law signed by the Governing Council due to the veto in the interim law granted to Sunnis and Kurds over a permanent constitution and what he viewed as a too-limited role of Islam in that the Law failed to enshrine the role of Islam in legislation, particularly in family matters. Consequently, the Shiite members of the Governing Council did not show up at the ceremony to sign the Transitional Law on March 5, 2004 (Phillips, 2005, pp.187–190). In reaction to Sistani's stance on the interim law, Muqtada al-Sadr quickly organized daily protests against the law, claiming to be acting on the behalf of Sistani (Packer, 2005, pp.321–322). Others went even farther and the acting President of the Governing Council, Ezzedine Salim, was murdered by insurgents in May 2004 (Phillips, 2005, p.175).

Sistani did, however, eventually become involved in the democratic process imposed by the United States if for no other reason than that true democracy would put power into his own hands in a country that is 60% Shiite. Sistani helped formulate "List 169" on the Iraqi ballot, which the Iraqi people referred to as the "Sistani List." "List 169" stood for a society based on Islamic values and religious authority and called for subservience of society to the highest Shiite religious scholars. Sistani also issued a fatwa that limited the religious duty to vote only for Muslim men and women (Packer, 2005, p.431).

Sistani and the Shiite clerical hierarchy also engendered support from the Shiite population after the fall of Saddam when they used their considerable resources that they receive from the giving of alms for the purpose of restoring municipal services in some places, paying salaries left unpaid by the American occupiers, and bringing some semblance of order and stability amid the anarchy that replaced Saddam's regime. In short, the Shiite clerics were able to accomplish in the areas of security and services in some instances what the Americans could not (Hashim, 2006, p.254).

Iraq as a Launching Pad for Global Jihad

Clearly, if the American forces were not in Iraq, most of the jihadists who are currently attacking Americans in Iraq would not be attacking Americans at all, simply because they would have no logistical means of reaching across the Atlantic to attack Americans to begin with if the Americans had simply stayed home. Furthermore, given that most of the foreign fighters in Iraq apparently have no previous background in terrorism, it appears that the American invasion and occupation is the motivation for their jihad, without which they would not have been compelled to wage jihad against Americans in the first place (Hashim, 2006, pp.150–151). These circumstances suggest that it is ridiculous to argue that the United States is fighting terrorists in Iraq so that it will not have to fight them on American soil. Furthermore, although foreign jihadists have clearly been streaming into Iraq since the American invasion, it is foolish to assume that they will all stay there. Instead, the insurgency in Iraq will surely provide the world with a new, seasoned group of dedicated jihadists who will be determined to continue their global struggle after the American military departs some time in the future, much as the Mujahadeen from Afghanistan continued their jihad elsewhere after the Soviet withdrawal. As CIA Director Peter Goss explained to the Senate in February 2005 (Quoted in Benjamin and Simon, 2005)

> Those who survive will leave Iraq experienced in and focused on acts of ur-
> ban terrorism. They represent a potential pool of contacts to build transna-
> tional terrorist cells, groups and networks. (p.59)

That being the case, the arguments of the Bush administration that America is fighting terror in Iraq so that it does not have to fight them on American soil appear to lack a firm foundation. Instead, it is per-haps most likely that fighting the terrorists in Iraq will actually help them build transnational "cells, groups, and networks" that will eventually bring them right back to American soil, just as planned by al-Zawahiri in Afghanistan approximately a decade ago.

Islamism in the West

O ver 15 million Muslims live in Europe and the United States, and the existence of such a large Muslim diaspora is one of the key elements that enable the spread of global Islamism, as Muslims in the West are brought into contact with each other within the dominant Western cultures. The Muslim diaspora also allows radical Islamists from other parts of the world to develop contacts and safe havens within the boundaries of the "far enemy" of the West itself.

The Muslim diaspora has also led to the growth of Western-based Muslim advocacy organizations, Islamic groups and publications, and all manners of Muslim associational groups. Most of these groups, organizations, and publications are not radical Islamist in character; however, the sheer numbers of Muslims and the sheer numbers of the groups and publications lead to the probability that some will be supporters of Islamism. Their presence in Western societies is likely to lead not only to terrorism, but also to culture clash in the more mundane subjects of burying the dead, translations of the Koran into Western languages, gay rights, polygamy, equal rights for women, and forced marriages (*Economist*, October 29, 2005, p.87). For example, in 1989 when Ayatollah Khomeini of Iran called for the world's Muslims to execute Salman Rushdie, the British author of a book against Islam (with no connections to Iran) entitled *Satanic Verses*, an ad hoc Muslim Action Committee in London called for the expansion of British blasphemy laws, originally passed to protect the Church of England, to be extended to other religions such as Islam. The British attorney general ruled that British law offered no grounds for any civil suit to withdraw Rushdie's book from circulation and Britain's Muslims responded by taking to the streets in demonstrations. One Muslim activist, Kalim Siddiqui, created an informal Muslim Parliament, whose members claimed to "legislate in the name of all Muslim believers in the United Kingdom" (Kepel, 2003 pp.188, 201). Although the Rushdie affair has faded from memory for many (though at the time it received more press than most other cultural clashes in the

West between Muslims and Westerners), and many at the time viewed it as extraordinary that the leader of an Islamic country was able to mobilize Muslims living in the West to political action, it has proven to be far less unique in the years, as contact between Muslims and the West has increased with globalization and the number of Muslims living in Western countries has increased.

Prior to the Rushdie affair, Muslims in the West exhibited a tendency to avoid conflict in their Western host countries (although there were major strikes among immigrant workers in France between 1975 and 1978 and Lebanese Hezbollah carried out bombings in Paris in the 1980s). The vast majority of Muslims viewed conflict with Western sovereigns as inconsistent with Islam and believed that they had no authority in Islam to demand that their Western infidel sovereigns implement sharia. The South Asian Muslims of the United Kingdom, for instance, tended to keep their own creed and apply the sharia to themselves in their own separate community within the United Kingdom without provoking the intervention of the state. In Germany, where citizenship is by blood rather than residence, the Muslim population was even more inclined to live in closed groups and apply their religious beliefs informally to their separate society within the society at large (Kepel, 2003, pp.192-198).

By the end of the 1980s as Muslim populations increased in the West, however, Muslims began to view their situation differently and began to make demands on European governments. In Britain, Muslims demanded halal (ritually slaughtered) meat in school lunchrooms and the creation of all-girls' schools. In 2005, there were legal battles in several European countries over the wearing of headscarves at school and in the workplace by Muslim women. In France, where French law restricts religion in public life and therefore the wearing of veils and headscarves in school, Muslims began to clamor for the right to wear their religious clothing in schools at the end of the 1980s (Kepel, 2003, pp.198-19). The French government claims that the wearing of Islamic headscarves in French schools is prohibited because of the European Convention on Human Rights that bans the degradation of women. Many of France's Muslim schoolgirls, however, protested that the scarf was not degrading, but a cultural preference. Simultaneously, a British court cited the same European Convention on Human Rights document to uphold an Islamic schoolgirl's right to wear an even bulkier covering known as a jilbab in British schools. In Germany, the German Land of Baden-Wurttemberg prohibits the wearing of Islamic headscarves by teachers, but not by students. In Denmark, a supermarket fired an Islamic cashier for wearing a headscarf on the grounds that it was a safety hazard that might get stuck in the till (*Economist*, October 29, 2005, p. 87).

If conflicts over headscarves were the most important issue, then perhaps the Muslim Diaspora in the West would not be so worthy of concern; however, the cultural conflict has also proven to be dangerous, violent, and present throughout Europe and the United States. For example, in 1995 and 1996, France experienced a series of eight Islamist attacks that left 10 dead and 175 injured. Included in the French attacks was a gruesome beheading of the Trappist monks of Tibehirine in May 1996 (Kepel, 2003, p.308). In 2001, Hamburg, Germany served as the logistics and planning base for the 9/11 terrorist attacks on the United States (Benjamin and Simon, 2005, p.82). In London in July 2005, 56 people were killed and 700 injured in Islamist bombings on the London transportation system. In Netherlands in November 2004, the country was shocked when Theo van Gogh, a well-known Dutch filmmaker, television producer, and writer, not to mention relative of Vincent van Gogh, was murdered in Amsterdam by an Islamic fanatic who shot him twenty times, stabbed him repeatedly in the chest, and slit his throat so badly that he was almost decapitated. The murderer, Mohammed Bouyeri, a Dutch-born Muslim of Moroccan ancestry, pinned a five page letter to van Gogh's chest with a knife that warned van Gogh's film collaborator, Ayaan Hirsi Ali and several Dutch leaders of a similar fate (Bawer, 2006, pp. 1-2). One day after the murder, 20,000 people demonstrated to denounce the killing and 30 people were arrested by Dutch authorities for inciting hatred against Muslims. Finally, in Spain in March 2004, Islamist terror bombings on the Spanish transit system killed 191 people and wounded over 1800 when ten bombs planted by Islamists were detonated in four different blast zones. The bombings led to a change in the Spanish government in the next election as the ruling party of Prime Minister Jose Maria Aznar were defeated. The tragedy also had global political implications outside the Spanish borders since the newly elected Spanish government subsequently withdrew 1300 troops from Iraq (www.danielpipes.org/article/2218).

Importantly, the Madrid bombings were not designed, funded, or executed by al-Qaeda or any other international Islamist organization, but were carried out by local Muslims in Spain who were at that time unconnected to any other international terrorist organizations, thus demonstrating the global impact of Islamist ideology separate from al-Qaeda and the international terrorist network (Benjamin and Simon, 2005, p.6). In the words of Benjamin and Simon (2005, p.7), "Madrid shows all too plainly that people who hold these ideas and want to act on them live in the heart of the West. Their number is growing, and so too is the danger they pose." The van Gogh killing later that year, the London bombings in July 2005, and the burning of more than 9000

cars in France by disgruntled French Muslim youths were grim re-
minders of the same lesson.

Afghanistan and Western Islamism

An increase in radicalization of Muslims in the West after 1990 was
undoubtedly aided by the end of the war against the Soviet Union in
Afghanistan and the global dispersion of Afghan jihadists to Western
locations throughout the globe. In the United States. in particular,
anticommunist zeal led to the granting of visas to members of the Afghan Mujahadeen, some of whom would later have connections with
al-Qaeda. For instance, in 1986, only two years after his release from
prison in Egypt for his involvement in the assassination of Anwar Sadat, the blind Sheik Omar Abdel Rahman obtained a visa to the
United States. through the CIA. In 1991, just two years before he
would be involved in the first World Trade Center bombing, Rahman
received a permanent resident's visa on the grounds that he was a
minister at a mosque in New Jersey (Kepel, 2003, pp.300-301).

Rahman, however, was far from alone. The area where he resided in
Jersey City by the end of the 1980s had become known as "little
Egypt." Rahman's accomplice in the first World Trade Center bombing, Ramzi Yousef, received an electrical engineering degree in the
United Kingdom prior to training for jihad in a camp in Afghanistan
in 1990. Yousef then came to New York City in 1992 with a fake passport he had purchased in Pakistan, with the idea of launching a terror
attack on the United States in retaliation for American aid to Israel.
Yousef's bombing of the World Trade Center killed six people and injured over a thousand while causing $500 million in damage (Benja-
min and Simon, 2002, p.12). Yousef temporarily escaped to Pakistan,
but was caught and brought to trial in the United States after one of
his associates returned to the car rental company from where they had
rented the vehicles used in the bombing, seeking his deposit. Yousef
also hindered his ability to remain a fugitive with letters to New York
newspapers, claiming responsibility for the attacks. In his letters,
Yousef demanded that the United States end aid to Israel, break relations with Israel, and pledge to end interference in Muslim countries
(Coll, 2005, pp.249–250). The Yousef case demonstrates how
Islamists in the West have been able to become interconnected with
global terrorism. Not only did Yousef train in jihadist camps in Afghanistan after the World Trade Center bombing in 1993, he flew to
Pakistan and stayed in a safe house funded by Osama bin Laden (Coll,
2005, p.278).

Yousef explained to the FBI that he felt guilty about the deaths in
the bombing, but his remorse over the deaths was overridden by his
desire to do whatever he could do to stop the killing of Muslims by Is-

raeli troops (Coll, 2005, p.273). In other words, Yousef's act was a clear case of the type of "ends politics" with which traditional conservatives are often associated. Yousef, of course, is not alone in his mindset. A month before the first World Trade Center bombing, Mir Amal Kasi, who received a Master's degree in English literature from Baluchistan University (Pakistan) in 1989, shot and killed two CIA employees who were waiting in their cars to enter the gates at CIA headquarters. Kasi had been convinced that the CIA was responsible for the deaths of thousands of Muslims worldwide, and he viewed his act as justified due to Muslim deaths at the hands of the CIA (Coll, 2005, pp.246-247). Kasi would later be apprehended in 1997 by Afghan agents working for the CIA in Afghanistan (Coll, 2005, pp.374-375).

Meanwhile, other jihadists took advantage of Western freedoms of speech and traditions of asylum, not only to obtain transport and residency in the West, but also to publish their Islamist propaganda under the cover of Western protection of free press. The radical Islamist group, The Egyptian Gamaa Islamiya set up a headquarters in Copenhagen, whereas the Algerian Armed Islamic Group (GIA), a group that has killed thousands in Algeria in an extended campaign against the government since a cancelled election in 1991, published its Al-Ansar propaganda in Stockholm. In 1994, the GIA proved that it is much more than an irritating propaganda agency in the West when four Algerian GIA terrorists hijacked an Air France jet with plans to fly it into the Eiffel Tower. French authorities fooled them into thinking they lacked enough fuel to make it to Paris and diverted them to Marseilles, where they were all shot to death by French commandos (Coll, 2005, p.275). The next year in Belgium, Belgian authorities seized a GIA training manual with a preface dedicated to Osama bin Laden that explained how to make bombs using a wristwatch as a timer (Coll, 2005, p.275). In the United Kindom, asylum was granted to so many militants from all over the world, that militants declared Britain a sanctuary where no acts of terrorism were to be committed. In particular, an Egyptian Islamist group known as Talai al-Fath (the Vanguard of Conquest) set up its operations in London (Kepel, 2003, pp.303-304).

Cartoon Wars

In September 2004, the Danish newspaper *Jyllands-Posten* published a dozen cartoons depicting the Prophet Mohammed. Given that numerous Islamist sects ban all images, photos, drawings, etc. of the human form, thousands (if not millions) of Muslims worldwide viewed the cartoons as a blasphemous abomination. To make matters worse in the eyes of the Islamists, one of the cartoons portrayed Mohammed with a bomb in his turban. The Muslim world both within and outside the West erupted in violence and demonstrations that Denmark's Prime Minister Anders Fogh Rasmussen summed up as a "global crisis that has the potential to escalate beyond the control over governments" (Quoted in the *Economist*, February 11, 2006, p.24). At least ten people died in protests following the publication of the cartoons, several in two incidents in Afghanistan when protesters attacked a Norwegian peacekeepers' base and an American military base. Western embassies in Syria, Lebanon, Indonesia, and Iran were also attacked. In Khartoum, Sudan, a crowd of an estimated 50,000 people took to the streets to demonstrate against the cartoons and shouted, "Strike, strike, bin Laden" (Quoted in *Economist*, February 11, 2006, p.24).

Governments in Islamic countries also joined the protesting fray, with Saudi Arabia, Syria, Libya, and Iran all withdrawing ambassadors from Denmark, and Iran placing an embargo on Danish imports. In both Yemen and Jordan, newspaper editors who republished the cartoons were arrested and their newspapers were shut down. In Syria, where protesters burned the Danish and Norwegian embassies, mass protests were evidently orchestrated by the government where witnesses reported government officials with walkie-talkies directing the crowds, and camera crews followed arsonists into buildings to film the torching of Western-associated buildings (*Economist*, February 11, 2006, p.25).

While most European Muslims exhibited calm amid the global storm of protests over the cartoons, the man that some credit as being the primary instigator of the unrest was a radical Muslim cleric from Denmark named Abu Laban, who toured the Middle East for the purpose of fomenting outrage over the cartoons. The fact that the initial rabble-rouser in the cartoon affair was a European Muslim is symbolic of the challenges facing the West in attempting to accommodate its Muslim populations. While free speech and free press remain lynchpins of democratic values, radical Muslims living in the West appear ready to compromise those values when they view them as conflicting with Islam. The chilling impact of radical Muslims living in the West on Western free speech and free press was exemplified in the Danish Cartoon affair, when British and American Newspapers were reluctant to reprint the cartoons due to fears of Muslim violence. Similarly, President Bush called on world governments to "be respectful" and Britain's foreign secretary denounced the cartoons as "insensitive and "unnecessary" (*Economist*, February 11, 2006, pp.24-25).

Islamists in Bosnia

In 1990, as communism was collapsing across Eastern Europe, an Islamist named Alija Izetbegovic began an Islamist political party in Bosnia known as the Stranka Demokratske Akcije (SDA). In the November 1990 elections, the SDA swept the Muslim vote in the democratic elections for the Presidency of the Yugoslav Republic of Bosnia-Herzegovina. Itzetbegovic was to become the first democratically elected Muslim President of a secularized country in Europe. In 1992, as ethnic and religious conflict raged in Bosnia between Muslims and Christian Serbs, some 4000 jihadists from Afghanistan and other Muslim countries around the world arrived in Bosnia to wage jihad, with financial backing from Iran. The International Muslim Brotherhood joined the fray by calling for jihad against the Serbs. Beginning in 1992, $150 million in aid began flowing into Bosnia from Saudi Arabia. Islamists both within Bosnia and internationally pointed to the ethnic cleansing in Bosnia carried out by Serbs as proof that Muslim assimilation in Western countries is futile (Kepel, 2003, pp.237-250).

The tactics of the jihadists that arrived in Bosnia, however, shocked Western sensibilities by their brutality. Photographs of Arab jihadists holding the severed heads of Christian Serbs or crushing them under their boot-heels caused international outcry against the Muslim warriors. Foreign jihadists also used the war as an opportunity to attempt to impose sharia in Bosnia, including the destruction of businesses they deemed un-Islamic, and forcing women to wear veils and men to wear beards. The attempts to impose sharia were generally disparaged in the European press and President Izetbegovic reacted by inviting all foreign volunteers to leave Bosnia in 1995 and allow themselves to be replaced by American peacekeepers. Although the jihadists were humiliated by the suggestion that they give way to the infidel Americans, most quickly departed from Bosnia with the result that Bosnia's Muslims largely returned to the practices of liberalism and secularism that typify most Muslim communities in Europe (Kepel, 2003, 250-251). Although the Bosnian case clearly represents the dangers of religious strife, by 2006 Bosnia also appears to represent the possibility that religious differences between Muslims and others in Europe can be overcome.

Islamism in Chechnya

For over a decade, a jihadist civil war has raged in the Russian enclave of Chechnya, between Islamists, who desire an independent Islamic state, and the Russian authorities who desire to continue sovereignty

in the area. In 1999, Chechen rebels launched incursions and bombings into neighboring Dagestan and carried out a series of bombings
in residential apartment buildings in Moscow that killed more than
300 people. In 2002, Chechen rebels seized a theater in Moscow and
took 800 people hostage. In December 2002, Chechen rebels blew up
the headquarters of the Russian-backed Chechen government and
killed 80 people (Clarke et al., 2004, pp.45-46). In September, 2004,
the conflict experienced its most horrific event when Islamists took
more than 1000 people hostages in a school in Beslan. By the time the
siege was over, 300 civilians were dead, more than half of them children (Benjamin and Simon, 2005, p.20). The Chechen rebels are
linked to al-Qaeda and share bin Laden's goal of creating an Islamic
state and waging jihad against the West (Clarke et al., 2004, p.46).

Muslim Assimilation Problems

Although Muslims in the West may be overwhelmingly secular in outlook and supportive of core liberal values as a group, these are omi-
nous signs that Muslims in the West are becoming poorly integrated
into society and are retaining a separate Muslim identity based on religion rather than nationality. In the words of Benjamin and Simon
(2005),

> Most of the Continent's (Europe's) Muslims arrived in the 1950s and 1960s
> as workers to fill postwar Europe's labor shortage, and they stayed on in
> countries that, for the most part, neither expected nor wanted to integrate
> them into their societies. It soon became apparent, however, that there was
> no easy way to send these workers back or to stanch the flow of family
> members seeking reunification with loved ones—let alone to stop them
> from having children. As a result, Europe has sleepwalked into an awkward
> multiculturalism. Its Muslim residents, many of them now citizens, live for
> the most part in ghetto-like segregation, receive second-rate schooling, and
> suffer much hither unemployment than the general population. Those who
> do work are more likely than their non-Muslim counterparts to have low-
> wage, dead-end jobs. Indeed, it is this marginality that helps to explain the
> appeal of radicalism. (p.82)

Benjamin and Simon's conclusions are supported by employment
data. In Britain, for instance, unemployment among the Muslim
population is three times that of the general population and four times
the average for Muslim women (*National Statistics Online.* July 26,
2006, http://www.statistics.gov.uk/cci/nugget.asp?id=). In one British poll,
80% of British Muslims indicated that they view themselves as Muslims first and foremost, rather than as citizens of the United Kingdom
(Benjamin and Simon, 2005, p.52). Furthermore, it appears that there
may be a movement toward greater religiosity among Europe's Muslims. In one poll in France, for example, the percentage of Muslims

who identified themselves as "believing and practicing" increased by a full 25%, between 1994 and 2001 (Savage, 2004, p.31).

Greater religiosity itself clearly may open the door for increased radicalism, but this is especially true in Europe, where its Muslim population remains marginalized and not well integrated. Europe's ghettoized and marginalized Muslims, not surprisingly, tend to feel that they are persecuted by the larger non-Muslim majority across Europe. Survey data reveal that one third of Britain's Muslims report that they or someone they know has been persecuted because of their religion. Similarly, two thirds of British Muslims agree that antiterrorism laws are applied unfairly against Muslims and the same percentage agree that Britain's Muslims are politically underrepresented (http://image.guardian.co.uk/sysfiles/Guardian/documents/2004/11/30/Muslims-Novo41.pdf).

The propensity to radicalism is further enhanced, however, by the fact that there is a shortage of home-grown clerics in Europe, necessitating the import of Muslim clerics from the Middle East, North Africa, and South Asia, many of whom may have more radical views than those typically held by Western Muslims (Benjamin and Simon, 2005, p.84).

The tension between Muslims living in the West and the general populations should perhaps be expected to worsen in the near future, as more than one million Muslims immigrate to the West annually. Furthermore, the birth rate of Muslim population is triple that of the native European populations; consequently, Europe is expected to be 20% Muslim by the middle of the twenty-first century (*Economist*, November 25, 2004, p.28). Globalization and advanced communications technology in the West have the potential to exacerbate the probability of further cultural conflict, since it allows the West's Muslims to reach across state borders to both other Western Muslims and those Muslims living in the Islamic realm, and thus forge a global Muslim identity that supersedes national identities. Whereas much of this interaction is most certainly positive for Western Muslims and Western societies in general, the globalization of communications technology has also thus far proven to be a boon to radical Islamism in the West.

Burning France

In October and November of 2005, France erupted in an explosion of Muslim (and other immigrant) violence when two young Muslims, Bouna Traore, 15, of Malian background, and Zyed Benna, 17, a Muslim of Tunisian origin, were accidentally executed at an electricity substation near Paris, where witnesses stated that they were fleeing from police (an allegation that the French police authorities denied) (http://news.bbc.co.uk/2/hi/Europe/4407688.stm). Riots and demonstrations quickly spread from Paris to dozens of locations throughout France, including all fifteen of France's largest cities. The riots began on October 27 and escalated daily for twenty nights until almost 9000 vehicles had been burned in the violence and approximately $200 million worth of property had been destroyed. French President Jacques Chirac was forced to declare a state of emergency on November 8, which the French Parliament extended to three months, ending on the January 4, 1996 election in France. The French emergency law allowed local authorities to impose curfews, ban public gatherings, and conduct house-to-house searches in attempts to curb the violence (http://en.wikipedia.org/wiki/2005_civil_unrest_in_France).

Although the head of French intelligence denied that Islam was a factor for the unrest, instead citing high unemployment rates among immigrants in France from North Africa, the *New York Times* reported on November 5, 2005, that the majority of those involved in the riots were young Muslim males of North African origin (http://nytimes.com/2005/11/07/international/europe/07france).

According to the BBC, the riots were best explained as a reaction by Muslims against the negative perception of Islam in French society at large and widespread French social discrimination against immigrants. The BBC further stated that there was a "huge well of fury and resentment among the children of North African immigrants in the suburbs of French cities" and proclaimed that "Islam is seen as the biggest challenge to the country's secular model in the past 100 years" (http://news.bbc.co.uk/2/hi/europe/4445428.stm). Although no one died in the violence except for the two boys who provided the spark for the riots at the outset, and the riots may have been linked to poverty, unemployment, and discrimination as much as religion, the unrest in France served as another reminder that the potential exists for violence between large populations of marginalized Muslims and non-Muslim majorities in Western countries.

It also appears that discrimination and marginalization of Muslims in Europe, such as that in France, serve as a recruiting tool for jihadists. A report released by Dutch intelligence in March 2004 concluded that many Muslims in Europe are drawn into the jihadist network because they are outraged by the perceived discrimination and poor treatment that they receive in their adopted countries. Put more succinctly, the Dutch concluded that "the group of young people who feel treated disrespectfully is a major potential target for radicalization and possibly recruitment processes (for jihad)" (Quoted in Hashim, 2006, p.146).

Islamists and the Internet

In recent years, the global expansion of the Internet has meant that the Internet itself has become a major tool for Islamists in propagating Islamist ideology and winning converts to Islamism throughout the globe. Islamists take advantage of the freedom of speech and press that exist in Western societies, freedoms that are not present in the Islamic realm to the same degree, to publicize their propaganda criticisms of the West as morally decadent and engaging in a crusade against Islam. Some Web sites (like those of their Western counterparts) spew inaccurate propaganda that has little, if any, connection to reality. For instance, Islamist Internet postings after the American assault on Fallujah in November 2004 claimed that the United States had resorted to the use of chemical weapons because conventional weapons were insufficient to dislodge the insurgents (Hashim, 2006, p.168).

There are literally thousands of Islamist organizations with Websites, which if not based in the West, are certainly accessible to radical Muslims living in the West. According to Gabriel Weimann of Haifa University in Israel, the number of Web sites related to terrorist groups number over 4400 (Benjamin and Simon, 2005, p.60).

As of 2005, the most common subject of the Islamist Web sites are jihadist attacks on Americans in Iraq. Other Web sites, as explained by Benjamin and Simon (2005),

> Present cartoons, interactive games, fables, adventure stories—as well as images of children with real weapons playacting as terrorists. For adolescents, there are rap videos, like Sheikh Terra's Dirty Kuffar (infidel), which flashes images of Marines cheering as one of them shoots an Iraqi on the floor; a rolling list of the fifty-six countries that are said to have been the victims of American aggression since World War II; a Russian soldier being blasted by a Chechen guerrilla with an AK-47; and pictures of Colin Powell and Condoleeza Rice with the words 'still slaves' superimposed on them. As the heavy beat goes on, the rappers guffaw in the background while on the screen the destruction of the Twin Towers is replayed. (p.60)

The Internet essentially allows the jihadists to counter Western media dominance in a way that they otherwise could not. The usefulness of such Web sites to the Islamists for their recruitment is obvious. Web sites allow Islamists to recruit those with skills needed for their cause by placing advertisements for chemists, computer experts, electronics experts, etc. on line. Other Web sites provide prospective recruits with directions on how they may best make their way to the jihad in Iraq via Syria or other bordering countries (*Global Issues Report*, June 9, 2005).

Still other Web sites provide directions for bomb-making or the best ways to attack urban targets. For example, the Islamist Web site

Alm2sda.net provided detailed instructions on the types and characteristics of explosives that work best on Improvised Explosive Devices
(IEDs) as well as instructions on types of detonators and timers and
the best way to build a car bomb (*Global Issues Report,* May 20,
2005). Still others provide instructions on how to disable American
armored vehicles and tanks (*Global Issues Report,* March 22, 2005).
Other Islamist Web sites direct jihadists concerning what targets
should be hit. For example, in February 2002, an online article appeared explaining the advantage of bombing oil tankers. Perhaps not
coincidentally, the French tanker *Limburg* was bombed eight months
later (Benjamin and Simon, 2005, p.76).

Many of the groups that construct the Web sites, of course, are non-
Western, but many are posted on the Web by radical groups living in
the Western countries themselves. The number of organizations and
Web sites that are radical Islamist in character are simply too many to
mention in this space, but a few prominent ones will be noted here.

The Saviour Sect

One major Islamist group in the West is known as The Saviour Sect
(formerly Al-Muhajiroun), led by Anjem Choudry and Sheikh Omar
Bakri Mohammed. The name of the group (The Saviour Sect) is a reference to a statement ascribed to Mohammed in the Hadith, where
the Prophet stated, "My nation will be divided into 73 sects, all of
them will be in the Fire except for one (the saved sect) (Quoted in
http://en.wikipedia.org/wiki/The_Saviour_Sect). During 1998, Bakri Mohammed published the communications of Osama bin Laden, for
whom Bakri Mohammed claimed to be a spokesman. Al-Muhajiroun
gained global notoriety for its conference after the September 11, 2001
terrorist attacks where they praised the "Magnificent 19" in reference
to the nineteen terrorists who flew the jetliners full of passengers into
buildings in the United States. Among the items Al-Muhajiroun's
termed as its "vision," included the categorization of Islam as "a complete system of life," a call to persuade all Muslims to implement Islam, and to

> formulate a fifth column as a community pressure group which is well
> equipped with the Islamic culture, e.g. ruling, social, economic, judicial, pe-
> nal, and ritual systems in order to become capable of implementing Islam
> fully and comprehensively in society (http://en.wikipedia.org/wiki/Al-
> Muhajiroun).

Although the Saviour Sect's unapologetic Web site clearly states that
they do "not condone or incite any type of hatred whatsoever"
(www.thesavedsect.com/about.htm), the group posts articles on its Web
site that teach that Israel, the Jews, and the West in general are evil

enemies of Islam and it is the duty of Muslims to fight them
(www.ict.org.il/articles/articledet.cfm?articleid=484). It may also be true
that the Saviour Sect should not be considered a terrorist organization, and the group has not claimed responsibility for any terrorist
acts, as most Islamist terror groups tend to do, but the Saviour Sect's
propaganda does most certainly serve as a radicalizing agent, and
members of the Saviour Sect have become radicalized to the point of
violence since some have served as suicide bombers in the intifada
against Israel (www.ict.org.il/articles/articledet.cfm?articleid=484). In particular, two British members of the Saviour Sect were identified as
Hamas suicide bombers who killed three people when they attacked a
bar in Tel Aviv in April 2003. Furthermore, in 2004, Saviour Sect
members were arrested in London after police seized a warehouse
containing 1200 pounds of ammonium nitrate fertilizer (Clarke et al.,
2004, p.61).

Hizb ut-Tahrir

The Saviour Sect itself was essentially begun in 1996 as an offshoot of
Hizb ut-Tahrir (The Islamic Liberation Party), an international
Islamist movement dedicated to the creation of a united Khilafah (Islamic state) and the reestablishment of the caliphate consistent with
that of the seventh century. The head office of Hizb ut-Tahrir is not
Afghanistan, Saudi Arabia, or Palestine, but London, from where they
provide finance and recruitment to Islamist groups worldwide, including Hamas, Egyptian Islamic Jihad, and Hizbollah. Hizb ut-Tahrir
also supports other radical Islamic groups in the West, including The
Supporters of Sharia.

Where necessary, Hizb ut-Tahrir calls for jihad against infidels in
order to establish the Islamic state. Hizb ut-Tahrir opposes all existing
Arab and Muslim states (and all other existing governments, for that
matter) as apostates and favors a limitless Islamic state without national boundaries; consequently, Hizb ut-Tahrir has been banned in
current Islamic countries (Taji-Farouki, 1996). Hizb ut-Tahrir also
vehemently opposes the existence of the state of Israel and draws no
distinction between the state of Israel and Jews in general; consequently, Hizb ut-Tahrir has opposed all phases of the Palestinian-
Israeli peace process. Additionally, Hizb ut-Tahrir is decidedly anti-
Hindu, anti-Sikh, antihomosexual, antifeminist, antidemocratic, and
anti-Western. In fact, Hizb ut-Tahrir is so anti-Semitic that they deny
the Holocaust, arguing that the real holocaust is the killing of Muslims
in Palestine by Jews. One leaflet distributed by the group calls for the
killing of Jews wherever they are found, and another stated that "the
only place to meet Jews is on the battlefield." In spite of these radical

statements, Hizb ut-Tahrir also claims that they have "no relation-
ships whatsoever with any violent, terrorist, or sectarian organization,
nor does the party engage in violent or sectarian actions," an apparent
contradiction with the call to kill Jews (Whine, 2003, pp.1-8
www.guardian.co.uk/religion/story/02763.739813.00.html).

Supporters of Sharia

Unlike Hizb ut-Tahrir and the Saviour Sect, the Supporters of Sharia
are a Western-based Islamist group involved in more than just
Islamist propaganda, with direct ties to terrorism. The Supporters of
Sharia are associated with the radical Finsbury Park Mosque in London, the home Mosque for Zacarias Moussaoui, the so-called "twentieth hijacker," and Richard Reid, the American "shoebomber" (Whine,
2003, 5). The supporters of Sharia also have been linked to the kidnapping of sixteen Western tourists in Yemen in 1998 and a bomb
plot in Aden in 1999 (www.al-bab.com/yemen/hamza/hamza2.htm).

Like Hizb ut-Tahrir, the Supporters of Sharia also wish to reestablish the seventh-century caliphate and replace what they term as
"man-made laws" with the sharia. The Supporters of Sharia emphasize jihad as a Muslim obligation and claim to have supported Mujahadeen in Afghanistan, Bosnia, and Kashmir. In fact, the leader of the
Supporters of Sharia, Abu Hamza, claims to have fought in the Afghan
war, and lost both hands and an eye in an "accident" (www.al-
bab.com/yemen/hamza1.htm).

The focus of the Supporters of Sharia appears to be primarily on
what they consider to be apostate Muslim governments, which for all
practical purposes includes all Muslim governments in the eyes of Abu
Hamza. For example, after the death of King Hussein of Jordan, Abu
Hamza's Web site had a page dedicated to what Hamza viewed as an
apostate ruler under the heading, "Another one bites the dust," that
showed King Hussein, whom Hamza viewed as an apostate, with demonic horns on his head, surrounded by flames, apparently burning
in hell (www.al-bab.com/yemen/hamza1.htm).

Though Abu Hamza's main concerns are the apostate governments
in Muslim countries, he also poses a threat to Western governments
in his opposition to the introduction of Western culture into Muslim
countries, which he views as "polluting" Islam. Abu Hamza focuses on
Yemen in particular because he views it as the only Muslim country
that "has not surrendered to the United States of America," but he
views it on the verge of doing so; hence, Abu Hamza argues that jihad
in Yemen is necessary against those who would capitulate to the
Western cultural pollution. Abu Hamza argues that Muslims must
"explode in the faces of the snake" in Yemen, and in doing so hopefully trigger a jihadist domino effect over the entire Arabian penin-

sula. Abu Hamza views allowing Western involvement in an Islamic country, whether in the form of Western militaries, humanitarian aid, oil exploration, or tourism, as "surrender," and therefore opposes all contact with the West (www.al-bab.com/yemen/hamza1.htm).

The future of Abu Hamza and his organization is in question at the time of this writing, however, since Hamza was arrested in London in 2005 by British officials for using language construed as a solicitation to murder (*Economist*, February 11, 2006, p.9). When British officials raided his mosque, they found an arsenal of stun guns, tear gas, chemical warfare protection suits, false passports, knives, and radio equipment. The jury in Hamza's case was treated to extracts from speeches and sermons where he railed against adultery, democracy, and alcohol and declared that jihad was a religious duty, arguing that "Islam will never be dear to your hearts unless you sacrifice for it, until your blood comes out for it" (Quoted in *Economist*, February 11, 2006, p.26). Hamza also was quoted as saying that "Killing a Kaffir (non-believer) for any reason, you can say it is okay, even if there is no reason for it" (Quoted in *Economist*, February 11, 2006, p.26).

Committee for the Defence of Legitimate Rights

The Committee for the Defence of Legitimate Rights in Saudi Arabia (CDLR) was formed in Riyadh in 1993 in reaction to the decision of the Saudi government to allow the United States and other Western troops to defend the kingdom following Iraq's August 1990 invasion of Kuwait. The CDLR publicly questioned the Islamic credentials of the ruling family and championed the revival of puritanical Wahhabi religious principles and a return to strict sharia. CDLR leaders argued that what was happening in the Gulf was part of a larger Western plot to dominate the entire Arab and Muslim world. The CDLR was quickly banned by the Saudi government and its leading members were arrested and fired from their jobs. One member, Abdallah al-Hudhaif was beheaded following a secret trial; consequently, the group moved its home base to London in 1994. In 1996, the CDLR diminished in importance after a major segment split into the Islamic Reform Movement in Arabia led by Saad al-Fagih, which continues to disseminate propaganda against the Saudi government from London (www.hrw.org/backgrounder/mena/saudi).

Hilafet Devleti

Hilafet Devleti, also known as the Anatolian Federated Islamic State and "Kalifasstaat," is a German-based group founded in 1984 by Turkish native Cemaleddin Kaplan, who fled to Germany from Turkey, after being denounced as an "enemy of the state" in Turkey in 1983, a charge that would have carried the death penalty if he had not fled. Kaplan favored the creation in Turkey of an Islamic state modeled after the Islamic Republic of Iran under Ayatollah Khomeini. Followers of Hilafet Devleti in Germany wear traditional Islamic clothing, men wear full beards and turbans, and women wear full black Islamic coverings (www.im.nrw.de/sch/589.htm&...). Under Kaplan's son, Metin Kaplan, who took the reins of the group after his father's death in 1995, the group has called for a restoration of the caliphate and the overthrow of Turkey's secular government they view as apostate (www.ict.org.il/spotlight/det.cfm?id=245). Hilafet Devleti's published statement entitled, "The New World Order," states that (Quoted in Bakewell, 2000 (accessed online),

> Our goal is the control of Islam over everyday life. In other words, the Koran should become the constitution, the Islamic system of law should become the law, and Islam should become the state...Is it possible to combine Islam with Democracy and the layman's system on which it is based? For this question only one answer exists, and that is a resounding 'NO!'

Hilafet Devleti appears to be more than a mere propaganda organization, however, and is accused of having direct ties to violence and terrorism by German authorities. In particular, Metin Kaplan was suspected in the murder of his rival to power among Muslim extremists in Germany, Ibrahim Sofu, in 1996. Kaplan had publicly stated that "he would like to see Sofu dead," but German prosecutors could not prove that he had ordered the killing. He was, however, convicted of solicitation of murder and spent four years incarcerated for the crime in Germany (http://en.wikipedia.org/wiki/Metin_Kaplan).

In a separate incident in Turkey in 1998, Turkish security forces claim that Metin Kaplan and the Hilafet Devleti orchestrated a failed plot to bomb the mausoleum of Mustafa Kemal with a plane filled with explosives that they had planned to crash in to the mausoleum. Twenty three members of Hilafet Devleti were arrested in conjunction with the failed terror plot, and forty more were arrested in Germany during a demonstration involving approximately 500 followers of Hilafet Devleti, who were demanding Kaplan's release after his arrest for his part in the plot (www.ict.org.il/spotlight/det.cfm?id=245). In May 2004, German authorities evidently decided that they had had enough, and Kaplan's refugee status in Germany was revoked so that he could be extradited back to Turkey on charges of terrorism. In June 2005, Kaplan faced trial in Turkey and was convicted of plotting terrorist attacks against the Turkish government and given life imprisonment in Turkey, but his organization continues in his absence (http://en.wikipedia.org/wiki/Metin_Kaplan).

Jamaat al-Tabligh

The Jamaat al-Tabligh (Society for the Propagation of Islam) is concentrated primarily in Pakistan, but has a mosque in Queens, New York City that serves as a center for its activity. For example, the Queens mosque hosted a gathering of approximately 200 Jamaat al-Tabligh missionaries in 2003. The Jamaat al-Tabligh, like other Islamist groups, is dedicated to the purification of Islam and the return to the practices of Mohammed in the seventh century. Jamaat al-Tabligh rejects modernism, advocates segregation of women, and supports the Taliban regime in Afghanistan. The group is linked to al-Qaeda and helped John Walker Lindh, the American who fought with the Taliban in Afghanistan, to get to Pakistan and enroll in a madrassa (religious school) to study Islam. They also helped the al-Qaeda member Kamal Derwish recruit six Yemeni-American men in Lackawanna, New York for the purpose of traveling to Pakistan to engage in al-Qaeda training camps in 2001 (Clarke et al., 2004, pp.57-58).

Nida'ul Islam

Nida'ul Islam or "The Call of Islam" is an Islamist group based in Sydney, Australia. Nida'ul Islam's Web site contains interviews with Osama bin Laden, Sheikh Omar Abdul Rahman (who orchestrated the 1993 World Trade Center bombing), and members of the Taliban. A feature article on the Nida'ul Islam Web site is entitled, "The Termination of Israel: A Qur'anic Fact," in which it is argued that Israel's destruction is mandated by the Koran. In another article entitled "How the West Came to Dominate the Whole Wide World," the writers condemn Christianity and Judaism and claim that slavery was the Christian response to the spread of Islam in Africa. The writers also argue that capitalism is an invention of Jews and Christians to ensure Western domination of the world. In the words of Nida'ul Islam (Quoted in Cox and Marks, 2003),

> The globalization of trade in stolen goods was sanitized by the term, Capitalism. the trade was financed by the largest owners of capital, namely the (Christian) Church and Jews, underpinned by usury, sanitized by the term, 'interest,'... Little wonder that the capitalistic theories of Adam Smith–a Jew–are still popular under neo-colonialism. ... In 1947 Palestine was handed over to the Zionists. The never forgotten objective of the Church, the recapture of Palestine, had finally been achieved...the Jews returned under the New Secular Order, to dominate the socio-economic, political and foreign affairs of the Gentiles by indirectly ruling the Church. (p.64)

Other articles on the Nida'ul Islam Web site include "The U.S. War on Islam" and "Australians, Shooting for Israel." Although Nida'ul is not necessarily a terrorist organization, its inflammatory language is

clearly designed to encourage others to join in physical jihad against
Israel and the West. Nida'ul Islam's strategy has been referred to by
scholars as "the drip effect," which refers to a stream of constant negative criticism which gradually erodes belief among Muslims in the
values of Western societies (Cox and Marks, 2003, p.64). One may argue that the jihad (or the accompanying Western War on Terror) will
never be won on the battlefield, but in the hearts and minds of Muslims everywhere. Nida'ul Islam is engaged in a serious effort to win
the cultural struggle through the winning of hearts and minds, a strategy that thus far appears to be effective.

American Jihad

In general, the American Muslim community has thus far been less
hospitable to jihadists and less radical than their counterparts in
Europe. This is due at least in part to the fact that there are far greater
numbers of Muslims in Europe, although exactly how many Muslims
live in America is a matter of debate since the US Bureau of the Census does not collect data on religious affiliation. In order to get an approximate count, researchers are forced to rely on self-identification,
surname characteristics, and national origins, none of which are perfect measures. The best estimates appear to be that the United States
is home to approximately 3 million Muslim people, or a little more
than 1% of the American population (Benjamin and Simon, 2005,
p.289).

In general, American Muslims appear to be much more integrated
into American society than they are in Europe, where there is a tendency for Muslims to occupy low-wage jobs and reside in Muslim
ghettoes. In contrast, American Muslims are better educated, more
likely to be professionals, and more economically advanced. The average household income of American Muslims is higher than the median US household income and a fourth of American Muslim
households earn over $100,000 annually. Similarly, more than a third
of American Muslims have graduate degrees, compared with 8.6% of
the American population as a whole (Benjamin and Simon, 2005,
p.119).

The greater assimilation of American Muslims may explain why the
9/11 terrorists do not appear to have been part of a vast network of
Islamists within the United States. The *9/11 Commission Report*, for
example, documents a fairly solitary path of the 9/11 terrorists while
they were in the United States. The terrorists evidently did not make
contacts with other American-based groups of Islamists, and the terrorists apparently had more contact with individuals from foreign
embassies than with other American Muslims (*National Commission*

on Terrorist Attacks, 2004, pp.215-241). The behavior of the 9/11 terrorists suggests that if there were a radical Islamist network in the United States, the 9/11 terrorists were not associated with it, may not have known about it at all, and if they had, may not have trusted it.

Subsequent federal government efforts to thwart radical Islamism within the United States also have not revealed a vast Islamic terror network in the United States. For example, in spite of the recent American focus on terrorism, according to Eggen and Tate (2005, p.1), in almost four years after 9/11, only thirty-nine people were convicted of crimes tied to national security or terrorism in the United States, and of those, only fourteen had any links to al-Qaeda. Among those fourteen were the celebrated cases of John Walker Lindh, the American who fought with the Taliban, Zacarias Moussaoui, the so-called twentieth hijacker, and Richard Reid, the notorious shoe-bomber.

Other cases, however, reveal that though the radical Islamists in the United States thus far appear to be few in number, it is also true that some have indeed arrived, including a select few that are native citizens of the United States, such as John Walker Lindh. In another case of "American Taliban," in Lackawanna, New York (as mentioned previously), six Yemeni-Americans (The Lackawanna Six) associated with Jamaat al-Tabligh were arrested on charges of providing material support for terrorists after they had traveled to Afghanistan and attended an al-Qaeda training camp (Benjamin and Simon, 2005, p.117).

Other celebrated cases include that of Sami Omar al-Hussayen, a Saudi graduate student, who was charged in 2002 with raising funds for terrorist organizations, including Hamas, and managing Web sites that supported terrorism. Al-Hussayen was acquitted, but was quickly deported for immigration violations (Benjamin and Simon, 2005, p.124). In another case, Iyman Faris, a Columbus, Ohio truck driver with links to al-Qaeda, was arrested in 2003 for a ridiculous plot to bring down the Brooklyn Bridge by cutting its suspension cables with blowtorches. One could assume that a solitary Islamist on the Brooklyn Bridge applying blowtorches to the cables would have been quickly reported and arrested unless he was also a reincarnation of H.G. Wells' Invisible Man. Finally, in Virginia, a local imam, Ali el-Timmimi (the same imam who rejoiced at the crash of the space shuttle Colombia), was convicted in April 2005, and sentenced to life in prison for "soliciting others to levy war against the United States and contributing services to the Taliban" (Quoted in Markon, 2005, p.A01) after he had called on young American Muslims to join the jihad in Afghanistan five days after the 9/11 attacks. Nine others were convicted along with el-Timmimi and given sentences ranging from

four years to life in prison. The conviction of the el-Timmimi ring was
the first time since the conviction of Sheik Omar Abdel Rahman in
1995 (in the case of the first World Trade Center bombing) that someone had been convicted in American courts for his words rather than
for actually carrying out terrorist activities. Most disturbing in the
case to many, however, was the fact that el-Timmimi and five of the
nine convicted were Muslim American citizens born in the United
States (Markon, 2005, p.A01).

The el-Timmimi case is one of several indicators that suggest that
the Islamist movement in the United States, though small, like the
American Muslim population in general, may be growing. There are
numerous Muslim associations and organizations in the United States
that may have links to radicalism and terrorism. In particular, Steven
Emerson (2003) argues that there are links between global terrorist
organizations and nine American Muslim groups, which he names as:
the Muslim Arab Youth Association (MAYA), The American Islamic
Group (AIG), the Islamic cultural Workshop (ICW), The Council on
American-Islamic Relations (CAIR), The American Muslim Council
(AMC), the Islamic Circle of North America (ICNA), The Muslim Public Affairs Council (MPAC), the American Muslim Alliance (AMA),
and the Islamic Society of North America (ISNA). Similarly, Mohammed Hisham Kabbani, chairman of the Islamic Supreme Council of
North America, claims that over 80% of the more than 3000 mosques
in the United States are dominated by radical Islamist ideology and
that the ideology is beginning to spread into the American universities
(Cox and Marx, 2003, p.67). Kabbani also argues that there are numerous Islamic charity organizations in the United States who fund
Islamic extremism outside the United States. In the words of Kabbani
(Quoted in Cox and Marks, 2003),

> Our sources say that many, many millions of dollars have been collected
> and sent. They send it under humanitarian aid, but it doesn't go to humani-
> tarian aid...some of it will go to homeless people and poor people but the
> majority, ninety percent of it, will go into the black markets in these coun-
> tries and buying weapon arsenals. (p.67)

It should be noted, however, that Kabbani's contentions are disputed
by the AMA, AMC, CAIR, MPAC, ICNA, and ISNA, who together with
the American Muslim Political Coordination Council and the Muslim
Students Association of USA and Canada issued a statement condemning Kabbani's arguments and demanding an apology, which
Kabbani refused to offer (Cox and Marks, 2003, p.67).

American authorities have known about the problem of the diver-
sion of funds from Islamic charities in the United States to radical and
violent Islamist causes, at least since the first Persian Gulf War. During that conflict, the Saudi Ambassador to Pakistan informed the

American Consulate in Pakistan that Islamic charity organizations in California and Texas were funding violent jihad in Afghanistan. The CIA and FBI were made aware of the information, but apparently did not follow up with investigations (Coll, 2005, pp.230-231). In another incident, Osama bin Laden once apparently wired $210,000 to a contact in Texas to purchase a private cargo jet for use in transporting weapons to Afghanistan (Coll, 2005, p.269).

The issue of aid to terrorists from American Muslims is just one more difficulty that American policymakers now face in their quest to stem the threat of global Islamist terrorism. One of the difficulties in stopping such "humanitarian" aid from going to terrorists is that many legitimate Islamic charities may be linked through multiple connections to terrorist groups, even sometimes without their knowledge. This is partially due to the fact that the lines between legitimate Islamic charities and terrorist groups become blurred, because many successful terrorist groups, such as Hamas in Palestine and Hezbollah in Lebanon, also perform social welfare functions, providing food and necessities to the impoverished. For American Muslim groups to therefore claim that the funding of Hamas is the funding of a legitimate charity organization is not completely false, but ignores the fact that the same organization that helps the poor, also engages in horrific acts of terrorism (Sayyid, 2003, p.xv).

American Islamism and the War on Terror

Almost immediately after the terrorist attacks of 9/11, President Bush launched a comprehensive "War on Terror" that included everything from an invasion of Afghanistan to the increased screening of passengers at airports, to restrictions on financial institutions and greater surveillance of American residents. The impact of the President's War on Terror is in dispute, with the President claiming success and his political opponents claiming otherwise, and it is possible that it remains too early to provide comprehensive conclusions concerning the impact of the War on Terror and Islamism in the United States. It is worth noting, however, that in one substantial academic study, New York University's Center on Law and Security concluded that President Bush's legal war on domestic terrorism has thus far been largely unsuccessful in curbing the spread of Islamism. In the words of the New York University's Center on Law and Security, Bush's effort (www.law.nyu.edu/centers/lawsecurity/publications/terroristtrialreportcard.p df.)

> has yielded few visible results. There have been relatively few indictments, fewer trials, and almost no convictions on charges reflecting dangerous crimes. Either the government is focused primarily on using arrests to ob-

tain information rather than conviction, or the legal war on terror, as fought in the courts, is inconsequential.

The post-9/11 era does, however, appear to be developing a mild back-lash in the American Islamic community against what some American Muslims view as discrimination and injustice against Muslims perpe-trated by the Bush administration during the War on Terror. In the words of one Chicago college student,

> Our new awareness is also a reaction to the treatment of Muslims in this country. After 9/11, the older generation who ran the show thought it best to lie low...As that happened, the younger generation was uncomfortable with this, especially at colleges and universities. We decided we must be-come active. (*Chicago Tribune*, September 14, 2003)

This particular student's new radicalism is perhaps an inevitable reac-tion to the fact that more than 750 immigrants in the United States, many of them Muslims, were arrested and detained by the Bush ad-ministration in the four years following the 9/11 terror attacks. Doz-ens were jailed for weeks or months without charges and without rights to counsel (*New York Times*, July 27, 2005). In some cases, the Justice Department of Attorney General John Ashcroft was clearly overzealous. In Detroit in 2002, for instance, Ashcroft announced the arrest of a supposed "sleeper cell" of terrorists in Detroit that were suspected of being connected to the 9/11 attacks. The only conviction, however, was for a minor immigration offense, and even that was later overturned. The charges, it later was discovered, were based on misin-terpretation of some pieces of evidence and the exclusion of some ex-onerating evidence (Benjamin and Simon, 2005, p.121). Similarly, FBI agents arrested a Muslim American lawyer in Portland, Oregon in 2004, on suspicion of collaboration in the Madrid bombing earlier that year. The condemning evidence that led to the man's arrest em-barrassingly later turned out to be nothing more than his son's Span-ish homework (Benjamin and Simon, 2005, p.122).

Other actions of the Bush administration that have spurred resent-ment among American Muslims (as well as those around the world) include the detention of 6000 Muslims at Guantanamo Bay, Cuba, without charges, and without rights under either the US Constitution or international law. American Muslims generally view Guantanamo Bay as evidence of how the United States has made the "War on Ter-rorism" into a "War on Islam." The reports of torture and prisoner abuse, as well as the reports of flushing a Koran down the toilet, have become potent symbols to American Muslims (as well as for the global body of Muslim believers) of an anti-Muslim campaign by the gov-ernment of the United States (*New York Times*. May 21, 2005).

In such an atmosphere, the potential exists for the ignition of Mus-lim hostility and violence in the United States similar to that experienced in recent years throughout Europe. Survey data suggest that almost 75% of American Muslims "either know someone or have themselves experienced an act of anti-Muslim discrimination, harassment, verbal abuse, or physical attack since September 11" (Benjamin and Simon, 2005, p.122).

American Culture Wars and Crusade

Another factor that may contribute to the Islamist threat in the United States is the fact that the United States is much more religious than its European counterparts and therefore perhaps more likely than European countries to be viewed by Islamists as waging a "crusade" against Islam. In the words of Ahmed Hashim (2006), the United States is a

> self-professed moralistic country that sees the world in black and white rather than shades of grey, and it conducts crusades. Its victory in the Cold War reinforced that, as did the terrorist tragedy of 9/11. It is in effect, as currently constructed, congenitally incapable of waging effective counter-insurgency (against radical Islam). (p.320)

President Bush is perhaps the most important contributor to the Islamist perception of the United States as crusaders due to his invasions of two Islamic countries and several statements he made, where he essentially framed the War on Terror as a "crusade." Three days after the 9/11 terrorist attacks at what Bush declared as a "National Day of Prayer and Remembrance," Bush proclaimed in dichotomous language similar to that of the Islamists that "our responsibility to history is already clear: to answer these attacks and rid the world of evil" (Quoted in Phillips, 2005, p.16). Similarly, in an address to a joint session of Congress in January 2002, Bush proclaimed that "We will pursue nations that provide aid or safe haven to terrorism. Every nation in every region now has a decision to make. Either you are with us or you are with the terrorists" (Quoted in Phillips, 2005, p.16). Again, the dichotomous "with us or against us," black or white, dichotomous thinking mirrored that of Bush's Islamist adversaries. Finally, in January in his State of the Union Address, Bush provided Islamists with perhaps their "smoking gun" proving that the United States is bent on destroying Islam, when he referred to the American invasion of Afghanistan as a "crusade" and declared that "Liberty is God's gift to every human being in the world" (Quoted in Phillips, 2005, p.16).

Bush, however, is not alone in his "crusade," and it is most likely that he used the term because many Americans view it as positive, rather than negative. Currently, approximately 60% of Americans say that religion "plays an important role in their lives" and 80% claim to have experienced "God's presence or a spiritual force." Furthermore, over one fifth of Americans identify as attending church more than once a week, whereas three-fourths of Americans report that they attend at least once a month (Anderson, 2004, pp.143-156). For these Americans, accustomed to fervently singing "Onward Christian Soldiers, marching as to war, with the cross of Jesus...") without any real consideration of possible interpretations, Bush's call for a crusade was simply a call to the restoration of goodness and justice. For Islamists, the call to Islamic jihad has literally the same meaning.

Much like the jihadists, America has a long history of couching its military struggles in terms of religious moral crusades. In World War I, President Woodrow Wilson famously proclaimed that the United States was going to war to "make the world safe for Democracy." In the Civil War, both sides essentially claimed that God was on their side, and the Union even began putting "In God we trust" on their coins in 1864 to suggest that the faith of the Union was superior to that of the "godless" South (Thomas, 1960, p.359). The Union's "Battle Hymn of the Republic" could hardly be more religious and the words speak of the civil war as a religious war, eerily similar to the way that Muslims speak of jihad in the twenty-first century. For example, the opening and closing lines to the first verse and the chorus read (www.cyberhymnal.org/htm/b/h/bhymnotr.htm)

> Mine eyes have seen the glory of the coming of the Lord, he has trampled down the vineyard where the grapes of wrath are stored...his truth is marching on...glory, glory hallelujah.

As if the message were not clear enough in the first verse, the final verse of the hymn is not only religious, but proclaims the war itself to be an act of religious martyrdom that very well parallels the views toward jihadist martyrdom of radical Islamists (Quoted from www.cyberhymnal.org/htm/b/h/bhymnotr.htm).

> In the beauty of the lilies Christ was born across the sea; with a glory in his bosom that transfigures you and me; as he died to make men holy, let us die to make men free, while God is marching on.

During the cold war of the 1950s, Congress endeavored to show that God was on the side of America when it directed the President to create a national day of prayer, designated "In God We Trust" to be the National Motto, placed "In God We Trust" on American paper currency, and inserted the words "under God" into the American flag salute. In casting the War on Terror as a religious crusade, Bush was merely falling in line with a long American tradition.

Bush, however, was not intending to speak to the Islamists, but to the religious right in America, which is largely credited with the election of George W. Bush in both 2000 and 2004. Support of this core group would be necessary if the President were to carry out a military campaign against radical Islam. There are multiple reasons for the marriage between the religious right and the George W. Bush administration, but the faith of the President himself appears to be an important factor and the President has made clear that he shares their values. For example, Anthony Evans of Dallas, a fundamentalist minister and confidant of George W. Bush, explained to a British journalist in 2003 that one of the impetuses for Bush's consideration of running for President in 2000 was Biblical teaching and direction from God. In the words of Evans, Bush "feels God is talking to him" (Quoted in Phillips, 2004, p.232). Similarly, journalist Bob Woodward wrote (based on his interviews with Bush) that "the president was casting his vision and that of the country in the grand vision of God's master plan" (Woodward, 2002, p.67). Likewise, presidential advisor David Gergen told the *New York Times* (Quoted in Phillips, 2004, p.233) that Bush "has made it clear he feels that Providence intervened to save his life, and now he is somehow an instrument of Providence." Finally, Bush as much as admitted that he viewed his Presidential role as part of a Divine plan at the National Prayer Breakfast on February 6, 2003, when Bush stated,

> We can be confident in the ways of Providence. ... Behind all of life and all of history, there's a dedication and purpose set by the hand of a just and faithful God. (Quoted in Phillips, 2004, p.239)

In Bush's case, however, the incentive is perhaps even greater since Bush owed his ascendancy to the White House perhaps as much to the religious right as to any other group. In each religious category in the 2000 election, whether evangelical, mainline Protestant, Catholic, or even Muslim, the higher the religiosity of the person, the more likely it was that they supported George W. Bush. For example, 84% of high-commitment evangelicals supported Bush. Similarly, Catholics, formerly a strongly Democratic demographic, supported Bush by approximately 60% (Phillips, 2004, p.223). With these kinds of Christian religious connections, it should not be surprising that Islamists view the President as the head of a Christian crusade against Islam.

As President, Bush has acted accordingly and remembered those who put him in the White House by placing religious right conservatives in numerous key positions throughout the federal government. Bush appointed Kay Coles James, formerly dean of the Robertson School of Government at Pat Robertson's Regent University, as head of the Office of Personnel Management. David Caprara, a former director of the American Family Coalition, an affiliate of Sun Myung Moon's Unification Church, was appointed the head of AmericCorps VISTA. Moon himself, a Bush supporter who controls the conservative pro-Bush newspaper the *Washington Times*, sponsored an Inaugural Prayer Luncheon for Bush on January 19, 2001, where propaganda on the Unification Church was distributed. This partiality to Reverend

Moon is in spite of the fact that Moon is often condemned by other evangelical Protestants for asserting that he wants to take over the world, abolish all religions except the Unification Church (certainly including Islam), abolish all languages except Korean, and abolish all governments except his own, one-world, theocracy (Phillips, 2004, p.235). Although Moon merely sponsored a Prayer Luncheon and was not appointed by Bush to a position in government, Bush did nominate J. Robert Brame III, a former board member of American Vision, a group that favored putting the United States under Biblical law and opposed women's rights, to the National Labor Relations Board. Additionally, to chair the Food and Drug Administration's Reproductive Health Drugs Advisory Committee, Bush appointed W. David Hager, a person who recommended specific scriptural readings and prayers for headaches and premenstrual syndrome. Finally and most famously, Bush appointed John Ashcroft, a devout Pentecostal Christian who had his own head anointed with Crisco cooking oil before being sworn in, as Attorney General (Phillips, 2004, p.226-227).

Bush was not alone among Republicans, however, in catering to the religious right. Other leading Republicans during the Bush years have tended to make statements favorable to the Christian right and support the policies they champion. Republican House majority leader Tom DeLay, for instance, exhibited his own consistency with religious right thinking when he assured a Texas Baptist audience that God had elevated Bush to the presidency in order to "promote a Biblical worldview." According to Benjamin and Simon (2005, p.269), DeLay's importance in Middle East policy is such that the White House asked for his clearance on President Bush's June 2002 speech on American policy in the Middle East, where Bush declared support for a Palestinian State. DeLay also refers to the Israeli-occupied territories in Palestine by their Biblical names of Samaria and Judea and argues that they rightly belong to Israel (Phillips, 2004 p.230). On a visit to Israel, DeLay said of the West Bank, "I don't see occupied territory; I see Israel" (http://www.timesonline.co.uk/article/o,,11069-1561077_2,00.html).

Similarly, Dick Armey, DeLay's predecessor as Republican House majority leader, endorsed the transportation of Palestinians from Palestine to any other countries that would take them. Not to be outdone, Republican Senator James Inhofe of Oklahoma proclaimed to his fellow senators that Israel was entitled to the occupied territories "because God said so" (Armey and Inhofe quoted in Benjamin and Simon, 2005, p.270). Again, with such leadership in Congress and the Executive branches of the federal government, it is perhaps little wonder that Muslims in America and worldwide tend to view recent American policies as an anti-Muslim crusade.

Aiding the Islamists in their contention that the American invasion of Iraq and the accompanying War on Terror are anti-Muslim crusades is General William G. "Jerry" Boykin, an American General in charge of the hunt for Osama bin Laden and other top terrorist targets. Boykin is an evangelical Christian who has cast the US War on Terror as that of a Christian nation locked in battle with Satan, and declared that his Christian God was bigger than that of the Muslims (obviously not understanding that Muslims and Christians worship the same God). Furthermore, Boykin told one group that "George Bush was not elected by a majority of the voters in the United States. He was appointed by God" and that the jihadists "will only be defeated if we come to them in the name of Jesus" (Quoted in the *Los Angeles Times*, October 17, 2003, B17).

Meanwhile, the leaders of the Christian right itself would spend the years of Bush's first term flailing from one anti-Muslim issue to another and inflaming culture war against Muslims in the process. For instance, noted evangelist Franklin Graham offended Muslims by referring to Islam as "wicked" and "evil." In his best-selling book, *The Name*, Graham characterizes Christianity and Islam as "eternal enemies," and joined in a "classic struggle that will end with the second coming of Christ" (Quoted in *Washington Post*, September 2, 2002, A3). Furthermore, in spite of the fact that Christians and Muslims both worship the God of Abraham, Graham argues that Christians and Muslims do not worship the same God, the two being as different as "lightness and darkness." Moreover, Graham characterizes the War on Terrorism as a religious war between "evil and The Name" rather than a conflict between Islamists and the West (*Washington Post*, September 2, 2002, A3). Meanwhile, the Reverend Jerry Falwell referred to the prophet Mohammed as a terrorist, and Dr. Jerry Vines, Pastor of the First Baptist Church in Jacksonville, Florida, declared that Mohammed was a "demon-possessed paedophile" (Worldnetdaily.com, June 15, 2002). Not to be outdone, Reverend Pat Robertson referenced Mohammed as a "wild-eyed fanatic, a robber, and a brigand" (Phillips, 2004, p.230).

A central focus of American Christian fundamentalists in terms of foreign policy is American support for the territorial integrity of Israel to the exclusion of a Palestinian presence. To some Christian fundamentalists, it is a threat to God's ultimate plan for Israel if the United States is to mediate the Arab-Israeli conflict. For an example of such a position, one need look no further than the words of Reverend Malcom Hedding, whose group, the International Christian Embassy is the headquarters for Christian Zionists in Jerusalem, who stated (Quoted in Lampman, 2004),

> We stand for the right that all the land God gave under the Abrahamic covenant 4,000 years ago is Israel's...And He (God) will regulate the affairs of how Israel comes into its allotment which is hers forever...Palestinian statehood is also irrelevant, since there is no such thing as a Palestinian. (p.1-2).

Another American Christian fundamentalist group, known as the "Cattlemen of the Apocalypse," have spent their time since 9/11 shipping cattle to the Holy Land in an attempt to breed the Revelation-prophesied red heifer that would signal Israelis to rebuild their Holy Temple and thus usher in the "end times" (Phillips, 2004, p.230).

Exhibiting a different Israel-centered view, John Hagee, a well-known Protestant fundamentalist minister and televangelist in San Antonio, announced that his congregation would give over $1 million to Israel for the resettlement of Jews from the former Soviet Union to the West Bank and Jerusalem in the Israeli-occupied territories of Palestine (Phillips, 2004, p.230). Simultaneously, still another religious right group raised money to hire lawyers to defend Israelis who were arrested for planning to blow up Jerusalem's Al-Aqsa Mosque" (Phillips, 2004, pp.230-231). Another fundamentalist Christian group, known as the International Fellowship of Christians and Jews, claims to have raised as much as $100 million for Israel, $20 million of it in 2003 and 2004 alone. Furthermore, it has sponsored the resettlement to Israel of 100,000 Jews from Russia and Ethiopia, in anticipation of the apocalypse (Benjamin and Simon, 2005, p.269). Given these prevalent pro-Israel sentiments of American evangelical Christians and given the fact that President Bush won 78% of the Evangelical Christian vote in 2004, Bush's Middle East policies have been predictably pro-Israel, reflecting his support base, a fact not missed by Muslims, whether in the United States or abroad.

Finally, the Muslims' perception of the Iraq war as a crusade has been bolstered by the American Christian missionary efforts that have accompanied the American invasion and occupation of Iraq. In the words of Kyle Fisk, Executive Administrator of the National Association of Evangelicals (Quoted in the *Los Angeles Times*, March 18, 2004, p.A1).

> Iraq will become the center for spreading the gospel of Jesus Christ to Iran, Libya, throughout the Middle East. ... President Bush said democracy will be spread from Iraq to nearby countries. A free Iraq allows us to spread Jesus Christ's teachings even in nations where laws keep us out.

Similarly, Christian missionary in Iraq Tom Craig (Quoted in the *Los Angeles Times*, March 18, 2004, p.A1), stated that he and other evangelicals were in Iraq because "God and the President have given us the opportunity to bring Jesus Christ to the Middle East." Nine evangelical Churches opened in 2003 in Baghdad alone. For support for the contention of the Islamists that the American invasion of Iraq is a crusade against Islam, they need little else, since American Christian evangelicals openly admit that a modern-day "crusade for Christ" is indeed their purpose. With such attitudes, a significant reactionary Islamist movement among American Muslims (not to mention those worldwide) should perhaps be the most logical expectation. A successful strategy against global Islamism undoubtedly requires that Americans understand the Islamist mindset as much as possible and rid themselves of black and white ideological predilections. The prevalence of the crusade by the religious right in America suggests that a very large segment of Americans, perhaps a majority and including the Presidential administration of George W. Bush, are incapable of doing so.

· EPILOGUE ·

Islamism Since 9/11

The reaction of the masses in the Muslim world since the terrorist attacks of 9/11 has been decidedly sympathetic to the Islamists and opposed to the policies of the United States under the George W. Bush administration. Polls of Muslims in the Middle East in 2002 revealed that most Muslims did not believe the 9/11 attacks were carried out by Muslims. Instead, it was commonly believed that the attacks were most likely carried out by the CIA. Meanwhile, the globally recognized head of al-Qaeda, Osama bin Laden, thoroughly demonized in the United States for his role in the 9/11 attacks (and others), remains quite popular in the Islamic world. For example, in the largely Muslim Nigerian city of Kano, seven out of ten male babies were given the name "Osama" by their parents in 2002 (*BBC News.* January 3, 2002, http://news.bbc.co.uk/2/hi/africa/1741171.stm).

Meanwhile, the insurgency in Iraq has continued unabated, demonstrating that President George W. Bush's War on Terror has done little, if anything, to erode the prevalence of radical Islamist ideology either in the place Bush chose to make as his number one battlefield in the struggle against Islamism or, for that matter, anywhere else. Instead, Islamism and Islamist terrorism appear to have grown both in Iraq and elsewhere. Statistics from a RAND Corporation database show 5362 deaths from terrorism worldwide between March 2004 and March 2005, a figure that is almost double the total for the same twelve-month period before the 2003 invasion (*Amarillo Globe News.* July 10, 2005, p.1). To read that figure (that does not include the deaths in Iraq) and conclude that the United States is winning the war against radical Islam perhaps requires an ideology as impenetrable as that of the Islamists themselves. Unfortunately, the characterization of the War on Terror as a "long hard slog" appears to be much more accurate. The suggestion, however, that the "slog" can be won by the sword, rather than better ideas, flies in the face of statistical evidence and suggests that the American War on Terror is no less ideological than the jihad of the Islamists. Furthermore, America's invasion of

Iraq has only served to unite diverse groups of radical Muslims, including radical Shiites under Muqtada al Sadr and radical Sunnis under Abu Musab al-Zarqawi, against the American invasion and occupation of Iraq (Phillips, 2005, p.219). To make matters even worse, it is difficult to argue that education can eventually correct the ideological thinking of the Islamists since the policies of the Bush administration clearly demonstrate that better education has not released American policymakers from their own ideological thinking. Consequently, the culture clash between the West and the Islamists may be expected to continue almost indefinitely.

Islamism, however, should perhaps be expected to fail in the long run for the same reasons that Christian theocracy failed in the seventeenth century, after hundreds of years of bloodshed. Essentially, Islamism ignores the sociological reality that people will not and cannot all completely agree in the realms of religion and politics; hence, their vision of a world united under one set of Islamic laws can only be viewed as a fantasy. Moreover, some Islamic states, such as Indonesia, the world's most populous Islamic state, have instituted principles of cultural pluralism and religious tolerance in their constitution. In fact, the words "Unity and Diversity" are inscribed in the Indonesian National Emblem (Cox and Marks, 2003, p.1).

What is obviously needed in the world of Islam is a true Muslim "Enlightenment" that breaks the bonds of dogmatic fundamentalism, with all of its religious zealotry, crazed conservatism, and intellectual backwardness, and opens up the realm of Islam to new ideas and the kind of free thinking that has existed in the West since the Enlightenment. Islamic scholars must also begin to look critically at the inherent contradictions contained in the Koran, much as Western scholars have critically dissected the Bible. Only when Muslims can look at the verses in the Koran calling for jihad, and conclude that they are not obligated to go kill those with whom they disagree, can the calls to jihad fall on deaf ears. The fact that Christians generally have been able to ignore Jesus' call to kill his enemies (Luke 19:27) for centuries, suggests that Muslims too may be able to some day ignore the calls for jihad.

Whether or not such an "Enlightenment" is possible in Islam, and if so, how it may be achieved, are questions that remain unanswered as yet. Islamists are openly critical of the teaching of science, since it subverts Islam, and of critical history classes, because they might suggest that passages in the Hadiths may be apocryphal; hence, any critical analyses of Islamic history are condemned as un-Islamic (Sivan, 1985, pp.6-8). Furthermore, those that question Islam, such as Salman Rushdie and Farag Foda, find themselves subject to threats and assassination, whether they reside in the Islamic world, as Foda did in

Egypt, or in the West, as Rushdie did in the United Kingdom. In any case, it is clear that there are no safe havens for those who would criticize Islam, thus stunting the possibilities for any kind of Enlightenment. Again, however, the same could be said of Christian attitudes toward science and history in the Middle Ages, so perhaps Islam can follow a similar path. It is worth noting, however, that fundamentalist Christians often still oppose science, whether it be stem cell research or Darwin's theory, and American Christian groups often condemn the writings of "revisionist" historians who write anything inconsistent with what they view as the great patriotic "Christian" history of the United States. Again, fundamentalist Christians and Islamists are more alike than they think.

An Islamic Enlightenment would also necessitate a rigid separation of religion and state that represents a violation of some of the fundamental principles of Islam itself. Whereas Christians during the European Enlightenment could point to Jesus' "Render unto Caesar, what is Caesar's and unto God, what is God's," thus providing a religious foundation for the separation of religion from the state, one must look much further in Islam to find a similar religious parallel.

In conclusion, one of the foremost things that the Muslims must do is to find a way to move away from the literal and inerrant interpretation of the Koran, or innovation and rational thinking will remain forever hindered. After all, if all of God's will is explained in the Koran and God's will is all that one needs to know, then mere thinking outside of the Koran can be viewed as impious. In short, Muslims thus far seem not to have grasped the necessary separation of religious law from any actual social order. Unless that separation is achieved, the almost inevitable result will be some form of absolutism through the alliance of political and religious power. It is a lesson that Christian society has had to learn and relearn, often painfully, but which is clearly at present unlearned in the realm of Islam, and the fact that the Koran remains beyond criticism is at the root of the problem. Although it may be argued that the fact that the Koran remains beyond criticism is clearly part of the strength of Islam, that strength has been gained at the cost of being able to openly examine not only Islam, but anything else as well, thus stunting intellectual growth.

The logic of both Islam and fundamentalist Christianity is that if God is truly God, then no critical examination of his Revelation is possible, since the Revelation itself represents the will of the Omniscient and Omnipotent, the one and only God. When this logic is pursued, however, the religious fundamentalists are cut off from any meaningful intellectual inquiry, dialogue with other faiths, or even dialogue among themselves. In such cases, the lack of critical analysis renders the claim of the religion to be the fulfillment of God's will to be a vicious tautology and void of reason. For the Islamists, the argument is essentially that God said it, I know it to be true because it is in his book, and I know God's book to be true because it says it is in his book; therefore, the issue is settled and it cannot be questioned. As long as this type of tautological "reasoning" remains prevalent, the cultural conflict between Islam and the West can be expected to continue.

Bibliography

Abu-Rabi, Ibrahim M. *Intellectual Origins of Islamic Resurgence in the Modern Arab World*. Albany: State University of New York Press, 1996.

Ajami, Fouad. *The Arab Predicament*. Cambridge, UK: Cambridge University Press, 1981.

Ahmad, Jalal Al-e. *Gharbzadegi*. Translated by John Green and Ahmad Alizadeh. Costa Mesa, CA: Mazda Publishers, 1982.

Aiken, Henry D. *The Age of Ideology: The Nineteenth Century Philosophers*. New York: Mentor, 1956.

Amarillo Globe News. "Letter to Editor," June 28, 2004, p.8a).

_____."Terrorism Deaths Increase." July 10, 2005, p.1.

_____. "Robertson: Stroke Was God's Wrath." January 7, 2006, p.4A.

Anderson, Brian C. "Secular Europe, Religious America." *Public Interest*. Spring 2004, pp.143-156.

Armstrong, Karen. "Was it Inevitable—Islam Through History," in James F. Hoge, Jr., and Gidon Rose, eds., *How Did This Happen? Terrorism and the New War*. New York: Public Affairs, 2001.

_____. *Islam: A Short History*. New York: Random House, 2000.

Atlanta Journal-Constitution. January 3, 2003, p.1

Auster, Bruce B. "The Recruiter for Hate." *U.S. News and World Report*. August 31, 1998.

Baer, Robert. *See No Evil*. New York: Three Rivers Press, 2002.

_____. *Sleeping With the Devil*. New York: Crown Publishers, 2003.

Bakewell, Joan. "The Believers Who Despise Our Ways." *New Statesman*. May 29, 2000. (Accessed online at www.newstatesman.com/200005290011).

Baltimore Sun. "Shiites Target of Attacks in Iraq." January 22, 2005, p.1.

Bawer, Bruce. *While Europe Slept: How Radical Islam is Destroying the West from Within*. New York: Doubleday, 2006.

BBC News. "Osama Baby Craze Hits Nigeria." January 3, 2002. http://news.bbc.co.uk/2/hi/africa/1741171.stm. (Accessed online July 27, 2006).

Bearden, Milton. "Afghanistan, Graveyard of Empires," in Fredrik Lovegall, ed., *Terrorism and 9/11: A Reader*. Boston, MA: Houghton Mifflin, 2001.

Benjamin, Daniel, and Steven Simon. *The Age of Sacred Terror*. New York: Random House, 2002.

_____. *The Next Attack. The Failure of the War on Terror and a Strategy for Getting it Right*. New York: Henry Holt, 2005.

Bergen, Peter L. *Inside the Secret World of Osama bin Laden*. London: Weidenfeld and Nicolson, 2001.

Berlet, Chip. "Dances with Devils." *Political Research Associates*. www.publiceye.org/Apocalyptic/Dances_with_Devils_1.html; http://www.publiceye.org/Apocalyptic/Dances_with_Devils_2htm., 1998 (Accessed online, July 26, 2006).

Berlin, Isaiah. "The Bent Twig: A Note on Nationalism." *Foreign Affairs*. Vol 1, 1972, pp. 1-28.

Bickerton, Ian J., and Carla L. Klausner. *A Concise History of the Arab-Israeli Conflict*, Updated Fourth Edition. Upper Saddle River, NJ: Pearson Prentice-Hall, 2005.

Bloom, Mia. *Dying to Kill: The Allure of Suicide Terror*. New York: Columbia University Press, 2005.

Borisov, Sergey. "Osama Baby Boom in Nigeria." *Pravda*. http://english.pravda.ru/main/2002/01/08/25036.html, 2002. (Accessed Online, July 27, 2006).

Boston Globe. "Study Cites Seeds of Terror in Iraq." July 17, 2005 (Accessed online, July 27, 2006).

Bradford, William. *Of Plymouth Plantation 1620-1647*. New York: Random House, 1981.

Bradley, John R. *Saudi Arabia Exposed: Inside a Kingdom in Crisis*. New York: Palgrave Macmillan, 2005.

Bradshaw, Michael, George W. White, and Joseph P. Dymond. *Contemporary World Regional Geography*. Boston, MA: McGraw-Hill, 2004.

Burke, Jason. *Al Qaeda: The True Story of Islamic Terror*. London: I.B. Tauris, 2004.

Chicago Tribune. "Muslims Get in Touch With Their Faith, Culture." September 14, 2003, p.1.

Clarke, Richard A., Glen P. Aga, Roger W. Cressey, Stephen E. Flyn, Blake W. Mobley, Eric Rosenbach, Steven Simon, William F. Wechsler, and Lee S. Wolosky. *Defeating the Jihadists:*

A Blueprint for Action. New York: The Century Foundation Press, 2004.

Cockburn, Andrew, and Patrick Cockburn. *Out of the Ashes: The Resurrection of Saddam Hussein*. New York: HarperCollins, 1999.

Coll, Steven. *Ghost Wars: The Secret History of the CIA, Afghanistan, and bin Laden, from the Soviet Invasion to September 10, 2001*. New York: Penguin, 2005.

Cook, David. *Understanding Jihad*. Berkeley, CA: University of California Press, 2003.

Cox, Caroline, and John Marks. *The West, Islam, and Islamism*. London: Civitas, 2003.

De Blij, Henry, and Peter Muller. *Geography: Realms, Regions, and Concepts*. Tenth Edition. New York: John Wiley, 2002.

Diamond, Jared. *Guns, Germs and Steel: The Fates of Human Societies*. New York: W.W. Norton, 1999.

Diamond, Larry. *Squandered Victory. The American Occupation and Bungled Effort to Bring Democracy to Iraq*. New York: Henry Holt, 2005.

Dunn, Charles W., and J. David Woodard. *American Conservatism from Burke to Bush: An Introduction*. Lanham, MD: Madison Books, 1991.

Eatwell, Roger. The Nature of the Right, 2: The Right as a Variety of Styles of Thought." In Roger Eatwell and Noel O'Sullivan eds., *The Nature of the Right*. Boston, MA: Twayne, 1989.

Economist. "Inequality: For Richer, For Poorer." November 5, 1994, pp.19-21.

_____. "Honor Laws." June 21, 2003, p.48.

_____. "Iraq After Ayatollah Hakim's Murder," September 6, 2003, p.39.

_____. "Rebuilding Iraq." September 13, 2003, pp.21-23.

_____. "Failure Begins to Look Possible." November 1, 2003, pp.14-15.

_____. "New Fuel for the Culture Wars." March 5, 2004, p.11.

_____. "A Survey of Retirement: Forever Young." March 27, 2004, pp.3-4.

_____. "A Matter of Trust." April 3, 2004, pp.24-28.

_____. "Bloodshed in Iraq." April 10, 2004, pp.21-23.

_____. "Lexington: A House Divided." May 8, 2004, p.34.

_____. "A New Splurge of Torture Papers." June 26, 2004, p.23.

_____. "Iraq's Christians: Less Safe than Before," August 7, 2004, p.39.

_____. "Iraq: The Struggle for Order." September 25, 2004, pp.57-58.

_____. "Special Report: Afghanistan." October 9, 2004, pp.21-23.

_____. "Special Report: Iraq." May 7, 2005, p.21.

_____. "A Civil War on Terrorism." November 25, 2004, pp.28-29.

_____. "A Bloody New Year in Iraq." January 1, 2005, pp.31-32.

_____. "The World This Week." January 29, 2005, p.7.

_____. "Cartoon Wars." February 11, 2006, p.9.

_____. "Special Report: Islam and Free Speech." February 11, 2006, pp.24-26.

_____. "Muslims in Europe: Confusing and Confused." October 29, 2005, p.87.

_____. "Afghanistan: The Illusion of Empire Lite." June 24, 2006, pp.13-14.

Eggen, Dan, and Julie Tate. "U.S. Campaign Produces Few Convictions on Terrorism Charges; Statistics Often Count Lesser Crimes." *Washington Post*. June 12, 2005.

Emerson, Steven. *American Jihad: The Terrorists Living Among Us*. New York: Simon and Schuster, 2003.

Esposito, John L. *Voices of Resurgent Islam*. Oxford: Oxford University Press, 1983.

Ford, Peter. "Europe Cringes at Bush 'Crusade' Against Terrorists. *Christian Science Monitor*. September 19, 2001.

Freeden, Michael. *Ideology: A Very Short Introduction*. Oxford and New York: Oxford University Press, 2003.

Gabriel, Mark. *Islam and Terrorism*. Lake Mary, FL: Strang Communications, 2002.

Gergez, Fawaz. *The Far Enemy: Why Jihad Went Global*. New York: Cambridge University Press, 2005.

Global Issues Report. "Hostile Arabic Website Continues Militant Training Encyclopedia." March 22, 2005.

_____. "Hostile Website Provides Instructions to Make IEDs and Car Bombs." May 20, 2005.

_____. "Website Offers Instructions for Crossing Syrian-Iraqi Border: 'This is the Road to Iraq.'" June 9, 2005.

Goodwin, Jan. "Buried Alive: Afghan Women Under the Taliban," in Fredrik Logevall, ed., *Terrorism and 9/11: A Reader*. Boston, MA: Houghton Mifflin, 2002.

Gordon, Michael R., and Bernard E. Trainor. *Cobra II: The Inside Story of the Invasion and Occupation of Iraq*. New York: Pantheon, 2006.

Gunaratna, Rohan. *Inside Al Qaeda: Global Network of Terror*. New York: Columbia University Press, 2002.

Haas, Ben. *KKK: The Hooded Face of Vengeance*. Evanston, IL: Regency, 1963.

Halliday, Fred. *Two Hours that Shook the World, September 11, 2001: Causes and Consequences.* London: Saqi Books, 2002.

Hashim, Ahmed S. *Insurgency and Counter-Insurgency in Iraq.* New York: Columbia University Press, 2006.

Hassan, Nasra. "An Arsenal of Believers: Talking to the 'human bombs.'" *New Yorker.* November 19, 2001.

Hersh. Seymour M. "Target Qaddafi." *New York Times Magazine.* February 22, 1987.

_____. *Chain of Command: The Road from 9/11 to Abu Ghraib.* New York: Harper/Collins, 2004.

Hiro, Dilip. *Iraq: In the Eye of the Storm.* New York: Nation Books, 2002.

Hoffman, Bruce. "Holy Terror: The Implications of Terrorism Motivated by a Religious Imperative." *Studies in Conflict and Terrorism.* Vol 18, 1995, pp.271-284.

Hoover, Kenneth. *Ideology and Political Life.* Second Edition. Belmont, CA: Wadsworth, 1994.

http://en.wikipedia.org/wiki/2005_civil_unrest_in_France. (Accessed online, July 27, 2006).

http://en.wikipedia.org/wiki/Al-Muhajiroun. (Accessed online, July 27, 2006).

http://en.wikipedia.org/wiki/Metin_Kaplan. (Accessed online, July 27, 2006).

http://en.wikipedia.org/wiki/The_Saviour_Sect. (Accessed online, July 27, 2006).

http://image.guardian.co.uk/sysfiles/Guardian/documents/2004/11/30/Muslims-Novo41.pdf. (Accessed online, December 1, 2004).

http://news.bbc.co.uk/2/hi/Europe/4407688.stm. (Accessed online, November 25, 2005).

http://news.bbc.co.uk/2/hi/europe/4445428.stm. (Accessed online, November 25, 2005).

http://news.bbc.co.uk/2/hi/middle_east/2751019.stm (Accessed online, March 1, 2003).

http://news.bbc.co.uk/1/low/world/south_asia?1585636.stm. (Accessed online, July 27, 2006).

http://nytimes.com/2005/11/07/international/europe/07france (Accessed online, November 10, 2005).

http://observer.guardian.co.uk/international/story/0,,1080989,00.html. (Accessed online, November 9, 2003).

http://people-press.org/reports/display.php3?ReportID=175. (Accessed online, July 27, 2006).

Huff, Toby. *The Rise of Early Modern Science: China, Islam, and the West.* Cambridge, UK: Cambridge University Press, 2003.

Huntington, Samuel. "Conservatism as an Ideology." *American Political Science Review*. Vol 51, 1957, pp.454-473.

_____. "The Clash of Civilizations?" *Foreign Affairs*. Vol. 72, 1993, pp. 22-49.

Ingersoll, David E., Richard K. Matthews, and Andrew Davison. *The Philosophic Roots of Modern Ideology*. Upper Saddle River, NJ: Prentice-Hall, 2001.

Ishaque, Khalid. "The Islamic Approach to Economic Development," in John Esposito ed., *Islam: The Straight Path*. New York: Oxford University Press, 1991.

Jeffrey, Arthur. *Islam: Muhammad and his Religion*. New York: MacMillan, 1958.

Johnstone, Ronald L. *Religion in Society: A Sociology of Religion*. Fourth Edition. Englewood Cliffs, NJ: Prentice Hall, 1992.

Jones, Howard. *Quest for Security: A History of U.S. Foreign Relations*. New York: McGraw-Hill, 1996.

_____. *Crucible of Power: A History of American Foreign Relations from 1897*. Wilmington, DE: SR Books, 2001.

Juergensmeyer, Mark. *Terror in the Mind of God: The Global Rise of Religious Violence*. Berkeley, CA: University of California Press, 2003.

Keddie, Nikki. *Middle East and Beyond*. London, UK: Taylor and Francis, 1988.

Kepel, Giles. *The Trial of Political Islam*. Cambridge, MA: Harvard University Press, 2003.

Khomeini, Imam. *Islam and Revolution: Writings and Declarations of Imam Khomeini*. Berkeley, CA: Mizan Press, 1981.

Kirk, Russell. "Libertarians: Chirping Sectaries." *The Heritage Lectures: Proclaiming a Patrimony*. Washington, DC: The Heritage Foundation, 1982.

Koh, Harold Hongju. "Rights to Remember." *The Economist*. November 1, 2003, pp.24-26.

Kramer, Martin. "Islam vs Democracy." *Commentary*. January 1993.

_____. *Arab Awakening and Islamic Revival: The Politics of Ideas in the Middle East*. Piscataway, NJ: Transaction Publishers, 1996.

Kristol, Irving. *Two Cheers for Capitalism*. New York: New American Library, 1983.

Lampman, Jane. "Mixing Prophecy and Politics." *Christian Science Monitor*. July 7, 2004.

Lapidus, Ira M. "State and Religion in Islamic Societies." *Past and Present*. Vol 151, May 1996.

Lewis, Bernard. *The Assassins: A Radical Sect in Islam.* New York: Basic Books, 2001.

_____. *The Political Language of Islam.* Chicago: University of Chicago Press, 1988.

_____. *The Muslim Discovery of Europe.* New York: Norton, 1982.

Lia, Brynar, and Thomas Hegghammer. "Jihadi Strategic Studies: The Alleged Al Qaida Policy Study Preceding the Madrid Bombings." *Studies in Conflict and Terrorism.* Volume 27, 2004, 355-375.

Loconte, Joe. "I'll Stand Bayou." *Policy Review.* May/June 1998.

Los Angeles Times. November 4, 2001, p.1

_____. August 11, 2003, p.1.

_____. October 17, 2003, p.B17.

_____. December 10, 2003, p.1.

_____. March 18, 2004, A1.

_____. February 9, 2004, p.1.

_____. September 28, 2004, A1.

_____. April 2, 2005, A1.

Manchester, William. *The Last Lion: Winston Spencer Churchill.* Boston, MA: Little, Brown, 1983.

Markon, Jerry. "Muslim Lecturer Sentenced to Life; Followers Trained for Armed Jihad." *Washington Post.* July 14, 2005, p.A01.

Mayer, Ann Elizabeth. *Islam and Human Rights: Tradition and Politics.* Boulder, CO: Westview Press, 1991.

Micklethwait, John, and Adrian Wooldridge. *The Right Nation: Conservative Power in America.* New York: Penguin Press, 2004.

Msnbc.msn.com/id/6409042/. (Accessed online, November 6, 2004).

Muller, Jerry Z. *The Other God that Failed: Hans Freyer and the Deradicalization of German Conservatism.* Princeton, NJ: Princeton University Press, 1987.

_____. *Conservatism: An Anthology of Social and Political Thought from David Hume to the present.* Princeton, NJ: Princeton University Press, 1997.

Murad, Khuram. *The Islamic Movement in the West: Reflections on Some Issues.* Leicester, UK: The Islamic Foundation, 1981.

Murphy, John F. Jr. *Sword of Islam: Muslim Extremism from the Arab Conquests to the Attack on America.* New York: Prometheus, 2002.

Nash, Gary B., Julie Roy Jeffrey, John R. Howe, Peter J. Frederick, Allen F. Davis, and Allan M. Winkler. *The American Peo-*

ple: Creating a Nation and a Society. New York: Harper and Row, 1979.

National Commission on Terrorist Attacks. *The 9/11 Commission Report: Final Report of the National Commission on Terrorist Attacks Upon the United States.* New York: W.W. Norton, 2004.

National Statistics Online. "Focus on Religion." July 26, 2006. http://www.statistics.gov.uk/cci/nugget.asp?id=.

New York Times. "Free of Hussein's Rule, Sunnis in North Flaunt A Long-Hidden Piety." April 23, 2003, p.A13.

_____. "Blair Defends the War in Iraq as Part of a Historic Struggle." April 10, 2004, p.A7.

_____. "Iraq's Anxious Sunnis Seek Security in the New Order." August 10, 2003, p.A8.

_____. "Radical Shiite cleric Urges Revolt." April 26, 2003, A1.

_____. "Zarqawi's Journey: From Dropout to Prisoner to Insurgent Leader." July 13, 2004, p. A8.

_____. "The Conflict in Iraq: Intelligence; A New CIA Report Casts Doubt on a Key Terrorist's Tie to Iraq." October 10, 2004, p.A13.

_____. "Tape in the Name of Leading Insurgent Declares All-Out War on Iraq Elections and Democracy." January 24, 2005, p.A10.

_____. "For Some in Iraq's Sunni Minority, A Growing Sense of Alienation." May 8, 2005, p.23.

_____. "Study by Muslim Group Says Bias Crimes Up 50% in 2004." May 21, 2005, p. B5.

_____. "Jihadist or Victim: Ex Detainee Makes a Case," July 27, 2005, p.A1.

Newsweek, March 26 1979, p.26.

Nursi, Bediuzzaman Said. "Twenty-ninth Letter—Sixth Section, Which Is the Sixth Treatise," in Bediuzzaman Said Nursi, ed., *Letters, 1928-1932.* Istanbul, Turkey: Sozler Nesriyat A.S., 1997.

NYPost.com/millenium/mill.2003.

Ochsenwald, William, and Sydney Nettleton Fisher. *The Middle East: A History.* Sixth Edition. New York: McGraw-Hill, 2004.

Packer, George. *The Assassin's Gate: America in Iraq.* New York: Farrar, Straus, and Giroux, 2005.

Pape, Robert. *Dying to Win: The Strategic Logic of Suicide Terror.* New York: Random House, 2005.

Philadelphia Inquirer. "Mosque Bombing Incites Sectarian Strife." December 12, 2004, p.1

Phillips, David L. *Losing Iraq: Inside the Postwar Reconstruction Fiasco*. Boulder, CO: Westview Press, 2005.

Phillips, Kevin. *American Dynasty: Aristocracy, Fortune, and the Politics of Deceit in the House of Bush*. New York: Viking, 2004.

Podhoretz, Norman. "Oslo: The Peacemongers Return." *Commentary*. October 2001.

Radi, Nuha al. *Baghdad Diaries*. London: Saqi Books, 1998.

Rashid, Ahmed. "Osama Bin Laden: How the U.S. Helped Midwife a Terrorist," in Fredrik Logevall, ed., *Terrorism and 9/11: A Reader*. Boston, MA: Houghton/Mifflin, 2002.

_____. *Taliban: Militant Islam, Oil, and Fundamentalism in Central Asia*. New Haven, CT: Yale University Press, 2001.

Rippin, Arthur. *Muslims: Their Religious Beliefs and Practices*. Vol 1. London and New York: Routledge, 1991.

_____. "Literary Analysis of Koran, Tafsir, and Sira: The Methodologies of John Wansbrough," in Ibn Warraq, ed., *The Origins of the Koran: Classic Essays on Islam's Holy Book*. New York: Prometheus, 1998.

Rokeach, Milton. *The Open and Closed Mind: Investigations into the Nature of Belief Systems and Personality Systems*. New York: Basic Books, 1972.

Rossiter, Clinton. *Conservatism in America*. Second Edition. Cambridge, MA: Harvard University Press, 1982.

Rothbard, Murray. *America's Great Depression*. New York: New York University Press, 1975.

Roy, Olivier. *The Failure of Political Islam*. Cambridge, MA: Harvard University Press, 1994.

Sachar, Howard M. *A History of Israel: From the Rise of Zionism to Our Time*. New York: Random House, 1996.

Said, Edward W. *Orientalism*. New York: Vintage Books, 1979.

Saint Louis Post-Dispatch. "War Strategy: Dramatic Failures Require Drastic Changes." December 19, 2004, p.A1

Sankari, Jamal. *Fadlallah: The Making of a Radical Shiite Leader*. London: Saqi Books, 2005.

Sargent, Lyman Tower. *Contemporary Political Ideologies: A Comparative Analysis*, Ninth Edition. Belmont, CA: Wadsworth, 1993.

Savage, Timothy M. "Europe and Islam: Crescent Waxing, Cultures Clashing." *The Washington Quarterly*. Summer, 2004.

Sayyid, S. *A Fundamental Fear: Eurocentrism and the Emergence of Islamism*. London and New York: Zed Books, 2003.

Schumaker, Paul, Dwight C. Kiel, and Thomas Heilke. *Great Ideas/Grand Scheme*. New York: McGraw-Hill, 1996.

_____. *Ideological Voices: An Anthology in Modern Political Ideas*. New York: McGraw-Hill, 1997.

Seattle Post-Intelligencer. "A Nation Sagging under the Weight of Sanctions: Caught in a Spiral of Poverty and Death." May 11, 1999, p.1.

Shadid, Anthony. *Night Draws Near: Americans In Iraq*. New York: Henry Holt, 2005.

Sivan, Emmanuel. *Radical Islam: Medieval Theology and Modern Politics*. New Haven: Yale University Press, 1985.

Skidmore, Max. *Ideologies: Politics in Action*. Second Edition. Fort Worth, TX: Harcourt Brace, 1993.

Smith, B.D., and J.J. Vetter. *Theoretical Approaches to Personality*. Englewood Cliffs, NJ: Prentice-Hall, 1982.

Smith, Huston. *The World's Religions*. New York: HarperCollins, 1991.

Smith, Wilfred Cantwell. *Islam in Modern History*. New York: Mentor Books, 1957.

Suha Taji-Farouki. *A Fundamental Quest: Hizh ut-Tahrir and the Search for the Islamic Caliphate*. London: Grey Seal, 1996.

Sunday Times. January, 2002.

_____. May 30, 2004.

Suskind, Ron. *The Price of Loyalty: George W. Bush, the White House, and the Education of Paul O'Neill*. New York: Simon and Schuster, 2004.

Syal, Rajeev. "Cleric Supports Targeting Children." *Sunday Telegraph*. September 5, 2004.

Taeharah, Pasha Mohamed Ali. *An Introduction to Islamism*. Bloomington, IN: AuthorHouse, 2005.

Talbot, David. "Terror's Server." *Technology Review*. February 2005.

Territo, Leonard, James Halstead, and Max Bromley. *Crime and Justice in America*. St. Paul, MN: West Publishing, 1989.

Thomas, Benjamin Platt. *Abraham Lincoln: A Biography*. New York: Knopf, 1960.

USA Today. "Iraqis Oppose New Governing Council." December 4, 2003, p.1.

Wall Street Journal. "Iraqi Resistance Strikes a Chord with Locals on Mideast Street." March 26, 2003, p.1.

Wansbrough, John. *Quranic Studies: Sources and Methods of Scriptural Interpretations*. New York and Oxford, Oxford University Press, 1977.

Washington Post. "Religion and the War Against Evil." September 2, 2002, p.A3.

_____. "CIA Warns Iraq Invasion Could Breed More Terrorists."
September 9, 2003, p.A3.

_____. "Iraqis Skeptical of U.S. Motives." November 12, 2003,
p.A3

_____. "In Sunni Triangle, Loss of Privilege Breeds Bitter-
ness."January 13, 2004, p.A1.

_____. "Clashes Rise in Southern Iraq." April 11, 2004, p.14.

_____. "U.S. Hopes to Divide Insurgency." October 13, 2004, p.1.

_____. "Dozens Killed in Iraq Violence." July 17, 2005, p.A1.

Whine, Michael. "Al-Muhajiroun: The Portal for Britain's Suicide
Terrorists."
www.ict.org.il/articles/articledet.cfm?articleid=484, May 21,
2003.

White, Jonathan. *Terrorism: An Introduction.* Belmont, CA:
Wadsworth, 2002.

Woods, Roger. "The Radical Right: The Conservative Revolution-
aries in Germany." In Roger Eatwell and Noel O'Sullivan, eds.,
The Nature of the Right. Boston, MA: Twayne, 1989.

Woodward, Bob. *Bush at War.* New York: Simon and Schuster,
2002.

World Bank. *World Development Indicators.* Washington, DC:
World Bank, 1998.

Worldnet.com. "Mohammed a Demon-Possessed Pedophile?"
http://www.worldnetdaily.com/news/article.asp?ARTICLE_I
D=27975. June 15, 2002.

Wurmser, David. *Tyranny's Ally: America's Failure to Defeat
Saddam Hussein.* Washington, DC: The AEI Press, 1999.

www.al-bab.com/yemen/hamza/hamza1.htm. (Accessed online, July
27, 2006).

www.al-bab.com/yemen/hamza/hamza2.htm. (Accessed online, July
26, 2006).

www.ansarnet.ws/vb/showthread.php?t=14236. (Accessed online, July
27, 2006).

www.cyberhymnal.org/htm/b/h/bhymnotr.htm.

www.danielpipes.org/article/2218. (Accessed online, July 27, 2006).

www.danielpipes.org/article/2579. (Accessed online, July 27, 2006).

www.datelinehollywood.com/.../2005/09/05/. (Accessed online, September 10, 2005).

www.godhatesfags.com/2006/07/25/. (Accessed online, July 25,
2006).

www.guardian.co.uk/international/story/0,3604,1374581,00.htm (Accessed online, July 27, 2006).

www.guardian.co.uk/Iraq/story/0,2763,1398636,00.html. (Accessed
online, July 27, 2006).

www.guardian.co.uk/Iraq/Story/02,2763,155369,00.html. (Accessed online, July 27, 2006).

www.guardian.co.uk/religion/Story. (Accessed online, July 27, 2006).

www.guardian.co.uk/religion/story/0,2763,739813,00.html. (Accessed online, July 27, 2006).

www.hrw.org/press/2002/03/turabi-bio.htm (Accessed online, July 27, 2006).

www.hrw.org/backgrounder/mena/saudi. (Accessed online, July 27, 2006).

www.ict.org.il/articles/articledet.cfm?articleid=484 (Accessed online, July 27, 2006).

www.ict.org.il/spotlight/det.cfm?id=245. (Accessed online, July 27, 2006).

www.im.nrw.de/sch/589.htm&.... (Accessed online, July 27, 2006).

www.law.nyu.edu/centers/lawsecurity/publications/terroristtrialreportcard.pdf. (Accessed online, July 27, 2006).

www.religioustolerance.org_ter7.htm. (Accessed online, July 27, 2006).

www.salon.com/news/feature/2004/12/16/iraqi_insurgents/print.html. (Accessed online, July 17, 2004).

www.sistani.org. (Accessed Online, January 12, 2006).

www.smh.com.au/articles/2003/08/15/1060936052309.html. (Accessed online, August 16, 2003).

www.thesavedsect.com/about.htm. (Accessed online, July 27, 2006).

www.timesonline.co.uk/article/o,,11069-1561077_2,00.html. (Accessed online, July 27, 2006).

www.ummah.net/ikhwan/. (Accessed online, July 27, 2006).

www.usip.org/pubs/specialreports/sr134.pdf. (Accessed online, July 27, 2006).

www.washingtonpost.com/ac2/wp-dyn? (Accessed online, July 27, 2006).

www.washingtonpost.com/wpdyn/content/article/2005/12/26.html. (Accessed Online, July 27, 2006).

www.wikipedia.org/wiki/Jean-Marie_Le_Pen#quotes. (Accessed online, July 27, 2006).

Zucchino, David. Thunder Run: Three Days in the Battle for Baghdad. London: Atlantic Books, 2004.

Index